CAGE TALK

INSIDE THE WORLD'S TOUGHEST SPORT

BY JIMMY PAGE

CAGE TALK

INSIDE THE WORLD'S TOUGHEST SPORT

BY JIMMY PAGE

IN MEMORY OF
Genevieve Butler (1977-2006) & Conrad Wells (1977-2008)
Two wonderful people who were sadly taken from this world too soon

CAGE TALK

INSIDE THE WORLD'S TOUGHEST SPORT

BY JIMMY PAGE

First published in Hardback in November 2008.

Hardback ISBN: 10 DIGIT: 09552648-63
Hardback ISBN: 13 DIGIT: 978-0-9552648-6-3

Editor: Matthew Freeman
Designer: Martin Jennings
Published by:
HNL publishing - A division of HNL Media Group
Suite 185, 6 Wilmslow Road, Manchester, M14 5TP. United Kingdom
Email: contact@hnlmediagroup.com

Distributed by:

UK	USA
PGUK - 8 The Arena,	Midpoint Trade Books.
Mollison Avenue, Enfield.	27 West 20th Street. Suite 1102.
Middlesex. EN3 7NJ.	NEW YORK-NY 10011

Front cover photo of Frank Shamrock (courtesy of www.frankshamrock.org).
Back cover photo by Jimmy Page & Frank Shamrock.

ACKNOWLEDGEMENTS

A massive thanks to the Kocen family, without your kindness this book would not have been possible. Thanks in particular to Peter for his patient tuition in the art of Ko Son Do.

Thanks also to my family: my parents, Chris and Lorna; sister Sarah, brother-in-law Noel and baby Nuala. You've always been there for me and I can't explain how much I appreciate it.

Many thanks to the following fighters, trainers, promoters and doctor with whom I have had some fascinating conversations over the last nine months – in no particular order:

Paul Daley, Mark Weir, Paul Kelly, Alex Reid, Frank Shamrock, Mike Bisping, Mark Epstein, Sami Berik, Paul Taylor, Francis Heagney, Ian Freeman, Kevin Randleman, Drew Fickett, Dan Hardy, Frank Mir, Gilbert Yvel, Heath Herring, Tim Sylvia, Curtis Stout, Rosi Sexton, Ross Pettifer, Alistair Overeem, Eddie Kone, Paul Murphy, Lloyd Clarkson, Rob Nutley, Dave O'Donnell, Andy Geer, Neil Grove, Neil Hall, Dan Hardy, Paul Kelly, Gaz Roriston, Mustapha al Turk, Dean Lister, Alexis Demetriades, Paul Ivens, Paul James, Jimmy Wallhead, Dave Jackson, Mario Neto, Tony Quigley, Lee Barnes, Henrique Nogueira, Andre Winner, Lee Livingstone, Leigh Remedios, Leon Roberts, Ashleigh Grimshaw, Jess Liaudin, Phil Baroni, Jason Young, Martin Kampmann, Clay Guida, Marc Goddard, Bob Scrieber, Maurice Smith, Tom Watson, Dan Mohavedi, Sol Gilbert, Grant Waterman, Sunny Dhoalki, Wesley Felix, Jeremy Bailey, Herb Dean, Yves Edwards, Matt Ewin, Rorion Gracie, Eddie Bravo, Nigel Whitear, Dr Andrew Curran, Jason Barrett, John Hathaway, Paul Marchent, Brad Pickett, Tom Blackledge, Alex da Souza, Roberto Atalla and Andy Walker.

Many thanks to the editor of this book and MMA Unlimited magazine, Matt Freeman; I sincerely appreciate your inspirational conversation and painstaking attention to detail. I would also like to thank the mighty editor of Fighters Only magazine, Hywel Teague for his encouragement and advice over the years; I owe you both a curry. Thanks also to the rest of the mma journo posse - Lisa James, Lee Whitehead, David & Danielle West, Robert Swann, Peter Hugh Jones and John O'Regan, as well as a massive thanks to the Evil Overlord of UK mma, Cage Warriors match-maker, Ian Dean.

Last but by no means least; I would like to thank my wonderful girlfriend, Jody, for gently bullying me into doing more writing when I was fed up. Your kind support has been invaluable – I'm so glad to have met you, young lady!

Photos courtesy of Jimmy Page, Frank Shamrock, Alan Orr and Cage Rage and www.sherdog.com.

TABLE OF CONTENTS

INTRODUCTION
BY MATTHEW FREEMAN

'Remember, men all naturally want to be tough guys, they want to be leaders of the pack. If guys turn up at our gym and want to fight, they get a fight. When you tie them up and you're smiling, you choke them out or you armlock them and they are forced into tapping, it breeds a certain sort of discipline, a certain sort of respect amongst these people...'

- Gracie-Jiu-Jitsu Black Belt, Eddie 'The Cyclone' Kone

Mixed martial arts (or cage fighting, as it is sometimes known) is now widely regarded as the most exciting, fastest growing sport around. The Ultimate Fighting Championship (UFC) regularly enjoys pay-per-view audiences in their millions and coverage in the mainstream press has even escalated to being featured in British broadsheets and mainstream television. But, it was not always seen like this: when mma first emerged in America it had to battle against notions of being a brutal form of human cockfighting, limited to small venues in backwater states that would turn a blind eye to what many conservative politicians saw as a blood-thirsty spectacle.

From those first underground events mixed martial arts quickly grew in popularity, capturing the imagination of the world and filling huge arenas with masses of loyal fans. The UFC has been a huge factor in the growth of the sport with its marketing moves and reality television shows that pit top class fighters against one another in elimination tournaments. But, it is mma itself which has made such an impact with its high octane, fast paced, white-knuckle form of entertainment. The unpredictable nature of the competitions, the technical complexity of its encounters and the sheer passion and spirit of its athletes has made mixed martial arts into the most exciting sport there is. It is the nature of the fights themselves that has attracted so many fans to the sport; as the athletes who compete become more refined in their techniques and better physically conditioned for the rigours that mma competition demands, the sport has fast become an art in itself.

Jim Page, a highly respected UK journalist, has produced a fascinating book that takes us on a journey into this world of mixed martial arts and those who compete in it. Using interviews from the some of the greatest fighters in mma, the author builds a picture made up from snapshots and insights to create a narrative about the sport of combat unlike any other. Moving from small venues in the UK where young, hungry athletes give their all in the cage to the huge glitzy arenas of America and Japan, Jim Page introduces us to the awe inspiring world of 'physical chess matches'.

Employing his vast knowledge of mma and letting us in on his conversations with those dedicated men and women who make the sport as thrilling as it is, Jim gives us a look into the intriguing and varied lives of fighters and promoters. Each chapter offers a unique perspective into mixed martial arts and its myriad elements from the multitude of winning techniques to the hardships of training and the highs of winning. A must read for any fan of the sport, Jim Page has produced a very real look at mma: the excitement, the entertainment, the thrill and unpredictable nature of its competitions but, more importantly, the brave and gutsy performances of those who chose to enter the cage and fight.

CHAPTER ONE
THE MORALITY OF MMA

'I just want to have some fights and make some money doing it.'
- Leigh 'The Bulldog' Remedios

There is no disguising the fact that mma is a rough, potentially injurious sport - a point demonstrated at almost every event as the combatants often throw wild leather in a concerted attempt to knock their opponent unconscious. As a result, it seems only reasonable to expect that the sport is likely to attract some profoundly offended critics along the way. Faultfinders repeatedly levy a repetitive stream of accusations at the sport, ranging from claims that it is merely a theatre for street fights; to assertions that it is simply too dangerous an activity to be allowed in a modern society.

Critics of the Sport

The British Medical Association is a group of medical professionals which would very definitely count itself collectively as a sincere critic of the sport, having made numerous public calls for the activity to be banned. To receive such damning criticism from an organisation with such vast expertise on the subject of human health should be a concern to everyone involved in the sport; however, instead of brushing aside the critics of mma, it makes clear sense to try and understand why the organisation came to this view and what can the sport learn from its assessment.

I contacted the BMA to see if they had a spokesperson that might be interested in discussing the organisation's position in this matter. Given our very different outlooks on mma, I did not hold a great deal of hope that anyone from the group would get in touch; so it came as a surprise to receive an email from Dr Andrew Curran, a neurologist and judoka with an unusually deep understanding of combat sports.

Speaking to an eminent professional, I began by nervously asking Dr Curran what interest the BMA has in sporting activities. 'There's two answers to that question,' he replied after a moment's careful thought, 'the first is the preventative answer, and the second is the health answer, if you like, and they both actually overlap. The BMA's interest in sport is, firstly, how can you use sport positively and, secondly, what aspects of sport are negative?

'The positive aspects are obviously those that show that good exercise taken three or four times a week is protective against heart disease, hyper-tension, things of that nature.' He continued, 'The negative aspect in sports is those that have the potential to do preventable harm, i.e. that if you don't do those sports, you won't experience a certain type of illness or injury.'

That sounds reasonable enough, coming from the chap who has to patch up these damaged athletes; so which sports does the BMA consider to be negative and thus should be banned, according to the organisation? 'The main two that the BMA are concerned about at present are; boxing and cage fighting.' Dr Curran replied. 'The issues around those are predominantly to do with the fact that they are both sports where the aim is to cause injury to the opponent and where that injury specifically affects the brain.'

Potential Brain Injury

Dr Curran continued with a sombre tone as he assessed the potential damage that a knock out blow could do, 'If you suffer a concussion, the neuro-biological event that has occurred is that you have put your brain into shock, you've actually disrupted your nerves cells to such an extent that your brain is not working properly anymore.'

In line with contact sports the world over, the experienced neurologist insisted that athletes must take time off to recover from a concussion or knock out, as is essential to the healing process. 'Whilst we don't have accurate figures for it, the general feeling is that after a concussion of that nature nerve cells take about six weeks before they are back in balance and are capable of taking another blow. If they return to fighting too soon after substantially injuring nerves cells, those nerves cells are not going to be in a condition to take further blows. Of course, in professional sports where people are being paid to get back in the ring, there is huge commercial pressure on them to get back in the ring again, but the problem with both boxing and cage fighting is that you may suffer repeated blows in the same bout.'

MMA is still a comparatively young sport and, currently, not a great deal is known about the long term neurological damage that can be caused by a gruelling career in the cage. However, it is well known that fighters who take on board huge levels of punishment in the boxing ring run an inherent risk of suffering some kind of brain injury. The most famous boxer of all time, Muhammad Ali is one fighter who, for all his balletic grace and defensive skill, took an extraordinary amount of punches to the head during his long career. Towards the end, Ali's speech was barely recognisable in comparison to that of the lucid young motor-mouth that he was in his earlier career. Sadly, the legend now suffers from Parkinson's disease, a common and very tragic condition.

'I know that a lot of people do try and attribute that to his boxing,' Dr Curran said, 'but there's no evidence for that. He may have suffered from Parkinson's anyway. It's certainly possible that the fact that he was boxing at the level he was and receiving heavy punches, it may have accelerated the process, but there's no evidence for that. Parkinson's can take over anybody, whether they are boxing or not. Actually proving that a boxer has got Parkinson's because they box is not possible.'

One injury, however, which the BMA attributes with some certainty to both boxing and mixed martial arts is a subclinical electro perturbation. 'It's a long term to say that if you repeatedly hit the brain you damage it', Dr Curran explained simply. 'The problem with brain injury whether it be from intent or by accident is you are born with a number of nerves cells that you are going to have in your whole life, which is about 150 billion, so you've got lots of them. But if you move them and if they are damaged or die, then whilst there's some evidence now to suggest you can replace a some number of those that are injured, it's only a tiny, tiny fraction of what is lost. The particular issue around repeated blows to the head is that injuries to the cells occur that are potentially in deeper brain structures where you have fewer nerve cells to compensate for ones that you've lost.'

MMA and Boxing

Receiving powerful shots to the head as part of a normal working day, there is no doubt that participants of both boxing and mma run an inherent risk of brain injury while pursuing this sporting interest. However, it is interesting to note that the BMA lumps mma and boxing in together as sports which should both be banned, without making any distinction between the two vastly different forms of competition. This point is taken on by Dr Rosi Sexton, a professional female fighter with two degrees and a Cambridge education.

'As far as head contact goes, it is certainly the case that getting punched in the head a lot isn't good for you.' Sexton began, 'I do think that mma fighters aren't at as much risk as say boxers for example because of the greater variety of the strategies and you're better placed to look after yourself. With boxing, you are forced to fight at a certain distance; if you end up in a clinch the referee will split you up and you'll go back to that same range again. If you get knocked down they'll give you a ten count; if you get up, they will throw you back in there again, so you've got people having multiple concussions in the same fight. That doesn't happen in mma because if you get knocked down and you can't protect yourself straight away, that's fight over.'

This position was echoed by Leigh Remedios, a veteran of no-holds-barred competition who is clear about which of the two sports he is more concerned about in terms of safety: 'I think boxing is mental, 12 rounds of being punched in the head. Its head trauma isn't it, not just getting your legs kicked, getting armbarred or being choked – you're being punched in the head repeatedly, but I'm not going to complain,' he added with impish chuckle, 'if you want to get punched in the head for 12 rounds, be my guest.'

Dr Curran conceded that the two sports were quite different both in terms of the variety of target areas and permitted techniques; however, the difference between the two with regard to safety is still unknown. 'The scientific answer is that no-one has yet studied cage fighting in depth, particularly the brain impacts. Bruised muscles and fractured bones are things that heal well; you can end up permanently disabled if you have a joint ruptured or damaged in the fight, but they will, by and large, heal. The issue as I say, for me certainly as a neurologist, gets down to brains cells, if you are doing anything which kills brain cells this is not a good thing to do and in both cage fighting and boxing, the head is a specific target.'

As you might expect, the message that fighters should stop competing and find alternative employment is not always going to be met with a politely considered response. A point demonstrated by American fighter, Kevin Randleman's initial outburst on the subject. 'This is going to really sound bad… but that doctor can suck my dick!' the furious wrestler barked in defiant frustration. 'He's a fucking pussy. I can't stand it when people try to ban what the fuck we're doing. Boxers get hit in the face fucking 15 times more in one fight, than I have in the last fucking five years!'

After a moment's reflection, Randleman cooled down and set about clarifying his point, 'The British Medical Association, well, honestly, they are right. They are 100% correct. I don't blame them because they are a medical institution, they are saving lives. Fighting, you can honestly say, is not something that is going to save your life. It'd save mine in a street fight – maybe yours – but these doctors are fucking pussies. They are looking at it from a medical stand point; I'm fucking making money for my family, this is what I do. I'm a smart intellectual, but I still enjoy fighting.

'I've never got injured badly from fighting and I'm still very articulate' Randleman continued, 'The occasional beer might slur my words, but, hey, I like to have fun too! But they are wrong' he said, referring back to the BMA, 'What about football, basketball? All these sports where people take shots and hit the floor should seem dangerous to these guys, so they should try to ban them all. Why aren't they trying to shut down auto-racing?'

Accidents and intent to cause damage

In terms of the number and seriousness of injuries sustained across all sports, 'The Monster' has a valid point. In fact, pugilistic sports only make up only a very small percentage of the overall number of injuries which occur each year across a range of sporting activities. I put the point to Dr Curran; does the BMA not seem to be taking a disproportionate interest in combat sports, when accidents taking place in cycling alone result in thousands of head injuries each year?

'I think the point you've just made is "accidental injury."' Curran replied, 'Whilst we would encourage people to cycle in a safe way, to wear helmets and take other precautions, cycling is not a sport undertaken to cause injury, and I would suggest it falls philosophically, into a completely different category.'

We were starting to uncover that the root of the BMA's objections to pugilistic sports lie in the intentions of the competitors. By calling for a ban on mma and boxing, the organisation is essentially voicing its understandable moral predisposition to protect the health of potential patients, rather than watch them injure one another in competition. I put the point to Dr Curran that he and his organisation were taking a moral position in the matter, rather than basing their view on any statistical review of a wide range of high risk sports.

'I think that all positions ultimately have a moral element in them,' Dr Curran fired back, 'I think it would be unfair, or judgemental to say that the BMA was taking a moral stance in this, as you seem to be implying. Sports that you mention such as rock climbing and all that stuff, I've actually done one or two rock climbs. Rock climbing, when done appropriately and professionally, is not a risky sport in that you are, if you are sensible, protecting and defending yourself against injury. I'm also a judo player – and judo is a physically robust sport, but it is not one where people are fully setting out to cause harm to other people. That cannot be said of either boxing or cage fighting.'

As a professional fighter, Rosi Sexton holds a very different view to that taken by the BMA. 'You're right when you say that it's a moral distinction, it's not a medical distinction and I don't think that medical practitioners are in a privileged position when it comes to making moral judgements, if you see what I mean. The thing is, in real terms, in concrete terms, what is the difference? You know that so many rugby players a year are going to get their necks broken, you know that. It might vary a little bit, but over a five year period, realistically - a certain number - it's going to happen. The same thing with cycling, over a certain period you're going to get roughly so many injuries. You might change bits to improve safety or whatever, but it's going to happen and I think from a medical point of view that's no different than if you have got someone that is intending to do damage.'

Offering a different slant on Dr Curran's insistence that rock climbing is safe when taking the appropriate steps to avoid sustaining injury, Sexton was adamant that a fighters' ability to defend themselves in the cage is a critical and often over-looked point in the safety debate. 'The flipside of having someone that is intending to damage you is that you are intending to keep yourself from being damaged. In rugby for example, if someone gets damaged, that's kind of beside the point. If I happen to get my leg broken while trying to score a try, well that's very sad, but that doesn't lose the team the match.'

'In mixed martial arts it does,' she continued, 'that's the whole point, to stop yourself from being damaged while you're trying to win the fight. I think that because of that in a way, paradoxically, makes it safer in some respect because people put a higher premium on their personal safety. We are developing techniques and studying techniques and training and that's all part of it. You learn defence as part of boxing, if getting knocked out didn't really matter, then fighters would be a lot more cavalier about leaving their hands down; but the fact that someone is intending to do you damage and the whole point of the fight is to not let that happen, that really makes people focus on keeping themselves safe. That at least compensates for the fact that somebody is trying to injure you. But really, I think that the intention thing is a bit of a red herring. Unless you can show that it makes the injuries more serious or more likely, I don't think that it really matters.

'I did a review of a paper by an academic in the states who was interested in the whole head injuries side of things and he was doing a pilot study about the frequencies of concussions in mixed martial arts and boxing. I had quite a lot of contact with him and it turned out that he was actually quite a big fan of contact sports and he was just concerned about the safety aspects. I certainly welcome moves to look at the safety side of things and to see what can reasonably be done to improve that, but I think that with any combat sport, to keep it real, you have to keep the head shots in. Once you take the head shots out it becomes something completely different. It would still be a valid sport, but you are not doing the same thing. I think that's what keeps you honest as it were, if you are fighting', she added, in reference to the fact that unrealistic fighting techniques are exposed very quickly when headshots are permitted in competition.

'I wouldn't say the sport was completely safe' Sexton clarified, 'I would say that moves to increase safety, having doctors present at events, doing medical checks, things like that, I think that is becoming more and more routine now and I think that's a great thing, that is the way forward with regards to the sport and again if fighters go in there with their eyes open and you know what could happen and you have to take that risk.'

In conclusion, Dr Curran echoed the importance of mma fighters educating themselves on the risks involved in their sport, as he offered his advice to any potential participants in the sport. 'As a judo player, I have actually trained with people who cage fight and find them extremely nice, highly skilled and very professional people and they are making their own conscious choices to expose themselves to the risks that they are exposing themselves to. I suppose what I would say is, for goodness sake, read up around the injury you might be causing yourself, particularly to the brain and then if you are going to make the choice, at least do it from an intelligent stand point.'

CHAPTER TWO
WANTED: PROFESSIONAL FIGHTERS

'I was competing and working at the same time and the stress of my work leant me a bit more towards mixed martial arts. I got to a certain age and thought; you only regret the things you haven't done.'
- Mustapha al Turk

Fighting for a living is an unusual job; the role is not advertised, there are no application forms to fill in and your caged interview takes place in front of a room full of screaming fans. Your application can be denied on the basis that you have been injured or knocked unconscious; and you may find that, without notice, your ambition to fulfil the role evaporates under a relentless barrage of punches. Without doubt, a career in the sport of mixed martial arts is an unusually tough path to tread.

To the uninitiated, making a conscious decision to set foot in the cage and receive payment for fighting is the move of a barbarian, determined to take out his primeval aggression on another equally angry, confrontational individual. This perception, however, is simplistic and inappropriate, considering the numerous avenues through which fighters discover their flare for competition and their inner desire to put themselves through the toughest test imaginable.

Traditional Martial Arts

After the mauling that traditional disciplines received in the early Ultimate fighting championships, traditional martial arts are often viewed by online critics as being backwards or impractical in comparison to the new and fashionable discipline of mma. However, these naysayers forget that traditional martial arts have been helping people to defend themselves effectively for thousands of years, and as such must offer some useful techniques to the modern fighter.

Top traditional martial artists such as karate fighter, Lyoto Machida and former San Shou competitor, Cung Le have demonstrated precise striking and delicate footwork in abundance, proving beyond question that the doubters have missed something if they are content to write off the traditional world in its entirety.

A prime example of a traditional martial artist bringing a life time of experience to the cage with him is UFC fighter, Dan Hardy who began training in Tae Kwon Do at a very early age. 'I was six years old when I had my first class. I started off training once a week and that soon became twice and then three or four times a week.' It got to the point where Tae Kwon Do on its own was not enough for the Nottingham youngster, 'I had to start mixing in different styles of Kung Fu and boxing and things like that. I've cross trained from quite and early age, just because, you know, I needed more time in the gym, I needed more time training.'

Many young athletes who show promise at an early age lose interest in their training when they hit their teenage years, deciding that a life of dedication is not for them and they instead discover the irresistible temptation to slip on a hooded top and begin terrorizing their local neighbourhood. For Hardy, however, training martial arts has always been central to his existence. 'I've trained all the way through, I've never really had any time off, I've never taken a full break from martial arts, it's always been in my life.

'When I first started Tae Kwon Do, I started at a club with three instructors. One of the instructors didn't get on with my mum and there was a lot of conflict there and he really didn't make it very enjoyable for me. The only reason I was training regularly for those couple of years was because I really didn't want to let my parents down', he said earnestly. 'They were really trying to help me out and get me into something that I would enjoy. I was really into the Ninja Turtles,' Hardy explained, 'so I was running around, kicking things, my dad made me some nunchaku, so martial arts was where I needed to be.'

After a rough start, Hardy began training with a new instructor and his lifelong passion for martial arts began to take shape. 'My parents didn't realise that I wasn't enjoying it as much as I could at first, but I just wanted to keep them happy and for them to be proud of me. After a couple of years, when I started to get a bit better, I was moved into the group with the other instructor, a guy called Mick Rowley. He's great, we're still good friends now.'

Hardy trained with Mick for near on 11 years, earning his black belt and several British Championships under Rowley's tuition. 'That was when I really started to enjoy it, when I moved to a new instructor, then my granddad starting going, so then I would go because my granddad started going, so he was also really quite influential in the beginning of my martial arts career.'

After scoring some notable successes on the domestic Tae Kwon Do circuit, Hardy took an incredibly brave step into the unknown as he made his way to train with some of the worlds' most dedicated, if not slightly imbalanced martial artists, the infamous Shoalin monks. 'Back in 2002 I think it was, I went to the Shoalin temple, up in the North of China. I spent two months training with the Monks. It was kind of crazy.'

Thousands of miles from his Nottingham home, Hardy was put through a torturous regime, but insists that the trip helped to forge his dedication to martial arts competition. 'To be honest, the main thing I learnt was mental discipline and strength. It was training between 10 and 12 hours a day, starting at 5 o'clock in the morning. I really was pushed to my limits. The main thing that I learnt out of that was that I wanted to compete, I wanted to do more. I wanted to follow the competitive side of martial arts as opposed to the traditional side, with weapons and the forms. Now, the mental strength and discipline is what gets me through the day – it keeps me focussed and keeps me training hard.'

The point at which professional fighters discover that they have found their calling in life varies greatly between individual pugilists, in the case of 'The Outlaw' his move to the paid ranks came as a natural progression. 'When I got back from China, I started to compete in amateur mixed martial arts tournaments and from that point, I realised that I could make a living out of doing what I wanted to do. I always dedicated all my time to martial arts anyway, so it really wasn't anything different for me and it just slowly progressed. Now I'm in a position where I don't have to work and I can just train and compete. It was just something which presented itself as I followed my dreams of training martial arts full time, it made itself available to me. I was really lucky.'

Considering himself fortunate for the opportunities he has received, Hardy credits his traditional background for giving him the balance of technical skills that he demonstrates in the cage. 'You can see fighters that are doing well, but they are the guys that started training and competing in martial arts later on in life, maybe since 14 or 15 and they are not quite as sharp, or as clean technically. I think that from the traditional martial arts I've got the technical sharpness, you could say. I think you can tell when people have been training since they were very young because things seem a lot more natural to them, things flow a lot better, their footwork is usually better and they don't tend to get hit a lot.

'That's what I find.' Hardy concluded, 'I had two fights, two weeks apart a couple of months ago and really didn't get hit hardly at all. I probably took about five or six shots between both of the fights. Tae Kwon Do and the other martial arts have given me the speed and the reaction time to get in and out and not take as many shots, which is going to be better for me in the long run as well. I definitely think that traditional martial arts have got some benefit; I just think that you have to be quite selective about what you take from them.'

Sportsmen in Stressful Jobs

London Shootfighter, Francis Heagney is a stock broker by profession and probably the only fighter in the sport who consistently wears a pinstripe suit to pre-fight press conferences. Like his well to do colleges, he is well spoken, friendly and articulate; however, whilst they might relax after work in their local wine bar, Heagney is on his way to the gym. 'I've kind of always had a stressful job,' he began, 'I've worked in finance since I left college. Training is definitely one way of unwinding; I never ever see the television. People talk about what's on television, I never ever see it.'

Dismissing the preconception that mma is a strange activity for such a high-powered professional to engage in, Heagney explained he had always been interested in rougher sports, but that he discovered mma by chance. 'I was always strong as a kid, I was always a lot stronger than my friends, so I guess I went to sports that I could use my strength in more. But, to be honest, finding mma was more accidental than anything else. When I was a kid, I boxed for 3 or 4 years, so I was a boxer originally because I had two left feet for playing Gaelic. I wasn't really any good at that so I stuck with the boxing. When I went to college, I wanted to do something, so I ended up playing for the rugby team.'

Francis played rugby for 12 years, but after this enjoyable run in a sport dominated by men twice his size, his luck ran out. 'I got a knee injury,' Heagney explained, 'so I couldn't really run any more. I had to find something I could do where I didn't have to run a lot, so I went to the gym. It was like an ordinary Fitness First in Ireland and I basically got so bored of going to there.'

Knowing with full certainty that weight training and circuits were not enough to satisfy his craving for competition, Heagney jumped at the chance to take up martial arts. 'This Australian guy came into the gym and he was doing classes in Thai boxing and I thought I'd give that a shot. I didn't know if there were any clubs or anything around, but I thought that would be a bit more entertaining than sitting there doing your reps in the gym, which is very boring after a while, so I went to his class.'

Heagney instantly caught the bug for training and spent six months picking up the basics of Thai boxing at the club. However, as soon as his interest began to pique, the instructor decided to move back to Australia - leaving a disappointed Heagney assessing his training options. 'I thought, as we had a nice bunch of lads together, why don't I try and keep the class going, see if people are interested in staying with one of the lads taking the classes because there were quite a few Eastern Europeans who were very good Thai boxers. One of them had taught before, so we had planned for him to take over the class, but the rent was a bit much.'

As it turned out, this premature ending to his pure Thai boxing training was a blessing in disguise, as bigger and better things were looming around the corner, in the shape of the Straight Blast Gym, run by internationally recognised grappling wizard, John Kavanagh. 'I heard about someone else called "SBG", so I met the guy and had a chat. He told me to come to the class he was running in this tiny room.'

Not the sort of person to turn down an opportunity, Francis went along, casting his initially sceptical eye over the grappling class. 'I took my stuff and came at the end of the class and had a look at what they were doing, it looked like they were just rolling around, it didn't look very interesting but the guy who was teaching the kickboxing, he said, "If one of those guys gets on top of you, you wouldn't believe this, but it would be impossible to get him off." I didn't believe him, so I went up and I had a look and I thought that might be interesting enough. John said, "Why don't you come back on Thursday and do some training?"'

That's a good question, Heagney thought, and with nothing to lose, he made his way back to the gym that very Thursday. 'From never doing it before, to just doing a couple of classes, it really got me going. It's like doing a 100 metre sprint when you've never grappled before, complete energy exertion; your arms just turn into rubber. It's like no work out you could ever do at the gym. Your muscles just get fully lactic; you know what it's like…'

Quickly getting over the initial, exhausting shock of grappling training, Heagney soon discovered that he had some handy, transferable skills from his Rugby playing days. 'Playing rugby absolutely, definitely helped me. From the stand up to the wrestling, to the getting people down, it definitely helped. It gives you great core strength. To be able to handle a body as such, in the rugby, you were doing a lot of tackling and stuff.'

Heagney also drew on his experiences as a young boxer in Ireland as he began to take his training more seriously. 'My coach from when I was a kid, boxing, he said to me "You're training now as a kid, you'll never lose that focus" because, to train properly for boxing, you have to have something within yourself to do that. Nobody is there to tell you to do your three rounds every single night, nobodies there to check you've done it or what time you do it at. You only get out of it, really, what you put into it. I kind of applied that to rugby as well and to jiu-jitsu.'

At the beginning of his alternative career in the cage, Heagney remained tight-lipped about his sporting preferences, but he insists that as long as he continues to set high standards in the workplace, he is unlikely to be met with any opposition from his superiors. 'Well, they are used to it now, I guess. They are happy enough with the work I'm putting out, so they are not really getting on my case. If I was coming in late, or taking time off to do this, that and the other, there would be a problem, but it doesn't restrict me.

'There are very few people in my business who really know what it is,' he continued, 'I generally just say, if I've got a muscle injury, that I've been doing jiu-jitsu and if I have a cut injury, I say I've been doing kickboxing. I kind of don't go into the details. My boss disapproves, but he's more concerned for my safety than anything. We get on quite well; it's kind of like that if you know what I mean.'

With a caring boss who openly has concerns for his safety, Heagney nonetheless remains quite clear that he is aware of the risks involved and is happy to roll the dice. 'The thing is, I don't see it as the same risk as other people do. Someone's said before that when you have a job, you are dealing in risk every day, measured amounts of risk. You become accustomed to living with risk, so my idea of something risky would be different to yours, if you know what I mean. If you are getting too many bangs to the head, of course, that's dangerous, but too much of anything is dangerous.'

Another London Shootfighter with a white collar, professional background is Mustapha al Turk, a fighter who used to earn his living in the glitzy world of pharmaceutical sales. 'My main sort of areas were allergy, cardiology, asthma. I was given a portfolio of products and I just used to have to go round to a geographical area and used to have to sell them to GPs and consultants. I used to have to do a lot of entertaining in the evenings, entertaining on the weekends, I was given quite a large budget to try and convince people to purchase my products – thank God, I don't do that anymore!'

Is there no sense in which the heavyweight terror misses his former profession? 'No. Not at all' al Turk replied as quick as a flash, 'Especially the politics, but wherever you go there are going to be politics. There's stresses wherever you go – there's politics wherever you go – but the paperwork, I used to hate paperwork, you know, I'd come back from training and I'd have a mountain of work to do. I'd be knackered and I'd still have to get through it, especially when it came to expenses. I don't miss it at all, no!'

Following a couple of years in which al Turk juggled his full work life with a passion for grappling and mixed martial arts, the talented grappler had an epiphany which would change his life forever. 'I was competing and working at the same time and the stress of my work leant me a bit more towards mixed martial arts. I got to a certain age and thought, you only regret the things you haven't done. I wasn't getting anywhere at work, things were going wrong and I just leant more towards mixed martial arts and decided to pursue the sport full time.'

The Entertainer

Man of many nicknames, Jason 'Bad Ass' Barrett is one of those people born to be on stage; indeed, 'The Punching Preacher' is as much at home in the pulpit as he is treading the boards. Though his razzmatazz style of pre-fight trash talking is not to everyone's taste, in stark contrast to mainstream entertainers, 'Super-J' has proven on more than one occasion that he is also prepared to step up and gamble his teeth for the enjoyment of the paying crowd.

Adding a romantic twist to the tale, Barrett's infatuation with mma began on his honeymoon in 1996 when he saw a clip of Ken Shamrock in the Ultimate Fighting Championship. 'I remember thinking, "Oh my God; that is the nuts." The whole of my honeymoon, I spent going in and out of these shops, "I'm looking for this programme, it's called the Ultimate Fighting Challenge." I managed to get number one and number two, I remember bringing them back to the UK and all my friends would come round my house and we'd watch them, we loved Ken Shamrock and one of my friends started getting videos from Brazil."

As a group of young men who had grown up watching professional wrestling on television, the parallels between sports entertainment and this new phenomenon were irresistible. "What we did was we started up our own little federation, we used to go up the park,' Barrett said, cracking up with laughter, 'We used to put money in and basically, we used to challenge each other. We used to fight and we used to go for it, we used to be trying armbars, kneebars, punching – but there was no punching to the face, everything else was allowed.'

Hyping themselves up for these light-hearted, but incredibly dangerous bouts, the group of friends began practising the art of smack talking in painstakingly choreographed interviews. 'Me and my mate Michael, we used to film them. We used to get our camcorders, we used to do interviews, sitting on the bonnets of our cars and we used to talk in these American accents. Looking back on it, I'm cringing now!' Barrett added with another bout of hysterical giggling.

The novelty soon wore off, however, when Jason suffered a nasty knee injury, 'A friend of mine put me in like a kneebar or something and even now, to this day, in winter it gives me a bit of trouble, I can't squat too heavy either because he fucked up my knee, which is when you realise that you're in the park at the end of the day.'

Time passed, but 'The Brockley Bomber' always harboured a hankering for competition and in an ironic turn of events, the same friend who injured Jason's knee in the park brawl put him in contact with Dave O'Donnell, head trainer of the Elite Fighting System in South London. 'I went down there and basically blagged my way into Cage Rage.' Barrett admitted, 'They liked my stand up, my big mouth and all the rest of it. My debut was right on the big stage, it was at Wembley against Dave Lee, who at the time was 6-1 and it was my first fight ever, but again I've always got this feeling like I can beat up everyone. I was always pretty handy, so I just thought, "Yeah, I'll go in there and beat him up." It was my first fight and I got fucked on.'

Since that lopsided submission loss, Barrett has returned with some success; however, by his own admission, he is not the most skilful fighter to ever step into competition. 'I always liked the entertainment side of it, sport is also entertainment. People buy into a personality, they buy into a character. So when I give it all of that "Bad Ass" and give it all that in the interviews, it's all just a façade but it adds to the entertainment. Love me or hate me, it adds to entertainment. You get known, I get stopped all the time in the street, shopping or something and you get the odd person that says "Hang on, you're Bad Arse, in't ya?" and have a laugh with you, because of that entertainment factor.

'One thing I used to love about Bad Boy Bailey' he continued, 'and why I really wanted to fight him, was because I know he's also an entertainer, not the best fighter in the world, neither am I, but we'll get in there, we'll have it and we'll bring that entertainment factor. There's going to be a load of girls with 'Bad Boy' written on the T-shirt.'

In what turned out to be an underwhelming clash Barrett picked up a disappointing disqualification loss for pulling his opponent's long dreadlocks; however, he remains convinced that a bit of pre-fight hype and cage-side banter can mean the difference to the fans' enjoyment of the event. 'Our promo apparently still gets downloaded the most off of the Cage Rage website. I was on there today; people look at it and leave their little comments. I always like to jump on the microphone. I always like to have a little chat with the fans. I always like to have a chat with my opponent or say something funny, do something. People think that sports personalities in general can be a bit dull, they can get a bit boring, that's why I think that the WWE does so well is because people buy into the whole character of it, like a male soap opera, you buy into it.'

The Doorman

Until the relatively recent introduction of stiff new registration laws in the UK, Doormen or 'bouncers', have suffered from an alarmingly bad reputation for dishing out unnecessary violence. Though this reputation was undoubtedly earned for the many by the few bad apples in the profession, Neil 'Goliath' Grove was quick to point out at the start of the interview that he is nothing like the traditional, misconstrued image of a doorman. Going on to explain his involvement in mma through his professional life on the door, Grove began, 'It's not because I'm someone who likes fighting or is a street brawler or anything like that, even when I was working on the door I was known as someone who never did fight.'

South African by birth, Grove worked in a bar in his native land before making his way to the UK in 1996. Finding himself in London and in dire need of employment, Grove accepted a job at a tough Irish bar in South London and turned up for his first shift on New Years Eve. 'I got there and I was all dressed up, ready to work in the bar and the manager said, "No, you'll be standing on the door."

'I said to him, "What? Are you serving drinks on the door?"'

'"No, you'll be doorman", he said to me'

Grove appeared slightly taken aback by this totally unexpected revelation, as he was a barman by trade and had never worked the doors. However, after hearing more about this new possible career move, he quickly changed his tune. 'I find out later on in the evening from another barman that what they got paid was £25 a shift and, on the door, it was £75 a shift – so there was absolutely no way I was going to work in the bar!' he said with a laugh.

However, the South African giant soon discovered that working the door in such a rough establishment was no joke. 'Being an Irish nightclub, there was a fight every Thursday, every Friday, every Saturday and every Sunday and the only way you could get in the clique of the doormen was to get stuck in.'

A peaceful man by nature, Grove was initially quite reluctant to get involved; though, as he became more comfortable with his environment, the rougher aspects of the job started to become second nature. After fulfilling his duties on a particularly physical night, 'Goliath' found himself in a spot of bother with his employers. 'I got stuck into a massive brawl, if you want to call it that. There was two of us against about 30 and we sort of knocked people out. They actually ended up turning the music off and putting the lights on to calm everybody down and if it wasn't for a friend of mine, Dave, who used to train with my sensei, Gavin Mulholland, I could have lost my job, but he said, "Instead of sacking them, why don't you introduce them to Gavin Mulholland and teach them how to channel their aggression?"'

Thankfully for Grove, the nightclub management took a lenient view and encouraged him to pursue his martial arts training with Mulholland. 'Doing the Karate stuff sort of taught me, rather than how to punch people and knock them out, to control and restrain, if you want to call it that. When you have the ability, with someone swinging at you to get out of the way and make a fool out of them, I suppose there's more to it than knocking them out.

'It sort of calmed me down.' Grove said with a smile, 'By the time I reached my blue belt, I was working in a place called "The Backpacker", and I was head doorman there, just purely because I had the confidence in protecting myself and I suppose it shows when you're standing on the door and I didn't have to fight – there were still fights, but it came a lot less.'

Grove met his wife in 2001 and moved to Essex, leaving the door in London to begin working in the local nightclubs. 'Living in Essex, Billericay, I found that the guys were a little bit harder than they were in London – I say harder, they just liked to fight! But I can honestly tell you that since I started doing the martial arts, I've got into less and less fights, basically because you could immobilise someone without getting yourself into more trouble. Even if there's four or five of them, it just became easier not to fight.'

Six short months after leaving door work behind in 2006, Grove became frustrated. 'I just felt there was something lacking, I didn't know what I was capable of and obviously, being such a big guy, a lot of the guys are smaller than me in the dojo and there's no real way of applying your skills on the smaller guys because you'll end up hurting someone. There was no way now of showing my ability; the stuff Gavin had been teaching me, there was no way of applying it. So I asked him,

'"Would you mind if I fight in the cage fights?"

'He said, "It would be great!"

'I suppose a lot of traditional martial arts teachers wouldn't condone fighting, it's all about protecting yourself in self-defence and all that, but because he had done some of that sort of fighting himself when he was much younger, he said to me, "Why don't you try it?" and within two months, Grove stepped into the cage for the first time.

In what was a daunting experience for the Grove, he remembered his mma debut against man mountain, Anthony Akore. 'I'd got Gavin and Lee in my corner and I was fighting this guy two pounds heavier than me, a massive, massive black guy. It was difficult getting over the fear of entering the cage… because when you're working on the door, you've got another five or six men to back you up in case things go wrong. Like a game of Rugby, you know, you've got 14 guys behind you to help you if things go wrong – it's a completely different kettle of fish when you step into the cage and I loved it! I actually loved the idea of stepping in there and testing myself.' Grove exploded to a fine start in his pro career as he scored a devastating knock out win over Pancrase London fighter only seconds into the contest.

CHAPTER THREE
MMA Is For Girls

'I'm a girl, I'm not any more physically capable than you, so if you want to do it you should just go ahead and do it and just give it a try.'
- Aisling 'Ais the Bash' Daly

On the whole, society tends to cast quite a disapproving eye on the activity of fighting; however, even amongst the most ardent pacifists, there is at least an understanding that confident young men have the capacity, or even, the inclination to vie for supremacy over one another in a physical exchange.

However, a vast accumulation of anecdotal evidence suggests that large swathes of the population are opposed to the idea of women taking part in combative sports for varying reasons, often finding it very hard to understand what would drive a woman into the cage to fight under limited rules. However, the fact of the matter is; female mma is gaining in exposure and following.

In the not so dim and distant past, the female side of the sport was consistently sidelined in favour of marquee match ups between established male fighters; however, as female mma creeps noticeably onto the radar of mainstream press, the world of opportunities for female combatants is ever-expanding. One fighter making the most of these new openings is rising star from Grimnagh in Ireland; Aisling Daly.

Starting out

Known as 'Ais the Bash' (pronounced, 'Ash') for over ten years, the plucky Irish fighter began training karate at an early age of ten, but she, like compatriot Francis Heagney, soon found herself on the mat, studying jiu-jitsu at the Straight Blast Gym under the watchful eye of John Kavanagh. 'I was a kid when I first started training and it was for fun and something to do, and when I started doing jiu-jitsu I just really, really enjoyed it. I was pretty much the only girl, I didn't really mind though because the guys I train with are actually really cool, it's not really a macho club, so I didn't have any problems when I started off. My coach was great when I needed help, if I wasn't getting something that the other guys were, he was really good. We got on grand in training; I felt like I fit in.'

The pink-haired punching machine quickly pushed her way up the jiu-jitsu hierarchy, contorting numerous male training partners along the way as she picked up her blue belt from SBG head instructor, Matt Thornton in 2006, before most recently earning a purple belt in early 2008. 'When I started competing I saw that I could be quite good at it, that's when I started thinking there could be a future in it. I'm quite a competitive person anyway, so I like the idea of pushing myself and trying to be the best and that kind of thing.'

As a lady competing in a small and often misunderstood fight sport, sifting through the feedback she receives in relation to her in-cage activities doesn't hold any particular problems for the youngster. 'The odd time, I get people who make the odd stupid comments, but it not actually to do with being female, it's more to do with mma in general, about it being brutal, or barbaric, having no rules and stuff like that. You get plenty of stereotypical comments from people - because you're female fighter, you must be very butch or you must be very masculine. But most of the time they are very surprised to see that I am a fighter, I don't look like the typical image of what they imagine a female fighter to look like. I'm very petite; it doesn't look like it should be something that I'm doing.'

Another lady in the world's fastest growing fight sport is the number one female fighter in the UK, the multi-talented, Rosi Sexton. 'When I started mma I wanted to fight and that was my reason for doing mma', she explained, having practised a number of traditional martial arts and become frustrated by not actually fighting. 'You talk about fighting a lot and you practise techniques, but whether I could actually fight, I had no idea. I'd never been in a fight and realistically, it was unlikely that I was going to get in a fight, unless I actually went out looking for trouble which seems a bit pointless when I got into martial arts because I wanted to learn how to defend myself. I think that's something you do see a lot in martial arts actually, certainly more so before mma came along. Originally, I just wanted a couple of fights to prove to myself that I could and then I got a bug for it and then I wanted to see how good I could be.'

Sport for the intelligent

Both Daly and Sexton have a deep inner determination to be the best that they can be in life: Daly cut short her studies to take up full time training, whilst Sexton chose to continue with her studies, attaining two degrees, Rosi feels that coming from an academic background has had only a positive impact on her martial arts endeavours. 'The thing I think a lot of people don't realise when they first look at mixed martial arts, is that really it is an intelligent person's sport. Contrary to the image it has some times, it's undoubtedly the most technical sport in the world. When you look at all of the individual components, you've got boxing, you've got kickboxing, you've got wrestling, you've got Brazilian jiu-jitsu; combining those elements, and each of those on it's own is a life time's study.

'Then you've got to combine all of those', she continued, 'and have the conditioning and the endurance, the strength, the mental toughness and the whole psychological game which is a big part of it, it's just a massive area of study. However deeply you go into it, there's always more to learn. I don't see myself as an academic so much as I see myself as someone who is interested in learning. I've got a bug for learning new stuff and mma is a good sport for that because there are always opportunities to be developing one area or another. It's something you could spend a lifetime doing and still have more to discover.'

Fighting and motherhood

This voyage of discovery took Sexton on a turn into uncharted territory as she continued to train throughout her pregnancy, even racking up numerous Olympic lifts as part of her hectic schedule. Working alongside pioneering mma trainer, Karl Tanswell, Rosi pushed her body harder than many athletes would dare. 'It's almost indoctrinated, "Ah, you're pregnant, you've got to look after yourself, be very gentle with yourself and not do anything strenuous." I think if you look into it and you look into the science behind it, there's a huge myth there and there's a lot of evidence that female athletes can train quite hard while they're pregnant and that can be massively beneficial for the health of both mother and the baby, psychologically and physically.

'Speaking to the midwives while I was pregnant, what they told me was that it was actually the women who were inactive tended to have more problems, the ones that sit around and don't do anything for whatever reasons. Whether it be because they are worried they might do themselves some harm if they go out and exercise and I think that's not the case.'

Pointing out that it would not be sensible for someone who had never previously done any exercise and suddenly starts doing quite a significant amount while pregnant, Sexton is convinced that it is actually more damaging to stop training, 'It's a lot worse for you to suddenly stop exercising if you're used to it. I think the healthy thing to do is just carry on and make sensible adaptations because there are some things that you do have to change during pregnancy. Obviously, anything with impact is a big no-no; anything where you might get punched in the stomach or anything like that, or falls, are something to look out for.

'In terms of actual exercise,', she continued, 'I had a personal trainer that I was working with while I was pregnant and he had worked with a few pregnant athletes before and so he knew what was doing, he worked me harder than I was expecting! I felt great for it, I know I felt better exercising than if I hadn't done that. [My son,] Luis has been very healthy and I'm convinced that it was healthy for me to do that.'

By continuing to compete, stepping back into the cage only a few months after the birth of her son, Sexton is challenging another of societal assumption - that the roles of mother and fighter are distinct. Asked if she experiences any difficulty in reconciling these traditionally separate roles, the well-educated Cage Warriors female champion gave a typically cerebral answer.

'I think the dilemmas I have are very similar to those that any working mum might have, whatever job you have to do. I think for most people it's true that there's some element of juggling involved. You've got to balance your work life and your home life and everything that goes along with that. Being a fighter, it's a different side to me, certainly, but I don't think that it's in conflict with the side that's loving and caring and puts Luis to bed at night; it's all me. We've all got different aspects to us, to our personalities, and I think one of the greatest things about the modern era is being able to express more than one of those aspects, being able to express lots of different parts of ourselves; by being able to fight, and be a mum, and be a student and an osteopath and whatever...

'I think that's a great opportunity and that's something that a lot of people in a lot of stages in history didn't have because they were stuck into a role where you have to do this, or have to do that. There wasn't that flexibility to explore different sides of themselves, I think that's something that we have and I think that's something that should be valued.'

Female MMA in the news

In the days preceding our conversation, Sexton was interviewed by the Manchester Evening News which syndicated the story out to the national press, bringing hitherto unheard of exposure to female mma. 'It was pretty good on the whole', she said, referring to the story which even surfaced in New Zealand's press, 'There wasn't much which made me cringe, which is progress. Either I'm getting better at doing interviews, or I'm getting better at being humiliated. There's always something a bit cringe worthy about it. It actually seems pretty ok this time, it's not how I would have written it, but it's full mainstream press, about mma, so I think on the whole, there's not much I can complain about!'

Asked whether this new interest from the main stream press serves as an indication that female mma has achieved acceptance, Sexton saw the good news in more general terms. 'I think that maybe it's a sign that mma on the whole is becoming more accepted and more mainstream. I think people know a lot more about it now than they did a few years ago. You don't get quite so many of the "Oh, is it really no-holds-barred?", "How many people have you killed in the ring?" kind of questions - I've never been asked that question,' she pointed out with a laugh, 'just to be clear, nobody has actually asked that!

'I think most people have seen something or know of the UFC, they are aware of "cage fighting", and it's becoming much more something that people are into, rather than looking disapprovingly at it, which is something that I think we had before, something for middle England to get up-in-arms about. But, I think there's a lot more genuine interest in it and what it actually involves. My experience is that female mma, over here anyway, has been pretty well accepted from the start, at least in principle.'

That is not to say that female mma has entirely eluded the spotlight of mindless publicity; usually a reputable and informative newspaper, 'The Daily Sport' offered its preview in the run up to Aisling Daly's fight with Aysen Berik - sister of UK journeyman, Sami Berik. In their less than charming piece, the paper put forward five reasons 'why girl fights are sexy'; also asking, 'What red-blooded British bloke wouldn't want to see two fit, athletic birds going at it in a cage?'

Daly was surprised to hear that she had made her debut appearance in the newspaper, 'I didn't see that. I don't actually remember doing an interview with them. I don't know how they actually got hold of it. I don't find stuff like that particularly good, if they are giving the wrong impression of the sport. I don't think we should be used for entertainment objects like we are. We are technical fighters; we are professional in proportion to the guys who fight, so I don't think that angle was the best one to take.'

Disappointed by the tone of the coverage, Aisling continued, 'Maybe with Cage Rage and all that they were wanting to sell tickets and thought that taking that angle would probably sell a few more tickets, thinking guys would be interested in that sort of thing, but it wouldn't be my approach. I'd like to be seen as an athlete rather than as some kind of object to be viewed.' At Cage Rage 25, however, Daly put on the showing of an athlete, rather than the performance of an entertainer as she took Berik to the ground, bashing her over-matched opponent to a referee stoppage in the first round.

The ramblings of a sex-obsessed tabloid aside, female mma has also recently seen a surge of mainstream interest in no small part due to the failed weight-cutter and talented Thai boxer, Gina Carano. No-one doubts the American has skills, but being the beautiful lady that she is, her images do tend to pop up rather more than those of other female fighters; in fact Carano once caused a mild stir of controversy by posing for a series of racy publicity shots. There is no doubt that the 'tits-get-hits' web marketing strategy does much to raise the profile of female mma with teenage lads, but does this portrayal of the sport have any kind of damaging effect?

'I'm not sure it's damaging exactly.' Sexton replied thoughtfully, 'It's not the way I'd like to see it promoted in an ideal world, but at the same time, from a promoter's point of view, it's no good doing something, promoting it the way you want to see it, if nobody is going to watch it. I think a lot of fighters look at it and say, "Oh, we don't want it to be seen that way, we want it to be seen as a sport", but then at the same time, we want to get paid for what we do and in order to get paid, you've got to have people who are going to watch it. So promoters have to sell it somehow and when you've got something which is basically a niche sport which nobody really knows about, you have to find some way of getting that interest.

'As far as the women angle goes, if you look at all women's sports, like it or not, female athletes are marketed on their image' she said, choosing her words very carefully, 'I don't think that necessarily has to be particularly explicit, but to a degree, if you look at a sport like mma, I mean all of the fighters are marketed on their image, whatever that might be. The guys are marketed on being tough and manly and you've got fighters like Gina who are marketed on being good looking women. As far as that goes, I don't necessarily think there's a problem with that, I think the problem comes when you've got women who are good fighters who are being missed or passed over in favour of somebody who is maybe worthy of less recognition, but is better looking. Then, that's a problem. I don't have a solution to that; I can certainly see why promoters do what they do, but if it is going to be a legitimate sport you have to base your rankings on talent rather than looks. I mean, the image has to be secondary to actual fighting ability.

'Gina is not particularly a good example,' Sexton clarified, 'she is undoubtedly a talented fighter. Whatever else you say about her, she's got skills. I think if you look at Kim Couture for example, in terms of somebody who has had a lot of publicity, when they have relatively little experience, certainly.'

Although Carano is without doubt the most talked about female fighter on the planet, according to Daly, the current EliteXC fighter has a path ahead of her before she becomes a figurehead for the sport. 'The fact that she's a pretty girl, it does get a bit more exposure, and it's getting the sport into the mainstream but I'd rather people didn't focus just on that. A lot of the time, people talk about her in terms of how well she looks, not in terms of how good a fighter she is. She is a very good fighter, she has some awesome Muay Thai skills, but I don't think she's quite up there as the face of women's mma. I don't quite think she's earned the title yet, there's plenty more female fighters out there like Tara LaRosa, Rosi Sexton, anybody like that who would be up higher in my estimation', Daly said, paying her SBG colleague a sincere compliment.

'I wouldn't put it down to her, it's not her fault, she has a company around her, she's working for and they tell her what to do and they look after her, make her fights and stuff like that that. She's just doing what she's told to keep her job, so I don't think it's her fault. She's looking after her own career at the end of the day, but I think in the long term, that's probably not going to be the best for the sport, I think maybe they need to branching out, which they are doing, obviously, now. I think they are getting more female fighters and they are opening up more divisions, but I don't think that they should focus on Gina as much as they do.'

Whiners and complainers

To what extent the marketing of female mma fighters has influenced the nature of online debate is unclear; however, for Sexton, the fact that female mma is largely dismissed or misunderstood by a large proportion of male online mma fans is more than evident. 'Click on any thread about women's mma and about 30-40% of the people on there will be going… "Oh, I'm not interested in women's mma, don't like it, women shouldn't be fighting, blah, blah, blah." I mean, going back two years and that would have been more like 70-80%, so a section of it has definitely improved recently. I think a lot of that is to do with EliteXC and getting that out there; so whatever else you say about what they've done, I think they've definitely made some progress.'

Sexton explained that, as a dedicated fighter among many ambitious female athletes, it can become frustrating when fans of the male side of the sport can be so scathing of their professional exploits. 'It's irritating; it's the kind of thing that makes you want to bang your head against a brick wall. Realistically, a lot of the criticisms are coming from people who haven't really seen much female mma and what they have seen, they've gone into it wanting to confirm their original opinion on it, that it's rubbish and I think a lot of that comes down to a cultural thing.

'If you look at the UFC's demographic for their fan base, a lot of it is basically young males and there's a whole ethos surrounding that where it's seen as being macho and masculine to view women as sex objects and not much else. I think there is this fear, if you like, that if they acknowledge that women may be able to fight, may somehow reflect badly on them, that it would make them less manly by saying that. I think that's the kind of thing you get going on these forums a lot of the time. If you look at it logically, if somebody is not interested in female mma, why would they be clicking on a thread about female mma?' she asked rhetorically.

'If I see a thread abut something I'm not interested in on a forum, I'll just ignore it, I won't go on it; I certainly won't go on it for the purpose of saying I'm not interested in it. That doesn't make any sense at all! – except if you see it as making some kind of macho statement. "Look at me, I'm so manly, I don't want to see women beating each other up." There is something there and I can't quite articulate the logic, maybe that's because the logic is slightly screwy in the first place.' She finished, marvelling at this nonsensical source of male inadequacy.

When people come out with statements to the affect that the cage is simply no place for a woman, Ais the Bash puts this view down to good old fashioned ignorance and holds little hope of converting genuine complainants. 'I'd just say that generally, they haven't seen any women's fights', she said in response. 'If you are referring to people who are fans of male mixed martial arts, but not female, I just show them some women's mma fights to show them how technical the women's fights are. If you are talking about somebody who isn't interested in mma at all it would be really difficult to change their mind. They have obviously developed an opinion over a long period of time so if even showing them fights doesn't help then it's really hard to change their opinions on it. Women fight in wars, women play all sorts of contact sports that men do. We're all supposed to be generally equal, so there's no reason why girls shouldn't be able to get involved in any kind of sports, not to mention mma.'

'I don't understand why people would be interested in boxing, but not like mixed martial arts,' Daly continued, 'they see mixed martial arts as being more brutal and violent stuff than boxing. When you go with the general statistics of boxing versus mma , there have definitely been more head injuries in boxing and deaths than there has been in mixed martial arts, but it's going to take time as mma becomes more mainstream, then female mma is going to start integrating into that. So it's going to take time, I don't see any quick fix to it.'

Accepting that a certain level of ignorance will remain among the uninitiated for some time to come, Daly tries her best to ignore unhelpful comments and focus on the task at hand. 'The way it is, when you're doing something like this, there's always going to be people putting you down, or trying to put you off it or just try to annoy you, kind of thing. So, basically, just don't listen to them, just keep going and don't think about what they are saying, like. If you dwell too much on it, it would probably affect the way that you perform and train and stuff like that. Just surround yourself with a good bunch of people who are supportive of you and it's pretty easy to ignore everybody else who is hating on you.' She added with a twist of jubilant defiance.

As a young, dedicated fighter with a string of impressive wins under her belt and an equally sparkling personality, in time, how would she cope with being a role model for aspiring female fighters?

'I would just keep being me and hope that would be good enough for people. I wouldn't exactly feel that I'm ready to take on the title.' She said, protesting modestly, 'I would definitely feel very proud to get other females into it, by just saying, well, "Look, well if I can do it then you can do it, there shouldn't be any reason why I should be different from you. I'm a girl, I'm not any more physically capable than you, so if you want to do it you should just go ahead and do it and just give it a try."'

CHAPTER FOUR
THE GAS TANK

'It doesn't matter if you are racing a Ferrari, if you run out of gas; you're going to lose to a Volkswagen bug.'
- 'New York Bad Ass' Phil Baroni

The diverse range of combat skills that an mma athlete needs to master in order to compete at the highest levels of the sport is only part of the story. Increasingly, fighters are beginning to realise that, alongside the required techniques drawn from various fighting arts, conditioning is crucial and can often mean the difference between success and failure, elation and concussion.

A fighter who feels assured that he has the gas to engage for up to 25 minutes of competition has a massive psychological advantage and can throw down with reckless abandon in comparison to a less well prepared opponent who might feel the need to hold something in reserve for later in the fight. Having the necessary fight preparation behind you is essential in the modern sport and many top fighters are now employing the services of professional strength and conditioning trainers.

The Professional
Sunny Dholakia is one such professional. A former competitive swimmer and cross-fit competitor, he has attained degrees in both chemistry and sports medicine, whilst also sailing his way through the multi-faceted examinations of the US National Strength and Conditioning Association. Upon completion of his studies, the Londoner began assisting athletes from a range of sports with their training, before recently deciding to focus his career on preparing athletes for mma competition.

'I've worked with rugby players and, more applicable to fighting, I worked as a civilian training instructor with the Royal Marines and Parachute Regiment, guys going for selection, so I handled their circuit training, what we call their short-term anaerobic fitness, fitness over 20 to 30 minutes, which is similar to what the fighters have.'

As a former cross-fit competitor, chin ups, press ups, step ups, treadmill runs are like second nature to the Wembley trainer and these applications are proving useful in the world of mma, 'I put my heart and soul, all my training and my studies, everything is geared towards ultimate fighting.' He said, explaining how he first came into contact with the sport. 'My first guy was Pierre Guillet – through him it just snowballed. Through Pierre I got James Zikic, through James Zikic, I started training Matt Ewin and then Paul Daley. Now we have Brad Pickett on board, we've got Ashleigh Grimshaw on board, this new, sharp kid, Jason Young, he's on board now', he said of the London plasterer who won the Cage Rage British Lightweight title just weeks after the interview took place.

As Sunny explains, however, each of his clients is unique and a different approach is taken with each of them to ensure they reach their maximum potential. 'You've got your introverted fighters like James Zikic, different approaches are taken to try and get them motivated, compared to extroverted fighters like Paul Daley, Pierre. A different method is used to get the most out of them. It doesn't always work, but when it does, it works well. More importantly, the schedules are set you see, six weeks out of a fight they are already really highly motivated, all I have to do is set schedules for them and go down there and supervise the session - especially, the sprint work, the really nauseating work, that's really hard to do on your own.'

When not preparing for a specific contest, most of the fighters maintain very decent standards of fitness by anyone's standards, before seeking the help of a professional several weeks before the fight to get into heavy fight preparations. 'It's basically split into phases of training; you've got your strength phase and what I call your speed-endurance phase. So it involves weight training from four to six reps, heavy weights done way, way out from a fight, eight weeks out of the fight. Then four to six weeks out from the fight I'll start to bring in high repetition speed weight training, circuit training basically. Then we use sledge hammers on tyres, we use powerballs for rotational power, we use hill sprints, things like that. Anaerobic fitness, high repetition close to a fight, low repetition work way out of a fight and then I put in intricate little things like powerballs, med balls and conditioning drills, burst punching sequenced over 20 – 25 minutes to get these guys ready for fights.'

Traditionally, it has always been seen as a fighter's chore to undertake hours of mind-numbing road work in preparation for a fight; but as Sunny explains, this aspect of a fighters training should take place in the off-season and only a very limit part in the eight weeks coming up to an event. 'That basic conditioning is done way, way out of a fight. Two-to-three mile runs should always be maintained as basics, that they know to do. The important thing is short, anaerobic fitness, which is what the sport is all about. So two to three mile runs is what we call your "steady state" training. That should be done, way, way out because without that they can't do the really, really hard circuit training. Maybe they will run once or twice a week [for the earlier part of their training] and then, four weeks down to one week out of a fight, we top up with very intensive circuit training.'

As a professional trainer, I imagined that he would have seen some fairly impressive turnarounds in fitness levels, so I asked him which fighter had made the most progress under his tutelage. 'Good question... they've all come to me pretty damn fit, Jim. Every single one has come to me able to do these tests, but within four weeks of working with them, their speed and endurance levels have been augmented for sure. Believe it or not, they all train pretty damn hard – my guys anyway. The guys I've been coaching have all come to me very, very fit, ready and I've just given them that extra five to ten per cent of fight fitness.'

Pushing fighters to the limit

Going on to reveal a few secrets of his trade, Sunny explained what he referred to as the hardest part of the training - taking his fighters to the 'Red Line'. 'About two weeks to a week out from the fight is the most intensive phase. It is when I pretty much take them close to black out; nausea or black out, whichever gets to them first. Looking in from the outside, it can come across as extreme, but you know what, ultimate fighting is an extreme sport, isn't it? So the conditioning needs to reflect that, so the conditioning is quite extreme. Hence the work I did with the special forces, the Royal Marines and the Paras comes into play, that real, real right to the end of the line training, to the red line as we call it.

'It's a very big challenge', he said of this unforgiving practise, 'You can't imagine, very stressful. As it is, they are working very hard in technical training and then they have my schedule to keep to as well. Non-one who hasn't lived it can imagine what it is that they go through. I know because I do a lot of fitness sessions myself, but I don't have to train Boxing, Muay Thai, Jiu-Jitsu together with it. It's excruciating, that's the only word to describe it. You can ask any one of my fighters, my conditioning sessions push you right to the limit, especially between three and one week out from a fight. I just progress it so that they get to week one knowing they can do that much more over 20 to 25 minutes.

'It's a combination of things involved', he continued, 'Hill sprinting is one of them. Hill sprinting is a very, very good way to red line an athlete, if it's done in the right manner. Obviously burst punching drills sequenced in the right manner. Speed endurance weight training - weight training over 40 to 50 reps with good posture and good technique - that builds a lot of lactic acid tolerance. What I try to do basically is put as much lactic acid in an athlete as possible and get the athlete fatigued over 20, 25 minutes without injuring them – that's the key. That's the key to being a good conditioning trainer, it's to push them right to the red line, but without injuring them... and over the last 16 years of being a conditioning coach, I've found that a method that works for me.'

However, not prepared to settle for a silver medal, Sunny is still looking for more challenging directions in which to guide his flock of willing clients: 'I'm still trying to be as innovative as the Americans, guys like Scott Ramsdale who is handling Sean Sherk and doing wonderful stuff. Sean Sherk's programmes are very good. Georges St Pierre is handled by a very good guy, there's a lot of very innovative training going on out there, I just want to make sure I keep up with it all, you know.'

Rising star of the UK scene, Andre Winner also counts himself as one of Dholakia's pupils and spoke with genuine feeling as he paid tribute to his instructor's dedication to training. 'Sunny has always got some good circuits and crazy stuff, he helps a lot with muscular endurance and the nutritional side of things as well, he's done a lot for us. When I want to get fit – really fit – Sunny's the man to see for the circuits, he gets you on the treadmills, sprints; he pushes you hard, it's not an easy session.'

Listening to a trainer adding layer after layer of fresh instructions to keep an agonising pace in the gym can be very difficult and having faith in your trainer can mean the difference between pushing yourself that extra mile, and giving yourself an easier ride. As Winner explains, however, has no trouble in taking on board instructions from Sunny: 'He's got your best interests at heart. Even though you're being pushed, you feel you can't do any more, inside it's like you're breaking, but he'll get you through it, he'll push you on. At the end of the day, he's there to help you – whether you like, or dislike it – he knows what he's talking about. His experience does it, I take his word for it, I respect him and have faith in him.'

Winner's technical coach, Lee Livingstone also makes sure the young fighter and the entire Rough House team stay on course with their fitness at his Bushido academy in Nottingham. 'A lot of people come here and we'll do five 5's [5-minute rounds] standing, light technical sparring. Sometimes we'll do it with mma sparring gloves, sometimes we'll do it, boxing with takedowns, but it's five 5's and for 99% of people who come and train in the squad session, it just blows their minds. Second or third round, they are like, "I've got to sit down, I've got to sit down."'

During the session that I visited on a cold day in February, the fighters did their five rounds of stand up sparring, before putting on the mma gloves and going for a further five 5-minute rounds of submission wrestling and ground-and-pound. Even after ten rounds of intense work, the assembled crew still had plenty of energy to enthusiastically rip the piss out of one another after the class, in a warm display of camaraderie.

'The one thing is stamina, we do work a lot of stamina', Livingstone said,

'We don't work it together; we've all got our own training regimes. I'll work four times a week on my own, Dan will do his, Paul will do his, with Sunny. Andre and Jimmy have got the Strength and conditioning coach at the [Leicester Tigers] rugby club, and we'll all do it. That is the underlining factor for this camp – stamina. If one of us has got a championship fight with fives 5's, we'll do seven, eight 5's in the gym so when it comes to the cage it's easy. One thing we'll always do, if we've got three 5-minute rounds, we'll always do five in the gym and then up the intensity near the fight. It surprises me because I think, "What are other camps doing?"'

However, keeping to such a torturous schedule is no mean feat and can lead to fatigue and the possibility of a sub-par performance. Sunny, however, has ways to help his charges back onto the correct path. 'If they've had a slightly off session, I try to ease things down and then build them back up again. I've never really had anyone who has had major problems with conditioning, they are all highly motivated because two or three of them have had really big fights over the last couple of years, especially James Zikic and Paul Daley who are my two most prolific fighters, I think Paul Daley is the most prolific out of all of my guys. All of the boys have been motivated to be honest.

'Yeah, you are going to hit a few hiccups,' he continued, 'but they get over that within a week or two. They may have slight injuries that you have to be careful about as well, whether it's the knees the lower back things like that. I just tailor it to what the situation is, you know, but I've been lucky so far, most of the boys have been injury-free and have been able to train 110% for each one.'

As fight time draws near, Sunny's job is done and he steps away as the athlete goes through his final technical preparations. 'I have them peak a week out of a fight, so the last week, I don't get involved, they are basically tuning up their range, their timing things like that. It depends from fighter to fighter, but I have them peaked a week before fight date basically and the last week they should taper off, so they are there with their technical coaches – my job ends a week from the fight.

'It's a high-pressure environment, very high adrenaline', he added, of fight day, 'Getting guys ready for competition, it's a time to be very focussed. I go through the nerves myself with them, I don't want to make any mistakes, I want to make sure I don't injure them, but at the same time deliver the highest level of fitness that I can do, you know.'

Mental Fitness

I brought the subject around to the abilities of his clients, asking in particular if any of them have exhibited any extraordinary, near-inhuman abilities; Sunny replied without hesitation, 'James Zikic - unbelievable mental fitness, unbelievable! People don't know how mentally strong he is; he never quits, he shows that in his fights.' A point which Zikic demonstrated with incredible clarity as he absorbed an massive number of low kicks over his incredible three round war with Chute Boxe representative, Evangelista 'Cyborg' Santos. The fight which left his thigh badly bruised from top to bottom, on both the inside and outside of the left leg.

'Zikic never quits', Sunny continued, 'and from the point of view of pushing right to that red line and through that red line, going to your point of black out over and over and over again – James really does stand out for me. With regards to discipline, they are all disciplined. Obviously Paul Daley is at an incredible level at the moment, he's young and fit and I look forward to doing great things with him as well, but all of boys to be honest with you, but mental fitness – James is the man.'

I asked Sunny to describe what he understood by the term, in the hope of building up a clear picture of Zikic's abilities. 'Mental fitness is the ability to suffer, over and over and over again over 25 minutes. For me, it's the ultimate in mental fitness because my conditioning tests a week out from the fight are over 25 minutes and between 15-to-25 minutes of that test, it's excruciating. The boys are required to go to that red line over and over again; whether it be sprints, or anaerobic things on the upper body. If you are not fit enough, you are going to vomit before you hit that red line, so the boys are built up over six or eight weeks so that they are fit enough that they don't puke before they get to that black out point, or close to a black out.'

Another trainer known for taking his charges out of their comfort zone is life long martial artist and trainer at the Wolfslair MMA Academy, Tony Quigley snr. 'Some of the lads are very self-driven and some of them are not, he said of his students which include UFC veterans, Mike Bisping and Paul Kelly. In a fight, if you're facing a good opponent, you're going to come out of your comfort zone, so I try to replicate that in the training. I'll burn them out before they fight,' he said, in reference to the tough sparring ahead, 'and give them that feeling that they've got nothing left, but they've got to go on. In the fight, if you get the feeling, you've been there before in training. I feel it helps.'

Just listening to the ways that he achieves this feeling amongst his charges was exhausting enough: 'The plyometrics, all the jumping and explosive stuff, but also the physical stuff, you know, making them clinch and after three rounds and then punch straight away without a rest. Up and down off the floor to replicate when a wrestler or a fighter with a jiu-jitsu background shoots and tries and take you down. Basically, I just try to give them the feelings that they are going to get in a fight and try and give them the fitness to get them through that.'

Amongst a torturous session of striking drills and exercises, Quigley signalled for the fighters to 'Do their sit ups', as if he were setting an insignificant task – one which turned out to be 50 sit ups, one of four sets, a nice little addition to the most intense three hour training session imaginable. 'I do the sit-ups because it's obviously good conditioning, it's core strength, going back to the traditional martial arts. I think core strength is very important so we do a lot of conditioning for taking blows, obviously, kicks and punches, elbows but also, in between, it keeps your heart rate up so when you start training again, you're already in your fight zone. With fit lads like this, your heart rate goes down very quick, so if I can keep it up, you're straight back in your high zone. The standard of fitness is very, very good, especially with the likes of Michael Bisping.'

As Quigley put the squad through a brutal set of circuits to round off the session; squat-thrusts and tuck jumps, press ups and legs raises. Bisping set himself apart from the rest of the squad hitting every single call on each exercise, no-one in a room full of super-fit athletes came close to keeping pace in the arduous routine. 'At the end of the day, as a trainer, you've got to find out what motivates people. What motivates one doesn't motivate another, so you've got to be good at man-management and know how they tick. When you're close to the lads, you start to get to know their personalities and through experience, you know what works well and what doesn't.'

As a fighter who has moved from camp to camp and has lacked a fitness mentor, Phil 'The New York Bad Ass' Baroni has, in the past, been accused of avoiding sections of his cardio preparation. However, as the American explains, in his fight with Kala Kolohe Hose, he was under a financial obligation to step into the cage without a full gas tank and suffered the consequences for taking this ill-advised route. 'I took like seven months off and I rushed into that fight on four weeks notice, it was an opportunity. It's a job, also, like everything else. I needed the money, I needed to get back in there and get the ring rust off. I misjudged my conditioning and I misjudged his toughness. The first round is how the rest of the fight would go if I was in top shape, but unfortunately I didn't have any gas in the tank.'

Baroni had an incredibly successful opening round, immediately dumping his foe on the mat and battering him with hurtful punches to the head and body. As the round wore on, the New York Bass Ass escalated his assault as he stood up to deliver a stream of knees and soccer-kicks on his hard-headed local opponent. However, Hose managed to ride out the storm and punished the exhausted former bodybuilder for the ensuing three rounds, eventually tagging Baroni with a right hand in the opening seconds of the fifth round and bombing him out on the mat for the win.

'It doesn't matter if racing a Ferrari, if you run out of gas, you're going to lose to a Volkswagen bug, and that's just what happened that night.' Baroni said, dismissively, 'I'm not really looking back at that fight anymore, it doesn't really matter to me, I know I'm the better fighter. If I had somebody exhausted in front of me for four rounds, I don't think they would last long. When we were both fresh, I had my way with him, I just should have been in a little better shape. It was bad judgement, but like I said, I needed the money.'

A round in the bank

When a coach feels confident that his athlete has made the correct preparations, however, it can be a wonderful feeling, as Sunny explained. 'It feels absolutely brilliant because I know that they can go 15 minutes at maximum work rate because we've done it in the gym over 25 minutes. If they were ever training for a five 5-minute round, then I'd be increasing the timeframe of the test to 35 minutes. It's what we call, "super-compensation", you prepare the athlete for more than he has to do on fight day. They come to fight day knowing that they have done more than they need to.

'James told me a wonderful thing a couple of years ago,' Sunny continued, 'he told me once that the conditioning is harder than the fight, harder than any fight. It prepares them and Paul and the rest of the boys will tell you the same thing. I like to ensure that the conditioning is as close to the red line as possible, so come fight day, it's not a problem. As long as they don't made mistakes technically, my guys, hopefully, don't gas.'

Achieving this added advantage that well trained athletes have going into the contest has become the focus for a great many aspiring mma fighters and as Sunny confirmed due to increasing list of booking, conditioning is a growing aspect of the sport. 'Nearly all the top athletes, most of the top fighters in this country have strength and conditioning coaches at some point I think. It's picking up here, in America nearly every decent fighter has a strength and conditioning coach, here in the UK, not as much but it's growing.'

Game plan

A UK fighter known for his both intense and intelligent preparations is Leigh Remedios, a fighter almost as famed for wearing his electric blue Speedos as he is for executing precise game plans in the cage. Speaking to him about a range of general issues relating to fight preparations I began by asking if it is necessary for fighters to have a set game plan, going into the fight. 'I think they are stupid if they don't. I think you have to train for the competition that you're in. If you don't train for the competition you're in, I think that's crazy. Look at Rob Olivier and Ronnie Mann; two totally different types of fighter. You're not going to train the same for both – you'd have to train defending the takedown for Robbie, you'd have to! And you'd have to learn to defend getting punched and kicked in the face if you're training for Ronnie Mann.

'Of course, Ronnie has got good wrestling and Robbie is a decent striker as well, but you've had to specialise. I'd work the whole game, I'd wrestle every week, do my boxing, do my kicking, do my jiu-jitsu, I'd do everything from MMA, but I would definitely train with a game plan in mind. You have to.'

Weights

Echoing Sunny's comments on weight training, Leigh continued, 'I personally stop training weights six weeks out from the fight. I have to weight lifts prior to the fight because I'm not a massive featherweight. A lot of guys cut from over 70 kilos down to 65. I walk around at about 67, 68. I used to do weights all the time, I used to powerlift all the time and I was walking around at about 71. But I don't like to lift weights anymore, I find I've got better things to do with my time and I'm getting old and it hurts. I walk around at 67, 68 and if I've got a fight coming up I'll lift weights and try and get up to 70-something and cut back down before the fight, but I'll come off weights six weeks before the fight.'

I once spoke with perennial UFC underdog, Jorge Rivera before his fight with Alex Reid at Cage Rage 10; he insisted that he never does weights in preparation for a fight, instead putting faith in exercises which manipulate your own bodyweight, such as press ups and pull ups. Remedios, however, holds weight training in marginally higher esteem. 'I think strength is a big part of a fight. It's not the most important, but it's better to have it and not need it than need it and not have it. If you're in the clinch and fighting for the takedown and the other guy is equally skilled, if you've got more strength, you're more likely to land on top of him. I don't do a lot of weights, but I do maintenance weights, I do 20 minutes a week and if I'm training for a fight, I'll probably do half an hour twice a week.'

'Weight cutting'

Remedios touched earlier on the process of 'cutting back down', or as it is commonly known, weight-cutting. A process which has been implemented by years for boxers and wrestlers, looking to gain an advantage by putting on significant amounts of weight in the 24-hour weight-gain window of opportunity between stepping on the scales at their division's limit and fighting on the show the following day.

Weight cutting involves the fighter maintaining a body weight that is significantly higher than his fighting weight and then shedding the pounds in the weeks preceding the contest through a mixture of diet and exercise and dehydration. Remedios has long been known as a master of this practise, but he shrugs it off as merely being an element of the sport. 'I was probably doing it before a lot of people were. I was fighting internationally. I started mma before a lot of guys, so I started competing internationally before a lot of guys and now I'm finding that everyone's doing it. I was competing at 70 kilos and the other guy was coming in at 78, so I had to really. I'm not a big bloke; I made a fuss about it on the [internet] forums, but it kind of stuck that I'm a weight cutter. I don't think I cut anymore than many other people.'

Referring to the actual process of shredding the weight, he continued, 'It's taken some trial and error and I've had some trouble in fights due to weight cutting, I'm not going to name the fights because I don't want to make excuses. But for me, I try to do most of it with diet, cutting my complex carbohydrates out, well, cutting my carbs out completely pretty much and making my portions a lot smaller as well. If I've got any pounds left to lose, I'd probably skip it off, but it's best to diet down. Over a week I find that I can lose about a pound a day.

'You will never have a problem putting the weight back on,' he assured me, 'your body has got its weight and it will want to put it back on again. I think how you put the weight back on is quite important; you definitely don't want to be stuffing your face with cream cakes and Coca-Cola. What you put back in is quite important I think, but it's never a problem, I just eat and drink, non-stop, for the next 20 hours or so.'

CHAPTER FIVE
FIGHT PSYCHOLOGY

"What the fuck is he doing? Is he letting me do this? Why isn't he getting knocked out?"

- Jason 'Shotgun' Young

Anyone can train in mixed martial arts, but not everyone can fight. In order to step into competition there is a certain degree of fight psychology that every competitor will have to master such that he can step through the cage door in the first place. Fear is in the heart of even the toughest of fighters in the run up to the contest; however, having the motivation to conquer this fear is what separates combat sport competitors as a separate breed of athletes.

However, overcoming the initial barrier of deciding to enter full contact competition is merely the first step into the world of fight psychology; the mental war between the fighters can often be the deciding factor in a contest and competitors will often use any psychological ploy at their disposal, at any stage before or during the contest, to upset the mental rhythm of an opponent to gain any possible advantage.

Motivation

The UK's best known fighter, Mike Bisping explains that putting on his game face is made easy by his deep commitment to bolstering the financial stability of his family. The Clitheroe fighter went through a range of unsatisfying jobs before making the jump into professional mma, at last finding an enjoyable profession that enabled him to provide for his family. 'They are my motivation to get up and do my runs at 6 o'clock every single morning, to train hard, constantly striving to learn; it's my family, that's why I do it, to try and make them a better life, which thankfully – touch wood – I'm achieving.'

A strong desire to make a financial return, however, is rarely enough to take an athlete to the top of their sport; there is no substitute for having the competitive drive to learn as many skills as possible and take on the best competition available. 'I've got two ambitions, one is to make a successful living and provide for my family, ultimately, first and foremost, but I also want to be the champion, everything's really based around getting the belt, that's what I want to do.

'I feel that I'm improving all the time, I know the areas I need to improve on and work on and I'm doing that. I don't think I'm the best fighter in the world, far from it. I know I've got a lot of faults, but I'm working on them, I'm determined and I'm on a mission – I want to have three fights this year and three knock outs.' At the time of writing, Bisping had scored two first round wins of his self-imposed three stoppage quota.

Confidence under pressure

Confidence is the very bedrock of fight psychology; squaring off with an opponent who exudes an air of real self-belief can be a sincerely daunting prospect. One fighter who has been accused of having a disproportionately high estimation of his capabilities is the 'New York Bad Ass' Phil Baroni; to the American, however, confidence is everything going into a fight. 'You've got to believe in yourself, you know, I had to believe in myself, it didn't really matter what anyone thought, or whatever anyone else was saying because they're not the ones in there fighting – I'm the one in there fighting, so all that matters is what I believe.'

Among his memorable wins, Baroni has certainly had his share of disappointing results and, as a motor-mouthed multiple UFC veteran, he has been harshly criticised by sections of the mma community. However, the flashy New Yorker proved in his fight with Ikuhisa Minowa at Pride Bushido 9 that he takes life very seriously when his reputation is at threat. 'My whole career was riding on that fight in my mind. I went on a 4-fight losing streak in the UFC. I tore my pec and rushed back against Evan Tanner, I should have taken some more time, but I felt I was being a man in that fight. Then the referee stopped it to check the cut and then stopped it when he was on top of me, not landing any shots. Before that, I had lost to Matt Lindland and the rematch and my career was just going down hill. I went from being ranked number two in the world, to being not ranked in top ten in the world. I was frustrated and I lost my job in the UFC' Baroni said, showing some discomfort as he recalled his unenviable position

'I saw it as an opportunity to get my career back on track. At the time, Minowa was on a four or five fight winning streak, he was a huge fan favourite in Japan and I saw it as an opportunity. They were bringing me in as the main event to fight him, but as an opponent, I was looking at it as an opportunity. I dug real deep in that fight – there was a lot of fighting within myself, when you win and you're on a winning streak, but when you lose you start doubting yourself and asking yourself questions. I answered a lot of questions in that fight - and I answered them by stomping on his head at the end.'

As an emotional fighter, Baroni often provides flashes of brilliance as a result of a professional rivalry or confrontation; in Japan, the American showed some of his most explosive skills after a pre-fight run-in with opponent, Ryo Chonan. 'I remember he was talking some stuff about me, saying that I wasn't that big of a deal as an American fighter, I wasn't an American champion and, after he beat me, he wanted to fight an American champion. That annoyed me; I didn't like the guy looking past me at all. That bothered me a lot – and then he gave me a crazy stare down too, he was staring me down, so I thought "I'm gonna bust this guy up!"'

Chonan had beaten rising star, and future UFC middleweight champion Anderson Silva months previously with an incredible, flying inside heel hook, and appeared to be a formidable opponent. 'That was a big fight for me,' Baroni remembered, 'that was a really big opportunity for me. He made it personal and, with me, that's something you don't want to do; make it personal. So I took care of him pretty quick, I hit him pretty hard.' He added in a wonderful understatement, bombing out the Japanese favourite in less than two minutes.

As part of his pre-fight preparations, however, Baroni revealed that he tends to use the mindset that each of his professional contests is a grudge match. 'It's personal because they are trying to take away from me what I've been working for, the goals that I'm trying to accomplish, that's what they're doing, they are standing in my way, so I can't let them take what I've been working so hard for. What I've made so many sacrifices for. It's always personal for me.'

Mind games

Unafraid to wear his heart on his sleeve, Baroni made no effort to curb his vociferous tongue in the run up to his EliteXC match up with arch-rival, Frank Shamrock and the ill-feeling between the two was exhibited plainly in the bout. After landing a pair of sharp right hands on his trash-talking opponent, Shamrock took the opportunity to exhibit some bold fight psychology of his own. Frank held his palms together to form a make-shift padded pillow which he placed to the side of his head, motioning to Baroni that he would soon be sleeping, unconscious under the weight of the punches he had coming.

Asked why he mocked Baroni in this way, the younger of the two famous Shamrock brothers had no idea. 'It just comes out,' he said, 'it's my brain telling me, "He's weak, get into his mind. He's distracted, make him more distracted." My brain just tells me to do things and, subconsciously, I find myself doing weird, funny things. I realised, it's because I do it in sparring; I have fun in sparring, I laugh and have a good time, I screw around. So whatever you do in sparring, you do in fighting and my personality comes out.'

Speaking to his New York opponent after the fight, Baroni swore blind that 99 out of every 100 times the pair met, he would destroy Shamrock. The winner of the contest had a theory to explain this usually bold statement.

'That's just how he gets himself together I think. I think truthfully, he's not as confident as he says he is. What people don't realise is that while styles make fights, experience and physical ability and mental desire and technical prowess can rule out a lot of things – that's why I can fight a Gracie or fight all these different guys who have real good strengths in all different areas. Nobody's submitted me, nobody's knocked me out, nobody's choked me out, nobody's ever really imposed their game so much that they were able to get rid of me. There's something to be said for that.

'Phil is the opposite,' Shamrock turned, 'he's been tapped, he's been choked, he's been knocked out, he's been stopped. There's a line where he really can't, or he's not willing, or he doesn't know how to go over – and I live over the line! He's just in a different world.'

Mind Control

The importance of seizing psychological control of your opponent is not lost on Team Titan fighter, Jason Young, who focuses his mind on memories of a tough childhood before his contests to stir up his competitive determination. In the run up to his Cage Rage Contenders 7 performance against Michael King, Young put on a ferocious display of bottled aggression and appeared to crush any semblance of optimism his opponent before the fight began, 'I think he touched me once in the whole seven minutes.' Young explained, crediting his pre-fight mental state as a main factor in his success.

'I looked at him like I wanted to kill him. Shall I tell you why? It's my sister, it may sound mad but my sister brought me up quite a lot in my life and she's the closest person to me, family-wise. Before that fight my sister had come up to me and she was psyching me up, she's the only person who can get to me, say a little prayer sort of thing. Then she'll say, "You've been through this, you've been through that, you've done this you've seen that, don't go in there and take it as a game." That just turns my brain straight on and when I go in there, I don't feel anything. I just wanna fight. At the end of the fight, yeah, I'll shake his hand, give him a cuddle and say, "No disrespect for all the looks and everything, but I've got to be in the game mentally to be able to fight."

'I try to stare at them to see if there's any fear in them', Young continued, 'I think I did see a little bit of fear when I was looking at [King]. He looked at me, he sort of looked at the floor and he looked around. I had a big crowd there as well, I sold quite a few tickets and that boosted me up a bit more as well. I said to my trainer as I was walking out, "I'm going to do everything, I'm going to elbow, I'm going to knee, I'm going to kick him in his head, I'm going to take him down, drop him down and ground-and-pound him." There was everything you could possibly do to someone. Everything; I think I broke his nose within the first minute, it was broke bad.'

King was under pressure and sustained painful damage early in the fight, he seemed to shut down mentally and stopped trying to attack the Titan representative in any way, instead his intimidated opponent appeared content to stand in his own corner and absorb a stream of high kicks from the talented youngster. 'It's like he allowed me to do it. I even stepped back halfway through the first round and I was thinking to myself, "What the fuck is he doing? Is he letting me do this? Why isn't he getting knocked out?", because I caught him on the button a couple of times and his legs went; it's like he wanted to stand there and get hit sort of thing.

'He didn't throw nothing back,' Young recalled, 'I'm not sure whether I scared him, or whether my first barrage of punches made him freeze. Maybe if he had hit me first, he might have felt a bit more comfortable.' As it was, in the second round, King was in line for more punishment as Young pinned him to the mat in a crucifix1 and laid in several hard shots to his opponent's teeth.

'As I was hitting him, I remember swearing, "Just fucking go out!", because he was strong. I don't know whether he's been doing chin exercises or took something before the fight because I gave him a battering and I've had fights in the street where people have gone down from less than that, a lot less than that. I don't know if he took something or if his adrenaline was keeping him up, I don't know at all, but he looked fucking battered at the end of it as well. He couldn't walk, after I spoke to him he was limping along, proper hobbling.'

Mental Terrors

The victim of a beating such as this can find it puts a noticeable dent in their fighting spirit and if the situation is not remedied one way or another, the cracks in their mental game can have a significant effect on his performances for years to come. Fighter and referee, Marc Goddard has previously been fenced in by psychological barriers which at one point threatened to call an early end to his career.

'It started in my second fight with James Thompson,' Goddard began, 'that's when the mental terrors began, so to speak. When I fought him, I just lost the plot mentally. We fought in his home town with a partisan crowd and it's the first time I'd really experienced fear, what to do with that fear, or - more importantly in my case - what not to do with that fear.' Virtually paralysed by his own bleak perception of the situation, Goddard was on the receiving end of an efficient, one-sided beatdown which temporarily shattered his competitive confidence.

'Since then I've blown hot and cold. I'd come back and have a great win and then just, excuse my language, fuck it up the next time and it was all a mental thing to be honest with you. Then when I fought [Robert] Buzz [Berry] at Cage Rage 14 a couple of years back, that was the last time and I just gave up. I was waiting for anything to happen in that fight so that I could just quit and get out of there. After the fight, I grabbed the microphone and I quit there and then in the cage. I was in a right mess beforehand and afterwards; tears and everything, it wasn't a nice place to be for me. But like I say, that's when I decided to leave it and go about addressing my weaknesses. I was always coming back; it was just a case of when.'

Thankfully for his legion of Birmingham fans, Goddard resumed his career in 2007, after seeking the services of a sports psychologist. 'I always knew I had the tools. I had to believe in myself and ultimately, that's what I learned to do. Then coming back last year, I had a good year last year, in terms of grappling and mma. I had a good quick win in my first outing back and then an absolute war with Ivan Serati and that was very enjoyable. To be honest with you, whenever I needed psychology, that was the time I needed it – it kicked in.'

Goddard ate some heavy leather in his opening fight with the tough Italian, before coming back in the second to bash Serati on the floor to earn a tremendously satisfying sense of redemption. Referring to his come back from the early shots, he continued, 'It was good to come out the other side of it and prove to myself that I could. That was my deciding moment as a fighter, I always knew I had it, and I just wanted to be tested in that way and I did and came out the other side, fortunately.'

Facing weaknesses

The public generally expects fighters not to show weakness of any kind, but as pugilists become older and more experienced, this determination to put on a good front can become displaced by a willingness to accept that all fighters have moments of weakness, in the hope of finding a way to come back stronger.

Frank Mir has known severe adversity in his career after a motorcycle accident in 2003 left him with a broken femur and unable to compete for 18 months. However, once back and able to compete with the sport's top fighters, Mir found that his struggles had followed him to the cage as he took on grappling champion, Marcio Cruz. The Brazilian was able to take top position and land a series of punches and elbows into the fallen champion's face; Mir did precious little to improve his position and was forced to absorb a string of shots to the middle of his face.

'It was actually a good fight,' Mir recalled, 'I got to learn about myself; I was kind of being a pussy. I needed to realise that when I was in a bad situation, the whole time I wasn't thinking about winning the fight, I was just thinking about feeling sorry for myself, my leg hurt and the shin. I looked for every excuse in the world to get out of the fight and it's a good thing, part of it is acknowledging that to myself. A lot of fighters don't like to acknowledge when they have a moment in their life when they are a pussy - and that was me really being a wimp. I can put the tape on and anybody with any intelligence can figure out that I didn't want to be there and that was humiliating to me, so I watch that fight all the time and have told myself that I'm never going to allow that to happen again, because how I felt after the fight was way worse than anything I was feeling during the fight.'

Back on the winning track

Perennial lightweight contender, Yves Edwards is another fighter for whom defeat in the cage has led to some painful soul-searching. Over the period of one year, Yves lost three straight fights, two by stoppage. Rather than letting this affect his future performances, he decided to find a new environment in which to focus his athletic potential, 'The losses affected my confidence, but not necessarily my confidence in what I was capable of. It had more of an affect on my confidence for that fact that I don't think I was doing the right things. I got away from training with really good guys, my team sort of split up and I really didn't have anyone to train with and I ended up doing a lot of training with my students and you can't compete at a high level, training with people who are just learning the game.

'So I decided that I needed to make a change and American Top Team, I had known those guys for years, they've always been real good friends of mine, so I just talked to them about it and they were more than happy to let me join their ranks and that changed everything for me. You're in there with Mike Brown and [Gesias] JZ [Cavalante] and Thiago Alves, Marcus Aurelio, all these guys that are so good at what they do and you're doing fine also, with them and against them, your confidence, everything changes. You get in the cage, or the ring and you look across the ring and you see somebody, he's just another guy. That part of the confidence is completely different for me now.'

His positive frame of mind coming to the fore, Edwards looked on the bright side of his losing streak. 'I think I lost against three really good guys, but I don't think I would have won three fights against three guys who weren't any good. I probably would have had a really hard time, but fighting these tough guys, I think that made me make a decision to change what I was doing rather than possibly give up on myself. Now my confidence is through the roof, knowing who I've got to work with, there's no-one outside of my team who can stop me, so I'm satisfied with the way the world is right now.

'A lot of fight game is mental' Yves continued, 'When you are mentally stronger than somebody else, you're going to have a big advantage and I think that a lot of the young up and coming guys, if they haven't competed at a high level in another sport all their lives, they're going to have problems; but right now, I don't think anybody is going to handle what I'm bringing to the table.'

With a wealth of experience behind him in his 11 year professional career, Edwards can afford to play the odd mind game with his younger opponents, either that or get a laugh out of the often tense pre-fight weigh ins. Usually comfortably under the 155 pound lightweight limit, Yves has been known to take a snack with him to eat on the scales in order to taunt his hungry and often weight drained opponent.

'It's quite funny,' he said of his cheeky antics, 'I thought people would either get annoyed or find it really funny, one or the other, you can't please anybody, so I figured I might as well please myself, get myself something to eat and maybe a few people would get a laugh out of it. I offer them some of my food, some guys will take the food, some guys will walk away. I don't know if that affects them, maybe they get pissed off a little bit or something, but it's best that they just relax, sit back and just prepare to fight me.'

CHAPTER SIX
THE RULES

'The concept of putting gloves on the people's hands? It's a very misleading idea, if you punch somebody with a bare knuckle, you'll break your hand, but if you put on a glove, you'll break the guys face.'

- Rorion Gracie

The original concept of 'vale tudo' fighting which spawned the modern sport of mma originally came from Brazil, where the two words simply meant; 'anything goes.' Under this rule system, the only impermissible techniques were biting and eye-gouging, leaving competitor's free to head butt, strike to the groin, kick a downed opponent in the head and purposefully gouge any cut that he may have suffered.

Incredibly, 'the rules of honour' as they were known in Brazil were successfully exported to the United States by Rorion Gracie, who throws his support behind the legitimacy of no-holds-barred fighting to this day. Gracie introduced the most fascinating spectacle in 1993 as he unveiled what would become the most successful mma organisation on the face of the planet in the shape of the Ultimate Fighting Championship. 'My initial concept was, no time limits, no points, no gloves, no judges to decide who won.' Rorion said simply.

However, this format for competition came extremely close to buckling under the strain of criticism as politicians began to demand that this new style of fight competition take on additional rules to curb the more brutal aspects of the sport and to improve fighter safety. For Gracie, however, this was the beginning of the end. 'When they started implementing all those rules, I said that's enough, I'm out of this, this is not exactly what I envisioned, so I felt it was the right time for me to move and I'm very glad I did, because the show today is completely different from what I originally made it.'

No-Holds-Barred

The implementation of the additional rules has a pronounced effect on the fight and in the Brazilian's view, these rules designed to increase fighter safety have had a negative effect, if anything making it a more dangerous competitive environment. 'It changes everything. Sometimes the guy who wins the fight is not necessarily the better fighter. You get a 5-minute round and the guy can have a perfect move locked in and after five minutes the referee can say "Stop the fight, start again. Rest for a minute." This is crazy; it's not like a real fight anymore - and the concept of putting gloves on the people's hands? It's a very misleading idea, if you punch somebody with a bare knuckle, you'll break your hand, but if you put on a glove, you'll break the guys face. The glove is not there to protect the person's face; the glove is there to protect the person's hand. It's much more dangerous, that's why half-a-dozen boxers die all over the world every year. Nobody has ever died in the UFC, or martial arts, my family has been doing this for 80 years.'

It seems unfortunate that Gracie has become so disillusioned by the sport which he initially brought to such great prominence, but the jiu-jitsu black belt can still take some satisfaction from having such a pivotal role in the rapid propagation of his family's art around the world. 'I mean, I'm happy that the show exploded, mixed martial arts all over the world, because like I said, my goal in 1978 was to make the whole world understand the necessity of learning Gracie jiu-jitsu. So I'm very happy that the message got across, but unfortunately the way the show has developed, when the people at home watch mixed martial arts, they don't think "Wow, I need to learn this." They think "Wow, these guys are very violent." The perception of the guys going in there now is that they are brutes and they beat each other up, full of steroids and muscle-bound, very strong and very powerful.

'That's not the message,' Rorion said, 'Gracie jiu-jitsu is for the little guy, that's why I specifically chose to put my brother Royce, who is a little skinny guy, to fight everybody [at UFC 1], because Royce was a good example that the little guy can defeat the big guy, that was the message, but once you start putting in rules and time limits and regulations, it doesn't work like that anymore. And of course, everybody becomes smart and they all start learning Gracie jiu-jitsu, it changed everything.

'My father who weighed 63 kilos in his fighting career – a very light person, 140lbs, he could never beat anybody in a 5-minute round, he just waited for the big guy to get tired and when the big guy got tired, then he defeated the man. For the person who is not in shape… otherwise you have to be very fast, very explosive, very strong and the majority of people are not like that. The majority of people see themselves as being out of shape, not very strong, and not being very limber or very co-ordinated – that's the people who can use the techniques of Gracie jiu-jitsu and then learn well how to defend themselves. Gracie jiu-jitsu is not a style of fighting for competition, it's a method of self-defence, the most effective method of self-defence in the world; I still believe that to this day.'

Referee and jiu-jitsu practitioner himself, Herb Dean is not enthused by the idea of a contest being fought in the modern era under the same rules used in the original UFC. 'I don't think it's good for the sport. I think the reason we are where we are today is because it's definitely a sport. It's not just a spectacle. The spectacle aspect of it appears and I enjoy that as well, but I think we are going to reach a lot more people and get a lot more people involved with it as a sport. I think it's better as a sport and not just a spectacle where you can go in there and brutalize people.'

'At the same time,' Dean continued, 'I'm kind of split on it because I've been involved in mixed martial arts from the very beginning, so I can understand that when it had very limited rules, you really got to get in there and see what worked. For the martial arts purist in me, I definitely respect people who do no-holds-barred and I can definitely see why it's so respected and why people want to do it. But at the same time, we have decided to make this a sport and it definitely would be bad for the sport.'

Cage Rage referee, Leon Roberts was slightly less gentle in his assessment of a old school vale tudo match taking place in the present day, 'Are you referring to bare knuckle, groin strikes, spiking opponents?' He asked 'If you are then I do have some concerns. Without the restrictions that are in place people would perceive a sport which we all love as too brutal and more like a street fight. With the regulations that are imposed and the strict rules that must be adhered to people can watch a combat sport that allows its competitors to demonstrate that what they are doing is MMA, it's an art. I am opposed to anything that brings controversy to a sport that so often unjustly receives way too much negative attention.'

Harsh reality

However, with a career stretching back to the very earliest days of the modern sport, UK fighter, Leigh Remedios has fought under the rules of honour on numerous occasions and sees no problem with the idea. "My first ever professional fight was in Raw Combat', the UFC veteran explained, 'I took the guy down and head-butted him in the face. He clinched me, so I nutted him in the face. He let go so I sat up, at the time we called it the avalanche, where you rain punches down until he turns his back. This was the mid-nineties, where you rain punches down, he turns his back and you choke him, pretty straight forward. He came in as a street fighter, so it wasn't a skilful match! I took him down, nutted him, punched him in the mouth, thanks very much.'

Another notable outing for the Ashford fighter on the no-holds-barred circuit came in the form of a weekend trip to Prague where the organisers went to what were at the time quite extraordinary lengths to ensure he was well looked after. 'They were pretty good. At the time it seemed amazing, nowadays most promotions treat you the same way, they treat you very well.

They were definitely ahead of the UK at the time in how they treated their fighters. They put me in a hotel, I got fed and everything else, I got taken out to movies, I was treated really well. Nowadays people over here treat you really well. Back in the day; not so much.

'Under the rules of the promotion,' Remedios explained, 'the only prohibited techniques included biting, eye-gouging and no slapping of the ears. You couldn't do a cupped hand to the ear otherwise you might burst an ear drum. During the fight, his corner -apparently, I was told this afterwards, I didn't know at the time - they were shouting out to him to hit me in the balls because I'm not used to it, I'm from the UK. But I'd fought before in no-holds-barred events, I was totally used to hitting people in the balls! So I took him down, tried to mount him, he defended it, so I punched him in the nuts! Well you're allowed to do it, so I did it!' he added unapologetically.

The low blows heard around the world

Perhaps the most famous incident relating to groin strikes comes from one of the original UFC contests when Keith Hackney took on the confident and bizarre Bond-villain, Odd-Job lookalike, Joe Son. The Giant Killer, who earned his nickname dismantling the 6'8" behemoth, Emmanuel Yarborough at UFC 3, started with a beautiful hook kick which whistled past Son's face. Son proceeded to goad the Illinois fighter, lowering his hands as if to challenge his opponent to commit himself in the stand up.

Joe Son soon caught his taller foe in a front headlock, negating the height advantage as forced Hackney back towards the fence. The older fighter was able to take the fight to the floor with a sneaky trip take down from which he landed in side mount, temporarily ensnared in an improvised guillotine choke by the Jo Son Do expert. So when did he realize that he had the option of striking to son's groin?

'All the time!' Hackney laughed. 'There was no biting, no eye gouging, but you could still do it and you'd get fined a thousand dollars, that's why it was no-holds-barred, you could still do it, but they didn't want you doing it. There was strikes to the groin thrown, there was strikes to everything and if that was going to loosen him up to let the guillotine go, the headlock go? You know what? Fighting according to the rules, so I didn't have a problem with it. I know it freaked some people out, but... you know...'

Within a few seconds of landing on the ground, Hackney began to fire off a stream of blows which had male viewers around the world wincing at the thought. Never a fan of wearing gloves for competition, the board-breaking karate fighter landed six precise full power shots directly to the groin area. At first Son appeared oblivious to pain like an over-the-top character from the world of pro-wrestling, but as Hackney continued to wail away, he knew that he would eventually see some form of reaction. 'He had a cup on so he was still protected, you're still going to feel something and I knew that eventually he'd let go and I'd work my way up to mount or whatever it came down to.'

A lot of observers were left confused by the ending as Hackney appeared to hold his opponent in place on the floor by the throat, but forced a submission from the stubborn Californian. Hackney cleared up the reason why Son called it a day. 'I got a finger choke on him squeezing his Adam's apple. Because a lot of stuff I did up to that point was geared towards the street as far as how I was training. The ground, I was still familiar with it but I wasn't familiar with the submissions because nobody really trained them anywhere that I knew of – but the grip was tight, I had my fingers almost touching behind the back of his Adam's apple. That's essentially why he tapped.'

Asked if he now misses the old style of rules which resembled a street confrontation to such a noticeable degree, the fighter-turned-trainer gave an even handed reply. 'I liked the rules the way they were, I enjoyed the fight, but I understand that they had to transition to be accepted by people and obvious they had to hook up with the boxing commission, do the rounds, judges, weight classes all that stuff, I understand that to put it on TV. I like where the sport is going, I'd like to see the fighters get paid more money. I like the acceptance that it's gotten, but in another respect, I look around now, everybody shaves their head, everybody gets tattoos, they wear all the gear and everybody thinks they're a fighter. As opposed to an art, it's an image thing now.

'I've enjoyed both,' he added, referring to no-holds-barred and mma competition, 'I like both. I think that if some of the rules were like they were a long time ago, I think about 80% of these guys wouldn't be in there. It's tough to fight three fights in one night, it's tough to fight somebody bigger than you. There's a lot of things they took out of the sport, but I enjoy where it's come to. I like the respect that it gets because a lot of the guys that are fighting and training are some of the best trained athletes in the world, and they weren't getting the respect that they should have been getting before.'

'King of the Yellow Card': Gilbert Yvel

As an introduction to the often maligned Dutch Wildman, Gilbert Yvel whose introduction follows on the theme on low blows as he recalled his encounter was a young Wanderlei Silva at Pride 11 'He didn't want to fight me because he was too light', Yvel said, of the noticeable weight advantage that he enjoyed over the Brazilian Axe Murderer. 'They gave him a lot of money to fight me, but he really didn't want to fight me. I second I gave him a low kick, I'm not sure if you can see it on the video, but he looked at his corner right away - and then he hit me right, straight in the nuts. You can tell me a lot of things, but c'mon!' he said, raising his voice in frustration at the injustice of what he considered to be a deliberate low blow.

The subject of a possible rematch emerged; 'Why not?' Gilbert said cheerfully, 'I was recently training at Randy Couture's gym, he was also there and he held me to two tough rounds and I was tired, he was like, "Come on, come on." We did a little kickboxing and I showed him a little something, so it was OK. All in all, he's like a really nice guy, but I think my weight is too heavy weight I'm like 110 kilos and he's probably 95.'

Whilst Yvel remains sure that he was on the receiving end of a deliberate display of cheating on that occasion, the notorious knee merchant has faced similar accusation himself in a career littered with controversial moments. One of his harsher critics, perhaps understandably, is American tough guy and mma pioneer, Don 'The Predator' Frye who remain convinced that the Dutch kickboxer gouged his eyes deliberately throughout their clash at Pride 16. 'Hell, that's just Gilbert, come on!' he laughed. 'It's a fight, that's the whole thing, it's a goddam fight and shit happens in the fight. You can't worry about it, you can't look at the referee and you can't whine about it, you just gotta keep going.'

Frye was equally as interested in re-matching Yvel, as the high kicker had been to face Wanderlai Silva for a second time. 'Sure, I'll fight him again. Hell, I want to fight everyone that I lost to, I want a rematch with them, so why wouldn't I give everybody I beat a rematch? It's only the gentlemanly thing to.'

I put Yvel on the spot and asked him straight out – 'Did you intentionally gouge Don Frye's eyes?'

'Let's say, "It was an accident"', was the somewhat evasive reply.

'Definitely an accident?'

'Definitely an accident,' he answered again, this time with a tone of slight annoyance. 'I was trying to push his nose away and my finger slipped. We have talked about it and we had fun about it, we're OK. Respect is the best.' He added, guiding me away from the topic.

I moved on with a question about the origins of his sometime nickname, 'The King of the Yellow Card'; 'I think it started with Don Frye. First of all, it was after 9/11, he came out with an American flag and his shirt and his song and everything, it was like I was the Taliban and I was fighting the USA! I got some yellow cards, maybe one was right, maybe two…

'In mma they favour the ground fighters and not really the stand up fighters, I was a stand up fighter and I didn't want to go to the ground. They didn't know what to do with me and I did some strange things and ended up with the yellow cards. They gave me a little bit, the role of the bad boy, you know? So that's why I always got the yellow cards.'

However, in easily his most famous foray outside the boundaries of the rules, Gilbert Yvel shocked the world in 2004 when he went too far by a country mile, knocking out a referee midway through a fight. To a sympathetic ear, when Gilbert tells the story, it almost sounds like he had a reasonable case for what most view as a thoroughly reprehensible act. 'This guy was like a promoter, the ugly side of the fight world, and he was the referee also and the trainer of my opponent', Yvel began. 'There was also this situation because the guy asked me the year before, "I've got this show... it's not a really big show, but if you fight on the show I can't give you a lot of money but it will help my show and I want to make it big in the world."

'You know, I'm not an asshole,' Yvel said, as if concerned that he may have earned a reputation to the contrary among some fans, 'I'm like "OK, you can't give me a lot of money, but treat me right." It's not like I'm a prince or a king, but if you ask me to fight on your show, you'd better treat me better than he did that time.'

Yvel and his team arrived in Finland at around 11 o'clock and to their frustration, the promoter and referee failed to show. 'He never arrived at the airport and made us wait for an hour. He came and then he went away and made us wait for another 45 minutes. Then we went to his gym for the weight check because I had to weigh 100 kilos or something and then he made us wait outside his gym for 2 hours which was a really messed up thing. 10 o'clock in the evening was the first chance I got a chance to eat, so although we were really pissed off with this guy, I went, "No problem."

'Then during the fight, he became the referee and he was trying to do a lot of strange things like a stand up, in the same position. 'Go on, this is not a rule! If you are on the ground and get too close to the ropes, they put you in the middle of the ring, but not standing up when you are bending backwards and almost falling out of the ring. Then he was like really favouring my opponent, trying to put me in a bad position and really trying to fuck me up. This during a fight, when you're all fucked up because you just want to destroy your opponent and then the referee started screaming, push you, pull you, push you and at that moment, it was a really bad thing for me to do, but at that moment, I just hit him on his face, you know.'

Gilbert landed a perfect short left hook on the multi-tasking official's jaw, sending him directly to the canvas. To his credit, the referee quickly bounced back to his feet, stumbling over to the ring-side officials to announce Yvel's disqualification. 'It's not good,' Gilbert said of the shocking situation, which was roundly booed by the live audience. 'I feel very sorry now, I'm a name and somebody to look up to, and then I hit the referee; that was one of the stupidest things I ever did.'

CHAPTER SIX: THE RULES

However, since this barbarous act which has seen the Dutchman black-balled by fight organisations the world over, Yvel has demonstrated that he is now able to keep a much calmer head to the most part as he demonstrated in a Chippenham nightclub after a local fight show, when a group of revellers tried their very best to get a rise out of him. 'I was there with some friends, a girl with us, she got into a fight with another girl, and I don't know, the girl who was with us pushed that girl and the guys with her looked ready for action.

'I just stood there in front of my girl and said, "You know what, you'd better back off, that's it." Then this local, I don't know what he wanted to do but he was standing in front of me and he was probably thinking about making a move, "If you want to make a move, do something, but I'm not the guy who is going to start something." Then, maybe he saw something in my eyes, but he decided to walk away and that was it. I'm not a guy who is going to fight on the streets. If you attack me? Aha!' he laughed, 'I fuck you up - but it's so stupid to start something, there's no reason.'

In my attempt to force Yvel to repent for his sins, I asked if he had any advice for any misguided younger fighters who might be tempted to punch the referee in frustration during a fight. 'Knock your opponent out!' He said simply, 'That's the only thing to do, don't hit the ref' Gilbert laughed, 'that's wrong. It's difficult, you know, everyone's got times when they think the referee is a fucker and they want to hit him on his face, but if you do it, you are way more fucked up than before. Knock your opponent out and after the fight, give your hand and say "You're an asshole", to the referee, but that's the only thing you can do.' He finished, chuckling in exasperation at his reckless former self.

'Dirty' Bob Schreiber

Another Dutchman and former street fighter, Bob Schreiber has also received his fair share of criticism for his past irregularities as he holds the dubious honour of being the only fighter in the history of the Pride Fighting Championships to kick an opponent to the head on the floor after the bell, but in the case of 'Terrible' Bob, to land an Ax kick on the back of the head of an opponent as he did to Daijiro Matsui at Pride 7. Referring back to the heavy illegal blow, Schreiber was penitent. 'Not very sporting, I think. Later on I saw the DVD and I went, "Ah, motherfucker... this is not very good for the sport", I thought.'

However, it was actually Matsui who was the first to throw an illegal strike as he kneed Schreiber in the face early in the contest – an illegal tactic at the time in the Pride organisation. This point was not lost on the Dutchman, 'That's true. I thought, "OK, if you want to play a game like this, you can get it from me." But later on when I saw the DVD, it was too terrible; that's the reason they call me in Japan, what do they call me?' he struggled, 'Oh, I do not remember, but it is not a very good name', he chuckled. The nickname of course was 'Dirty' Bob Schreiber, perhaps an appropriate moniker for a fighter with such an individual view of how the rules should be applied in mma competition.

'I never saw the sports from the moment that I climbed into the ring or the cage, I don't see this as sport; for me it wasn't a sport. It's sport when I'm training in my gym with my students and my colleague fighters; that's sport, but when I climb in the ring or the cage it's not a sport for me. Two people trying to kill each other in the ring or cage, for me that is not sport, if you know what I mean. I had many fights on the street also because I am working now for 23 years as a bouncer on the door by different discothèques and bars and I have had many, many experiences on the doors and on the streets. For me it is this thing, he came into the ring, or he came into the cage and tried to kill me, "OK, let's find out who win this." For me it is not sport in the ring or the cage.'

I asked 'Dirty' Bob if he felt he had received a fair nickname after his exploits in Japan, his answer was devoid of any protestation, 'I don't care. They can call me what they want, I'm not interested in what they call me.'

New Jersey State Athletic Commission rules

However, aside from some notable but somewhat marginalised organisations, modern promotions would not even dream of allowing kicks or knees to the floor which were allowed in Pride. In fact, a myriad of the nastier, or more damaging techniques, ranging from the scratching and twisting of skin to spiking an opponent's head into the floor are consistently outlawed as, barring a few minor differences between sets of rules on different promotions, the majority of shows tend to fall generally in line the New Jersey State Athletic Commission rules.

A referee who has given up the concept of enjoying a Saturday night out away from mma is Grant Waterman, who instead has officiated an mma show almost every weekend for the majority of his ten year career as the third man in the cage. Using the NSAC rules on almost every show he works, Waterman has a rare and well-informed view of their efficiency. 'MMA has evolved over the years and what they are trying to get is a balance between audience entertainment, sporting entertainment and the safety of the fighters. If you look at the track record, the success of the UFC and the record of safety, they've pretty much got it right.'

But can anything be improved? I asked Waterman's Cage Rage colleague, the deeply respected, Leon Roberts. 'I think these rules are well established and change would be difficult. I sometimes watch fights and if knees were allowed to the head of a grounded opponent I think several fights would have had a much different outcome. It puts a whole new dimension into the striking element, so perhaps this would be the only change I would consider.'

American referee, Herb Dean is another referee with a sincere interest in the smooth officiating of mma contests as he undertakes the role of an advisor to numerous athletic commissions in the United States. 'There are some things that we are always having discussions about, amending the rules and whatnot, we have times when we review them and discuss them and you know, there are arguments for and against different rule changes. We are always reviewing the explanation of the rules and also our procedure as far as what we are going to do, how we are going to enforce them, a warning here, or what are we going to do for this rule… Things can always be reviewed and change, so, those rules may not be totally fixed, they may be reviewed.'

The controversial 'Downwards elbow' rule

A rule which has been debated for years on internet discussion forums is the rules which prohibits the 'downwards elbow', an elbow thrown in a similar manner to which a trucker toots his horn - in terms of a clock, downwards from 12-to-6. 'People talk a lot about the elbow rule.' Dean said, 'That one is a little bit wordy as far as the history of where it comes from, I hear different stories as to why that rule was put in there. I wasn't refereeing at that level to be part of the rule-making process, so I hear differing stories on how it got in there. That rule is constantly under review. "Twelve-to-six strike with the point of the elbow", if anything it all, the way it's written is kind of strange.'

Waterman, however, is fairly clear about the origins of the rule and equally clear that he does not approve of the elbow strike being used in competition, 'One thing I do dislike is elbows to the head on the floor. If you look at the statistics, elbows don't cause more cuts than any other technique, but if you look at the cuts that elbows cause, especially if you're fighting someone who can throw a slicing elbow, designed to cut, it will go right down to the bone. That causes deep scar tissue which always has the potential to open up again and could end a fighter's career.

'I don't think, as an entertaining technique, that they are dynamic enough that you have to keep them in there.' Grant continued, 'It's great when you're watching it on TV, you're right up close to the action and can see the elbow being delivered. Some of Matt Lindland's fights, he'd hold his opponent down and use little short elbows, tapping away and you can win a fight using this sort of ground-and-pound wrestling technique, but if you're in the audience, you don't know what's going on. The referee's stopping it, the bloke stands up bleeding, "What's happened?" That's not very entertaining, so I don't see why it's imperative to leave them in there when you could take them out. You can watch Cage Rage fights [in which elbows are forbidden] and they are just as entertaining as UFC fights. No-one notices whether there are elbows or not.'

The 'strange' elbow rule is clear enough to the referee and promoter, 'The most powerful striking technique you can use, if you deliver it correctly, is an elbow. There are some situations like if a fighter were still standing, with his back against the cage, but he's lowered his knees a bit – the other guy's standing. He can jump up and use all of his weight to bring a downwards elbow down – that's a dangerous technique, on the collar bone, on the top of the head, you know that is a very dangerous technique. You see Kyokushinkai [karate] guys using this downwards elbow to break great big blocks of ice and allsorts, so without a doubt, it is a devastating technique,' he said of the point of the elbow strike, 'whereas from side mount there is no bodyweight behind it.'

As the sport progresses, the need to clear up disagreements and finalise a universal set of rules which can be agreed on by all promotions is a valuable goal in the eyes of referee judge and trainer, Neil Hall. 'I think an intelligent way forward would be with unification, because then it would prevent a lot of the differences of opinion. How this is going to come about I don't know because the promoters themselves [in the UK] – at the moment, there's no-one regulating what they can and can't do – they can have any rules they want really. It does happen that you go to one promotion and they've got a set of rules, you go to another promotion the next week and it's a different set. It can get confusing, not only for the referee but for the fighters themselves, which is where sometimes the accidental blows are made, "I didn't realise I couldn't do this strike, it slipped me mind that I couldn't do this strike in this position", or whatever, so unification would be a really good thing, I think.'

In order to ensure that a unified set of rules would be adhered to would require the establishment of a UK mma governing body – a possibility which has been eagerly discussed for years. However, it is very hard to imagine the drafting and subsequent ratification any kind of agreement which would allow all of the UK's promotions to co-operate. Hall has a more optimistic, and more than likely, better-informed outlook, 'I think not only is it a possibility, I think it's necessary. I think it will eventually have to happen, I think people are going to have to start getting on, they are gonna have to start talking to each other and making these things happen. I know we've been talking about it for years and people have had various attempts and not got on with each other, but they are gonna have to. If they want this sport accepted by everyone, it needs regulation, it needs unification, it's the only way that we're gonna get, really, where we wanna be, I think.'

The 10-Point must system in mma

Another problem that the sport currently faces, according to Hall, is the cumbersome, 10-point must system, which states that 10 points must be awarded to the winner of each round, with nine or less points being awarded to the loser, except in the rare case that a round is scored an even 10-10. Originally designed for the officiating of boxing matches fought over many rounds rather than the three or five round fights held by most modern mma promotions, the system is ineffective in the view of many experts.

'I think it's a poor system really,' Hall offered, 'it's a convenient system, it's easy. I don't think it's adequate for mma myself personally. You could ask me, what's my alternative then?' he laughed loudly, 'I haven't been able to work one out myself and I'd be a hypocrite if I said I had, but I don't think the 10-point must system covers enough. There's that many variables in mma, someone with a bit of a brain needs to have a look at this and think of a better way of doing this, I'm not suggesting that I'm the person to do that, but maybe myself and a few other guys could get together and come up with an alternative idea. The 10-point must system doesn't cover it, it doesn't cover it at all; it's too black and white.'

Ring vs. Cage

Drawing the rules section to a close, Marc Goddard set to rest one of the most heavily-debated subjects of the sport over the years in a couple of breaths, the argument as to which is better for mma; ring or cage? 'Personally, it's the cage, all day long. No two ways about it, like I said, the cage is the identity of our sport. In terms of my style of fighting, the cage suits me better, it's the influence and the bandwagon jumpers who jump all over it… it's not what we do and it's not what we fight in, it's just sometimes the way in which it's brought to the general public and like it or love it, the first word they associate with us is "cage". I'm sure if I was uneducated and I heard about the cage that would probably conjure up all sorts of magic to me. That's just the way it is unfortunately, I think it's just a slow process in terms of education and hopefully we can overcome that hurdle.'

CHAPTER SEVEN
THIRD MAN IN THE CAGE

'Some of these guys are so tough and they've got such an incredible belief in themselves that no matter how grim it looks from someone else's view, they think they can win. That's the belief that makes a fighter.'

- Herb Dean

Under whatever set of rules an mma fight takes place, the referee is under heavy pressure; as it only takes one wrong decision in an otherwise excellently well-officiated contest for one of the fighters to suffer an unnecessary injury. Officials from all sports are well used to unfriendly criticism; however, unlike most sports, due to the full contact nature of mixed martial arts, the safety of both fighters is placed firmly in the hands of the referee, who is thus presented with a world of responsibility unknown by football and basketball officials.

However, this important function largely goes unnoticed during a fight, as the referee skips round the outside in an attempt to maintain the correct distance from to launch himself in should the need arise to protect one or both of the combatants. Unfortunately, this leaves the referee in a difficult situation; if he does the perfect job, his works goes unnoticed, but if he makes even a hint of a mistake, the crowds boos and the online mma population quite often hangs him out to dry. Unwarranted criticism aside, the fact remains that the referee is the man on the spot to ensure fighter safety and thus has the most important job in the entire sport.

Who are they?

Cage Rage head referee, Grant Waterman is a recognisable figure on the UK scene who also finds time to fulfil the, usually quite distinct, roles of both doorman and college lecturer. Waterman gravitated to the sport of mma after briefly falling under the spell of some semi-fraudulent traditional martial arts instructors who had him believing that he was some kind of shiny-headed killing machine. Grant laughing as he looked back on an example of his early martial arts understanding.

'I was out one day with a few lads when I was young, 19 or something, I'd been doing karate for a while; one of these guys got upset with me and we were walking down the pavement and he punched me from behind – a Judas punch', he smiled.

'Everyone was drunk and I was convinced that if I had used my karate on him, I could kill him! I was that hypnotised, you know, back in the day, I was that suckered into it, I told the other guys, "Look, I really mustn't use the techniques that I know…", I was convinced – probably because I'd had a few beers as well – but it just shows you!'

Waterman soon found his way and took part in one of the UK's first ever mma contests, an 'exhibition bout' with old friend, Andy Foreman on a kickboxing show which took place in Portsmouth, back in 1997. 'There's no such thing as a demonstration is there?' he laughed, 'We got into a clinch and he did this crazy suplex on me, I landed on the back of my neck, got out of it and stood back up – it looked like it should have snapped my neck on the video!'

The fight received the biggest cheer of the night, but the mma scene in the UK was to remain in its infancy for some time to come. As he began to understand the circuit better, Waterman started to make more and more useful contacts, 'It's quite interesting for me because I didn't really have any friends who were into mma and when I started refereeing, I went to every single show on my own, so every time I went, I had to interact with people. I was a bit in awe at first of Ian Freeman, Lee Murray, Leigh Remedios and all this, you see them on the telly and when you've just started out you're a sort of newbie. I was quite respectful of them all, now that I know them, it's a different story!' he laughed, showing the back of his hand.

Back in the early days, however, Grant was not always on perfect terms with all of the characters involved with mma, but the process of getting to know them was an eye-opening experience. 'I've slagged a few people off on the internet, but I learnt my lesson quite quickly that sooner or later, you run into them. Internet forum, SFUK [Submission Fighting UK] was fantastic, back in the early days. It was such a laugh, it was so active, so busy and it was one of the only resources for mma discussion and online socialising, I thought it was fantastic. It was a shame when it died, there are other forums about, but nothing's really captured it. Because mma is not new anymore, it doesn't capture that – you're not learning about things that you don't know about, you know. It's just discussing things and taking the piss out of people, nothing new.'

'If it wasn't for things like SFUK,' Waterman continued, 'you would have had clubs, or a show up north that nobody down south knew about, you'd have a club in Wales, that no-one knew about and these things would have been going on. SFUK allowed people to learn from each other, you know, you're finding out how many people attended a show, what happened, what fighters are about. As a resource for putting a fight card together, a forum is quite a useful tool; for last minute drop outs, the internet is a fantastic tool – how do you get someone's email address? How do you get someone's email address that you don't even know exists? So SFUK, for putting shows together, I thought was essential. Everyone who's promoting in the UK now – bar a few – will remember and been a member of SFUK.'

Fellow UK referee, Marc Goddard also found himself gravitating to the growing sport of mma in its early years. 'Like the old cliché, I saw a few tapes of the early UFC's and fell in love with it since some of the very early shows, the old Grapple and Strikes, that's where I started and cut my teeth, the same place as Mark Weir, Paul Jenkins, Tom Blackledge, Ross Mason, Ronnie Mann, there's so many people who've come through that avenue, it's quite scary when you look back now. When I saw those competitions and started getting into the ground side of it, I thought, "You know, I'm gonna have some of that", and carried on.'

'The official thing came about by accident, I'm a fighter first and foremost, it just so happens that I'm a fighter who can ref, I'm not a ref who thinks he can fight. It was a couple of years ago. I was supposed to fight on the show, and I'd actually got injured a couple of weeks previous to that and that meant that I couldn't do it before the match was made but the promoter said how do you feel about reffing it? I reckon you'd be good. I said, "Yeah ok", and I went in there.'

'I've done well over 500 matches now,' Goddard continued, 'ranging from first time amateurs, they don't get any less of a commitment from me as when I'm reffing people like Monson, Hardy, Bisping, whoever they may be. A fighter is there to fight and what he deserves is my respect and obviously my protection, if they are fighting amateur or fighting professional for a world title, I can't take my eye off the ball at any time.'

Another vastly experienced referee on the UK scene is Leon Roberts, a coach at Mark Weir's Range Fighting gym with a genuine passion for the sport, who proves that you do not have to be the best fighter in the world to be an extremely competent referee. 'I refereed a show to help out a close friend and received some positive feedback and got asked by other promoters to work on their shows. I wanted to attempt to do something positive for a sport that I am very passionate about. I figured I could be an average fighter or an above average referee and the later seemed to me a smarter way to do something positive in the sport.'

Another referee who makes a massive contribution to the sport is Neil Hall, 'With the judging, I just thought, "I wouldn't mind having a go at that", so I sent out a request to a few shows asking if they would mind if I had a go and promised to do it for free. A few people got back to me and let me have a go. I liked most of it, there was only once or twice where I felt uncomfortable; but I love it actually.'

Hall spends every hour God sends training his fighters and promoting the sport; after competing himself and judging on the early Cage Warriors and Cage Rage shows, he knows mma inside out. 'If you're experienced, you've got a further understanding of the actual game. That's not to say someone who doesn't train can't do it, but I just think that it's probably a little bit better if someone has competed or is involved in training on a regular basis because you can see where the fight is going, you've got a better understanding of it.

'If they haven't actually trained themselves then basically they are judging everything on just viewing it, you know, watching it on television or video or whatever. They can learn the game, but it's just the subtleties they might miss and the timing of when the fighter is in danger or not, and, at the end of the day, it's the fighter's safety that we're looking at. There are no courses that I know of in the UK, it would probably be a good idea if we could get one together. If we could get the top guys, Grant Waterman, Marc Goddard, people like that and they could formulate some kind of course or training that we could start doing, I think it would be a great idea.'

Preparation for cage duty

As a referee, being prepared is a massive part of putting on a good performance. They will often put themselves through some kind of a physical warm up before the event is underway, but the psychological preparation to take charge of the contest is just as important, as Grant Waterman explained. 'I'm refereeing so often, I don't have to do the mental preparation like I used to. When I was refereeing once every month, once every two months, in the two weeks leading up to the fight, I'd get a load of old tapes out and watch them over and over to see what the referee was doing and just imagine myself refereeing that fight and tune myself back into refereeing. I'm refereeing almost every week now, so mma is just part of my life.'

'I try to keep myself fit.' Waterman added, 'I train in mma as well – I think that's imperative' he confirmed: 'You've got to keep up to date with techniques, you got to be aware of them. I'm not a great fighter, by any stretch of the imagination, but you've got to train all the areas, stand up, grappling and takedowns…

'What you've got to try and do, as a referee, is stay one or two moves ahead of what the guy is doing, seeing what he's setting up, where the fight is going to go so you can position yourself and anticipate when a fighter is going to be in a vulnerable position, if you train in mma and you are aware of techniques and you are aware of where a fight is going to go you can be much more aware of when a fighter is going to be in a vulnerable position and you've got to jump in to stop it.'

As Grant Waterman explained, gaining the correct perspective of the bout is half of the battle. 'Everybody watches a fight from a fighter's view point, what are they going to do next, who's going to get knocked out, where is he going to hit him? You should start watching fights down the gym and start thinking to yourself, "Where do you need to be to see the vulnerable points, when a fighter is in danger?"

'When you're watching a fight, and someone is in a kimura, you watch the submission; a referee needs to be watching the other hand, not the actual submission. You need to keep an eye on it to make sure there's no injury, but you've got to position yourself in a specific position to see if he's going to tap.

When guys are stood up, and they are circling, where should you be stood? - If they get banged, you need to see their eyes; you need to see their reaction, so where do you need to stand for that? You should be getting this mentality in the gym first; not thinking, "I'm going to referee a show and try it out." You need to get this mindset and get it right before you ever step on the mat and referee a proper fight.'

Being in position to watch out for competitors safety is something that Herb Dean has learned to do, whilst also developing an excellent technical understanding of how to save a fighter from damage in a submission hold. 'You should train and be familiar with all of the techniques used and keep abreast because it's constantly changing and evolving and different techniques that people are coming up with, you've got to keep up to date on what people are doing. We do a lot in the fight, we do stand ups, we stop fights, so sometimes people can be going for a backdoor escape and it looks like they are not fighting back and if you don't know what to look for, you don't see what someone's doing. Also, when you stopping the fight and someone is in a submission hold or whatnot, you want to have a knowledge of how the submission works so you can work against to protect the fighter. Kind of have a plan of what you're going to do, how you're going to do it. Are you going to take parts of the submission away or are you going to support the joint?'

When should the fight be stopped?

In mma competition, things can change fast – one strike, or the twist of a submission can immediately put a fighter out of the contest and at serious risk of incurring unnecessary damage. At this point, it is the referee's job to leap in and call a halt to the contest; a couple of seconds can mean the difference between a good stoppage and some kind of injury being inflicted on one of the fighters. Knowing exactly when to jump in and stop a contest is, therefore, the most important skill a referee needs. As Grant Waterman explains, there are ways of telling when a fight needs to be stopped.

'Unless they're tapping, it's usually facial expressions' he said, knowingly, 'The eyes tell a good story and if a fighter wants out, he will often look over to the referee to see what the referee is doing and perhaps gesturing, "Are you going to stop it?", because he's not going to tap.'

Neil Hall concurred, 'You can see it in their eyes to start with, that's the first sign that they start becoming not happy', he said in a wonderful understatement, 'The first sign is in the eyes, the second sign is body language, various postures that they go into suggest that they are not happy and you can usually tell when it's going that way. If it's a quick knock out, that's a different matter, if it's a ground and pound for example or something like that, you can see when a fighter's had enough. I think that's down to experience as well, looking for these signs, going back to the courses that we could do. You know, looking for these signs and these body postures that people are doing. It's just a feeling that you can get, you can just tell that they've had enough.'

Waterman described one of the postures his college refers to, 'When you're [on the bottom,] mounted and you want to bridge in order to escape, you've got to have your knees bent and your feet on the floor to bridge, to raise your hips up. If your legs go flat, you've kind of given up; you're accepting the pounding, as it were. Your knees have got to be bent to get out of mount position unless there's some new technique I've not heard about; if your legs to flat and limp, you've given up.'

Some fighters, however, simply refuse to show any signal that they are beaten and their fighting spirit will allow them to absorb potentially dangerous amounts of punishment. In situations such as this, the referee must make a judgement call as to whether the losing fighter is in a position to continue. 'The level that they have fought at before will determine sometimes how far you let it go', Waterman explained, 'Some fighters you know can take a lot of punishment, fighters like Sami Berik, for example, will keep being whacked all day long and can still pull out a win. Now, if you're refereeing two first timers, there's no way you're going to let those guys beat the hell out of each other for three 5-minute rounds; but if you're fighting for a world title then there's justification to let it go a bit further, you've got to give them the opportunity to turn a fight around. On the other hand, if it's amateurs or first timers you've got a duty of care to protect them more than the world class guys.'

In the world of professional mma, Nail Hall takes a quite different position, regarding the differing levels of punishment which may be received by a fighter under his jurisdiction. 'I don't really like to do that to be honest. I like to set a standard and stick to it to be honest because if you start having different guidelines for different people, I think personally, it's not the way to go. I understand that some guys can take more punishment than others, but at the end of the day, it's their safety that we've talking about. At the end of the day, if I see these warning signs that we were talking about I will say so to the fighter during the fight and give them chances that way.

'"You're in danger, you're going to have to do something about this"' Hall shouted, mimicking the warning he bellows at combatants under heavy pressure. 'Then, if I think it's over, it's over, whether it's a novice fighter or a more experienced fighter, safety is the most important thing. That's just my personal opinion, other referees might be different.

'There's got to be standardisation' Hall pointed out, 'If you want longevity from this – I want to be refereeing for a long time, I don't want to be seen as biased or in favour of somebody, giving people more chances than others – you set a standard, stick to it. If we have a discussion afterwards, we have a discussion afterwards.'

Rule breaking

Aside from their principle duty of maintaining fighter safety, a referee is obviously there to enforce a rigid rule structure. Unlike professional wrestling, mma fighters do not generally attempt to get round the rules in the hope that they will inflict some form of terrible disaster upon their opponent. Instead, the most common rule infractions are often the least significant to the outcome of the fight.

'Probably grabbing the fence', Grant Waterman said, referring to the most common infringement that he sees, 'It's a difficult one because there are a lot of cases where someone will grab the fence, but what you don't want to do as a referee is upset the momentum of a fight. It spoils the action and can upset both fighters. What you don't want to do is penalise one fighter for a foul, but in affect take an advantage from the other fighter. So there is a lot of cases where a fighter will commit a minor infringement and the referee won't do anything and the crowd wonders why. But if you actually stopped the fight and penalised the fighter, you'd actually be doing the other guy an injustice by taking away an advantage from him by stopping the action.'

Marc Goddard also confirmed that the rule breaking he encounters most often is far from dramatic or malicious, though professes to adopting a slightly sterner theoretical line with offenders, 'I see people grabbing the cage, pulling the shorts and hooking the glove. It's all little things like that you know. You can stamp that out there and then and if it goes any further it starts getting into the realms of deducting points and whatnot. It's always the small insignificant stuff, but when I say insignificant stuff, it can dramatically turn around the outcome of the fight; so if it does happen, I need to be on top of it. A rule's a rule, one rule is not bigger than the other, I've got to stress that, there's a list of rules that we adhere to. Obviously, someone grabbing the inside the glove is not immediately putting someone in danger, like blatantly standing up and soccer kicking them to the head.

'In all the matches I've done there have been a couple of disqualifications,' Goddard continued, 'but they were not horrendously vicious assaults, I just haven't encountered that. There's nothing which sticks in my head in terms of the fouls, most of the guys, they know me now, they all are good guys from good camps and they generally stick to the rules.'

A perfect example of the direction of a fight turning significantly on an apparently minor infraction came on the Bodog encounter between Fedor Emelianenko and the unfancied former middleweight wrestler, Matt Lindland. To the surprise of the entire crowd, Lindland was able to lift up his high-touted opponent and seemed on the brink of delivering a hard slam and landing in a dominant position. As it happened, a swift tug on the rope from Fedor reduced the impact of the takedown and allowed him to maintain an even keel in the contest, eventually turning the fight around to seal victory with an armbar.

'Infractions like that can have a huge effect.' Herb Dean stressed, 'One grabbing of a fence can definitely change the outcome of the fight, you know. That can change the way the fight ends up and it might have been that one take down that changed the whole course of the fight and it's prevented by grabbing the fence.'

Mistakes and criticism

Due to the highly pressurized environment in which they operate, referees often find themselves in the thick of controversy and face constant accusations that they have made terrible errors. Mistakes do happen, as any referee will tell you, but a referee who is able learn from his mistakes, and those of referees around him, has a good chance to take on board more of the finer details of his craft.

An often-seen mistake, in Grant Waterman's view, is the distance referees allow between themselves and the two fighters, 'It's quite difficult being able to judge how close, or how far away you should be, because if two fighters are moving around the cage, fighting, you've got to keep your distance because when they change direction, you obviously can't be in the way. You've got to be far enough away so that you're not getting in the way; but you've got to be close enough to step in and stop the action without having to travel too far so that they'd be a delay. Some referees I see, they're right on top of two guys, especially when they go to the ground. Larry Landless used to wind me up, with all due respect, he used to bang the canvas when two guys were on the floor grappling, he'd bang the canvas and tell them to work. He'd be shouting at the fighters, saying "Are you ok? Keep working, keep working" and he'd be banging the canvas. For the fighter who's grappling, that would put me off something rotten.

'Also, if a referee is too close,' Grant continued, 'if he's in your peripheral vision too closely, it could really put you off as well, but then I've seen other referees who are so far away, if a fighter gets knocked out, he has to run right the way across the octagon and the guy has taken two or three more punches before he's got there. It isn't because the referee hasn't reacted quick enough, it's because he's too far away.'

'The other big mistake I see is position of referees; you've got to be on the right side of a fighter, not only standing, but on the ground. You see it if one fighter is trying to apply a submission, a lot of people think that the referee's main viewpoint should be the arm that's being extended, or the leg that's being attacked, when actually, it's the other arm that you need to have sight of for one the guy's tapping. So obviously, you've got to keep switching view to see if there's any injury occurring, but the main point is to see if the guy's tapping so you can stop the fight. A lot of referee's are watching the submission, the guy could be tapping round the other side and he doesn't know about it, but he can't tap if his arm's being extended.'

'I may be biased but the referees in the UK are very experienced and competent and mistakes are few', Cage Rage referee, Leon Roberts said with a smile, 'but in other countries you sometimes see referees not knowing all the rules and allowing illegal blows. Also, sometimes refs will not play the advantage, so if one fighter puts an ankle lock on and receives a kick to the face, the ref should say he has seen it and allow the action to continue as the fighter who is applying the hold may well submit his opponent. If he jumps in straight away the momentum of the fight is ruined and the fighter has lost his dominant position. When there is a lull in the action or at the end of the round he can issue his warning or point deduction if necessary.'

As all referees are subject to criticism at some stage in their career, but Roberts is a rare example of a referee who has so far managed to avoid any kind of backlash from disgruntled cornermen. 'If I was often criticized I don't think promotions would use me. Some people will obviously not agree with a decision and go on the internet and say their piece, that's human nature and you are never going to change that. As a referee we leave ourselves wide open to criticism, however I think the UK is lucky to have high calibre referees who take their jobs seriously and all the fighters know we only have their safety and best interests in mind.'

'I don't think anybody likes to receive criticism, unless it's constructive.' Roberts added poignantly, 'This especially applies to when you are doing something that requires a lot of preparation and attention to detail. What I do not like too much is when a journalist or commentator criticizes you for something that they perceive you have done wrong because this influences other people who will often jump on the bandwagon, however, I understand they are doing a job and giving their opinion.'

'Everyone's entitled to criticise,' Waterman said, taking up the point, 'everyone's emotional at the end of a fight and I take everything on the chin. I encourage constructive criticism after every single fight, after every single decision I make; I love feedback, tell me what I've done wrong, tell me what you think I've done wrong, tell me what you think I could have done better. I'm not saying that I necessarily think people are right, but you take this feedback in and if enough people are saying the same thing, you've then got to decide whether you did make the right decision. If at the end of a fight, people are slagging me off, generally, it's because of their emotional state and 99 times out of 100, when they watch the video footage, I get an email or a phone call of apology anyway, so it's all good.'

The most controversial stoppage in the history of mma

After being roundly criticized for stopping the second fight between Tito Ortiz and Ken Shamrock, Dean fully accepts the fact that criticism is part of his profession; however, he has an excellent way of dealing with the uncomfortable views of others, 'You've got to stay in the mind state that - I'm there for a reason; to do what

I believe is the right thing and what the Commission decides upon and I'm there to enforce those rules and sometimes it's not going to make me a popular guy and sometimes people are going to be upset. If the fighters, who know that it was the right decision, decide to blame things on me, well, I'm here for that as well. I let the fighters know that I've got big shoulders, if you want to put something on me, that's alright. That's what I'm there for. The time when it begins to bother me is the time I need to walk away from this, you know? If I let the things that people say to me upset me.'

After his decision in the Tito versus Ken rematch, many people took issue with Dean, 'There were lots of times when I ran into a fan, and we'd talk it through from I guess a referee's point of view, then they usually end up agreeing with me. He'd taken five or six unanswered elbows; then I ask, did he seem to be in a position to stop the next elbow if I hadn't jumped in and the answer is, "No, he did not look like he was going to stop the next elbow." Well, how many are enough? What's the point I should have cut it off at?

'Basically, people are making a decision based on the fact that they wanted to see more of a fight.' Dean scoffed, 'Then they are making that decision based on the fact that Ken Shamrock recovers fast. But how fast you recover and what he's doing at the time are two totally separate issues – that's what I based my stoppage on and that's what I'm going to continue to base it on. No-one wants to have bottles thrown at them, but think about it, what could I have done differently, so the people aren't throwing bottles at me? But Ken Shamrock had taken some big elbows and was going to continue to take them and they were landing very hard, he was not defending them and I think that was a very good stoppage.

'It doesn't bother me that some fighters think that they can continue,' said Dean, adding a nugget of pure gold, 'that's what I expect of them. Some of these guys are so tough and they've got such an incredible belief in themselves that no matter how grim it looks from someone else's view, they think they can win. These people can be demolished and unconscious and they think, "If I could have had just one more second, I could have turned it around." That's the belief that makes a fighter, so I expect them to argue with my decision, I expect them to believe in themselves when it's evident to everyone else that the situation is hopeless. But, you know, I'm there to make my decision and keep it safe.'

Physical intervention

During his career, Grant Waterman has been charged with keeping fighters safe in the most physical sense of the phrase, not least when Geoff Hayes stepped in at late notice to take on the soft-looking, Rich Austin on the FX3 promotion. Fighting out of a good camp and with a bodybuilder's physique, Hayes was not the ideal opponent for Austin's debut fight.

Charging out of the corner with wild punches, Austin looked out of his depth and a thudding right hand from Hayes quickly knocked the hobby fighter unconscious. Hayes, however, full of adrenaline, rushed into deliver a series of crushing blows, completely ignoring Waterman's call to stop fighting. As it became increasingly less likely that Hayes would stopping attacking his downed opponent of his own accord, the south Coast referee grabbed hold of him with a tight bodylock and suplexed him across the cage, earning one of the biggest cheers of the night.

'I just remember that Geoff Hayes is a bit of as monster,' Grant chuckled, 'that's another situation where it's not a conscious decision, and probably a little bit of the doorman mentality comes into play there, he won't do what he's told, so you've got to do something physical. But afterwards, we all shake hands, you know, what happens in the cage stays in the cage, you know. That's how I feel.'

However, in situations when the fighter is not surrounded by red mist, Herb Dean feels confident that most fighters will stop of their own accord, 'I try to touch the guy, give him a chance to stop, I don't believe that you should tackle the fighters regardless of what they're doing. I think that when I go to stop the fight, I come in and when I touch them, I get a feel of what they're doing. If they are trying to stop, I let them stop; I give them a chance to be a gentleman about it. But if they are not going to stop, it's my job to keep that other fighter safe, that's the first job, the first responsibility of the referee, to prevent any unnecessary damage to the competitors. So I need to do whatever I can to prevent the people from taking damage after the outcome of the fight has been decided.'

Lies among lies

Another problem faced by mma referees surrounds the submission aspect of the sport. As alluded to when a fighter is caught in a hold and on the verge of submitting, it can often be very difficult for a referee to see when he is tapping out. The fighter's hand, or foot, can be shielded from sight by a combination of the opponent's body and a pile of interlocking limbs. If he feels his opponent may be about to capitulate, the combatant applying the submission will often have something to say to the referee; it is once again his responsibility to make a swift judgment call, should the fight be stopped? Or is the fighter lying?

'They advise me to say that their opponent has tapped all the time; that happens often.' Herb Dean said wearily, so used to being misled that he has devised a system to help him make the right decision. 'If he's tapped, then I need to see it. I tell them to continue the fight, you know. "He's tapping, he's tapping!" If he's tapping, I need to see it; if I don't see it, it hasn't happened. I'm going to check that fighter, obviously."

Grant Waterman has also heard his share of porkie pies, 'David Bielkheden, when he fought Phil Norman in Cage Rage, he told me during the fight that Norman had tapped. I didn't stop the fight, I just said "Carry on, carry on, I'll tell you when the fight is over." I looked and Phil Norman was holding a thumb up to me to say "Yeah I'm fine". In fact, Beilkheden did it again, and got up and walked off and said, "He's tapped" and I restarted the fight.'

Some fighters are just too brave for their own good and lie in order to cover up their own injury in an attempt to stay in the contest, a prime example of which occurred at Cage Rage 19 in the bout between two Brazilian jiu-jitsu black belts, Jean Silva and Danilo Cherman. 'Jean Silva had an upside down armbar and he was laying on top of Cherman's arm' Grant recalled, 'I couldn't see the arm. In that case, you're looking at the free arm to see if he's going to tap and he can't tap with that hand, you're looking for a foot to tap. 'If he suddenly looks like he's in excruciating pain, you've got to decide whether to stop the fight or not... "Surely he must be just about to tap", if he's grimacing.

'Jean Silva said to me, "I'm breaking his arm, I'm breaking his arm", and then just looked at me.

'I said "Carry on', thinking that if he's breaking his arm, this guy is going to tap, surely.'

Adjusting his voice for the magnitude of his next sentence, Waterman continued, with a tone of genuine astonishment, 'Cherman's face did not change one bit. His facial expressions didn't change. He got out of the submission, or Jean Silva let the armbar go and he carried on for another four minutes in that round - and used that arm to punch Jean Silva on the ground!

'At the end of the fight, his trainer said to me, "Can we get the doctor to look at his arm?" – it turned out that his elbow had been dislocated, his arm was broken - that was extreme. I think he was out of action for at least six months after that as well and he only got paid 400 quid for the fight. Only Brazilians have that mentality!'

With all the traps and pitfalls of being a professional mma referee are clear to see, Herb Dean summarized his feelings on the role he so enthusiastically undertakes and the praise he receives for continually making massive commitment to fighter safety, inside the cage walls. 'A lot of fans have a very good idea of what it takes and what a referee goes through. I think that overall, the fans are very respectful and pay attention to the referees, more so than in any other sport, because I think they realize how important the referee is in mixed martial arts. I'm very surprised by the respect and admiration the fans give to me and the attention I get, the notoriety, the fact that the fans pay attention to what we do.'

CHAPTER EIGHT
THE LIFE OF A PROMOTER

'In the old days I used to fight for free; in my first show, I had a main event fighter who's never fought mma before and he walked out with two grand [£2,000].'

- Marc Goddard

They say that moving house is the most stressful 24 hours that you are likely to have in life; however, as any fight promoter will confirm, there is nothing vaguely similar to the unrelenting pressure of putting on a 12-bout fight card. The stress begins weeks before the event as the initial preparations are made, invariably followed by panic-stricken last-minute rearrangements as fighters drop out due to injuries in preparation, before the anxiety piques in a stunning crescendo on a night which can bring either elation or financial ruin.

What motivates people to go through such stressful times and willingly take on these extraordinary financial risks? And what makes it all worth it? I somehow managed to pin down some of the most elusive figures on the UK scene to explain what it is like to live the rollercoaster life of a fight promoter.

The hobby which got out of control

Martial arts trainers and enthusiasts, Dave O'Donnell and Andy Geer decided to turn their hand to mma promotion after becoming disillusioned with the UK scene in late 2002 and what they saw as a poorly run and badly disorganised shows. 'We thought, "Let's just do one show, show them how to do it, give a guideline on how to do it,"' Dave O'Donnell said enthusiastically, 'Plus we were both in the entertainment business and it ain't just about putting a load of fights on, it's about running everything like an entertainment.'

The first Cage Rage event took place on 7 September 2002 at the Elephant and Castle Leisure Centre. 'It sold out,' O'Donnell said proudly, 'I think there was 1100 people there; no-one could believe how professional it was. We had Frank Shamrock there, Ian Freeman reffed for us at that time, so we had a load of celebrities and it was a massive, great night. I said after it, "We're never going to do it again!"'

Commentator, Rob Nutley was one of the fighters competing on the first event 'I think a lot of the exposure and the build up of the event was from a lot of friends and families being there to support the fighters and support the show. I know that I had around 70 to 80 people there, who had just to come and watch me fight because it was the fight time I had fought in the cage. Fighting in the centre of South London where, as well, a lot of fighters on that card originally were from the area, so promoting it in that area was pretty easy to do. It was a big thing, though if I'd fought at kickboxing or San Shou, I'd only attract 10 to 15, but because we was doing this "cage fighting thing", a lot more people turned up and a lot more people had interest in it.'

After the success of the first show, the temptation to put on another event was too much and before long, O'Donnell and Geer began working on an ambitious business for their new company. 'It was stressful', Geer said, weeks before stepping down as Cage Rage co-promoter for personal reasons. 'It was hard work, but at the same time, it was wonderful. When you have a good night, there's no job like it, but when you have a bad night, it's the worst job in the world! The biggest buzz we ever got was the first time we went to the Wembley arena and half way through the evening, when it was all rocking and rolling and the crowd was beginning to roar and we realised we'd nearly sold the place out!'

Cage Warriors co-promoter, Andy Lillis got involved in promoting for the love of the sport, but added his own business acumen into the mix, 'My background from years gone by was promoting raves,' Lillis said candidly, 'Yes, the illegal ones that were held in disused warehouses and farmer's fields and that kind of thing. Well, promoting is promoting whether it is for music or fighting.'

Lillis started martial arts at an early age, before putting his training on hold, as he picked up a rifle instead to join the Royal Marines. However, with his army career behind him, the Coventry entrepreneur started to make inroads into mma promotion. 'I had been friends with [long time Cage Warriors promoter] Dougie Truman for many years when he approached me with regards to investing into Cage Warriors and me and my business partner, Dean Griffiths, went along to a show in Sheffield. We liked what we seen and bought 50% shares in Cage Warriors. We then set up Warrior Promotions. Our first show was "UK versus France", in my home town and, at that time [May 2005], we pulled in the biggest attendance for a UK promotion, not bad for a first attempt!'

Berkshire-based promoter and keen martial arts enthusiast, Paul James took an even greater step into the unknown at the beginning of his career as a promoter - he and brother, Simon James invested heavily in their own venture as they set up the Free Fight Federation, better known as FX3. 'Basically, I've done promotion work for quite a few years now. I worked abroad and used to put on major dance events. I've always trained and been a big fan of the UFC and Cage Rage.'

The James brothers, genuinely some of the warmest characters on the UK scene, were forced to work hard every step of the way, investing heavily in their fledgling promotion and they struggled to get off the ground. 'I think, now that I've heard afterwards, I think everyone was very wary of us because these two brothers come along that no-one had ever heard of, and I think it was like "What the hell are you two up to?", but the response was really good. Cage Rage was very supportive, Dougie from Cage Warriors, he was very supportive, gave me advice. Everybody in the market, although it is quite a close-knit market, I think everyone saw that we were doing something for the good and everyone was very supportive and did try to help us out a lot.'

However, as a start up promotion, the initial FX3 event turned out to be far more expensive than they had anticipated and came as a significant financial hit to the brothers, who were forced to take drastic last minute steps to ensure that their show could go ahead. 'I can't tell you how much we lost on the first event, but I had to re-mortgage my house, so did my brother. It was that bad, we lost an absolute fortune. We just did not know what people would be getting paid, we had our own ring built; we spent absolutely thousands upon thousands on advertising it.'

The show sold out the 2,000 seat capacity Rivermead Leisure Complex, but that was of little consolation to the pair. 'It was very much because we were green behind the ears, we tried to run before we could walk basically and we lost a lot of money on the first event. Family and friends kept saying, "Don't have another one, you can't afford to…" I'll be honest, we lost a little bit on the second one too, not quite so much, but we learned a lot from that went back to the drawing board on the third event and, thankfully, perseverance kept us there and the last three events have made money. I think most promoters that you speak to will tell you that you do this because you love it and is does get under your skin, it does become part of your life, I think that's why we persevered even through loss of money, we just carried on doing it and thank God, it's now going in the right direction.'

Fighter, referee and promoter, Marc Goddard laughed as he outlined his reasons for setting up the Birmingham-based event, Amateur Mixed Martial Arts. 'Call me the Robin Hood of mma, mate, it's a bit of a laugh now, the guys who fought on the show will tell you; half of the ticket money goes straight back to the fighters, because it's all about them. At the end of the day, it may sound like a cliché but in the old days I used to fight for free. In my first show, I had a main event fighter who's never fought mma before and he walked out with two grand [£2,000]. People are struggling to get that now on the big shows.

'What I wanted to do', Goddard continued, 'was give those youngsters that platform, that level, there's a big crowd, 1,000 plus, they sell out every time. You get all the production, the MC, the ref, everything is there for them to cut their teeth and there's a good recognised rule set as well, which I produced pulling on all my experience of fighting and working on the other promotions.'

Council involvement

This set of mma rules may well work for Goddard's promotion, but quite bizarrely in this modern age of general acceptance that the sport enjoys, some local councils in the UK still regard mma as some kind of threat to the mindset of the public and have refused permission to allow promoters to hold shows on council owned property. Ultimate Force promoter, Paul Murphy recalled a brush which he had with Doncaster Borough Council. 'I had one major difficulty when we approached the Doncaster Dome – that is our home – but we had one major difficulty when they wouldn't let us in. They thought it was influential to people, predominantly youngsters, and that it was detrimental to the image they wanted to portray.'

Murphy attended a council meeting armed with a copy of both his most recent show, and of the most recent show staged by an American pro-wrestling organisation which enjoyed a monthly booking at the Dome. 'I took my kids to that show and it was one of the most shocking shows I've ever been to. I've got three kids and at the time the youngest was six. The show, it should have had an adult certification on it, it was full of bad language, full of chanting, swearing. The audience were like something off a hillbilly movie; I've never seen anything like it.'

Murphy stated his case at the meeting, simply by showing the footage. 'I showed our show, where it shows fighters shaking hands before and afterwards, explained the lack of injuries, different ways to win, so the onus isn't on striking the head and then moved onto the DVD of the wrestling and went straight to the scene where they pulled out a wall-paper pasting table, covered it in lighter fuel, covered it with what was apparently nails or pins or whatever, set it on fire and threw his opponent through it.'

'They also did a scene which was quite sickening,' Murphy said of a section of the action which involved a local disabled fan. 'They faked a severe injury to him; his American opponent publicly slated him, picked him up and slammed him. He pretended that he was dead and they the portrayed a funeral march carrying him out; my kids were mortified and my youngest was crying.'

Murphy showed this portrayal of violence to the shocked officials alongside footage of his event, comprehensively demonstrating the injustice of the previous council decision. 'They adjourned for a few hours and then told me that my show could go ahead.'

According to referee and Portsmouth promoter, Grant Waterman, this lack of understanding remains a massive hurdle to the sport. 'Even now, to this day, ignorance with local councils and the general lay person is vast. You mention mixed martial arts, they haven't got a clue what you're on about, they've never heard of it and they go, "Oh, is that that wrestling thing?" It's amazing, when you're involved in a sport or an activity so often, as I and you are, you're living it, you can't believe that no-one's heard of it. So even now, I've got this constant explanation going on with lay people about what I do and what it is. I've had meetings on meetings, I've written letters on behalf of many people regarding the safety of mma and how much safer it is than other activities, other sports and trying to justify its existence.

'Funnily enough, just recently, I ended up having meetings with the council.' Grant said, having been refused permission to stage a show at the 2,000-seater, Guildhall in Portsmouth. 'They didn't want to promote cage fighting, Cage Rage, anything that had the word "Rage" in it, because the definition of Rage is uncontrolled violence; which is ridiculous. So I wrote to my local MP and on my behalf, he wrote to the council and just recently, I've been allowed to use the Guildhall. As it turns out, after looking at it properly, it's not an ideal venue so it's been a bit of a wasted venture but it became a matter of principle in the end!'

In contrast, Marc Goddard anticipated that Birmingham local council would have an issue with the use of a cage, rather than the self-discipline or otherwise exhibited by the athletes in competition. As a result, the amateur promoter opted to stage his event in a ring, avoiding conflict with the council altogether. 'The cage, it's kind of like a double-edged sword. The cage is the identity of this sport and I've got some very good friends from some very good organisations and they have the word "cage" in their title. It's mma, mixed martial arts, but that's not decrying on anyone who's built their name on the cage – look at Cage Rage, Cage Warriors, Cage Gladiators, all fantastic shows, but it's just that Birmingham council have got a problem with the cage, I remember this from a friend of mine trying to put shows on. It's that whole stereotypical thing and they made it really difficult for them and they had to change venues about three or four times. Those are all the things that I just wanted to get away from and avoid.'

The endless woes of a promoter

However, promoters the world over will tell you there are certain problems that you face when putting on an event, one of which is fighters withdrawing from the contest at the last minute. 'You do get pull outs', Goddard said, 'but when you've got fighters who are earning the money that they are earning on my show, you tend not to pull out!' However, as he explained, Goddard has a sixth sense for telling when fighters are unlikely to show up on fight day.

'You know who's serious and who's not. You get so many people who are like, "I wanna do this, I wanna do that", and you get back in touch with them and you never hear off them again. Those guys go on the blacklist as it were. I tend to work with the same people. There's gyms I keep working with and they send down teams of guys, they are professional, they know what they're doing, they've got guys who are just looking to start out in the sport and establish themselves. We do get headaches and stuff, but fighters pulling out is the least of it, although I shouldn't really say that. To be honest with you I'm amazed that my phone is in one piece at the end of the day, but there you go.'

Goddard may have been fortunate so far, but as Grant Waterman laughed, some problems are more-or-less unavoidable as a promoter. 'There's always problems with hotels after the show', he said. 'Fighters want to let off steam because they haven't had a drink for a couple of months… and there's people smoking strange herbs. One of the hotels we used complained to me when I went down to pay the bill that they had had one of their replica Roman sofas stolen from the foyer. It must have been a 4-man lift, they had security guards and everything, but they didn't notice that a sofa got stolen', he mused with a broad smile.

A newcomer to the world of promotion, but no stranger to the UK mma scene, Jeremy Bailey recently inked a deal to co-promote the FX3 organisation alongside the James brothers. As a fighter himself, the 'Bad Boy' understands better than most where a lot of fighters get their anxiety from and the stressful repercussions for promoters. 'If you've got 15 fights on, you've got 30 fighters, obviously they've all got their needs and fighters come first, but to be honest with you the first thing I done was I rung up [Cage Rage promoters] Dave and Andy and was laughing, just apologising – I said, "You know what, I didn't realise I was such a nightmare!"' He laughed.

'You got 30 fighters coming after you from the same angle, all asking for the same things. But I really am enjoying it and something which sticks in my mind which Paul [James] said to me, that it's really weird how, after this massive buzz, the morning after the show, you feel a bit down. I laughed at him when he told me, but I remember ringing him on the Monday morning after our first event as a team, I just felt like I was depressed. Just a massive build up for two or three months before the show, the show went off, that was great and it was just like a horrible, horrible come down. You just feel lost like you've got nothing to do.'

Cage Warriors co-promoter, Andy Lillis, has also developed a love of promoting and has remained involved in the sport through some difficult times. 'My bank manager and my wife, think I'm mad. My wife has stood by me through the good times and the bad, even signed the papers when I remortgaged our family home, she has been a real rock to me and supported my every move regarding Cage Warriors. Ask me why I stay involved? It's a passion. When I see how much the fighters put into achieving their goal it hits me like a hit hits a junkie. When I see people like Mike Bisping and Dan Hardy reaching the highest point of their careers and realize that I had a hand in directing their career and getting them to where they want to be, and then all the money in the world cannot take that buzz away.

'I get a bit down when fighters don't show their appreciation at all the hard work and time effort and money that promoters put into showcasing fighters' Lillis continued, 'Despite what people think there are not pots of gold at the end of the MMA rainbow, not all fighters are like this maybe only a very small minority, but it's that small minority that make a lot of hard work for a show. I am not going to go in to how much work it takes let alone money, and then we get fighters that just do not turn up, send you a text saying, "My mummy said I can't fight anymore", then turn their phone off and fighters not making weight when they call themselves professionals. Apart from that, everything else I take in my stride I'm used to the knocks and always bounce back.'

Paul James has faced similar hardships over his testing first few years of promotion, 'If I'd known how hard this was, I wouldn't have done it full time, I don't think. Now I'm into it, it is kind of my life and if someone had said to me at the beginning that this is what it was going to be like, I would never have taken it on. It's extremely hard to run.

'Six weeks before the event happens you're working round the clock: the running around, the chasing around trying to deal with the fighters is one of the big things now. There's so many shows happening around the UK and Europe, the fighters are getting double-booked or they are fighting too close to the fight cards. That's a massive problem. The promotional side of things, the cost involved with it.

Double-booked fighters and the costs of advertising are just a part of what an event organiser can expect: 'Just trying to run everything like a professional event, trying to do pre-day weigh-ins, put people in hotels. It's a lot of work, you're running around continuously. Even the day of the actual event, policing it properly, making sure there's no trouble happening, it's a very, very stressful time, I don't think I actually enjoy it until the following day when I sit down and watch the DVD. I probably lose about 7-8 kilos in weight, day before, day of the event, just running around. It's very stressful, but it's very rewarding, if it wasn't rewarding we wouldn't still do it. I think the stress levels are the worst thing about it, but it's definitely worth it.'

At the inaugural FX3 event in June 2005, Paul was looking particularly under fire, but it wasn't until my conversation with him two years later that I realised exactly why he had a look of thunder on a night which turned out to be hugely entertaining. 'We didn't have enough money two or three days before the event to pay for it, I had to re-mortgage my house, which is always a problem.

'At the beginning, I couldn't handle myself, I was so green,' he confessed, 'I didn't know what I was doing and I learnt the hard way, but I think now I plan it a lot better, I make sure that everything is organised very well. The money is there before we start to do an event, in case there are any problems, we can pay the athletes, the judges and for the cage and so forth, we do manage it a lot better now, we do manage it as a proper company.'

With his organisation on the up, James already has a variety of happy memories to look back on. 'Obviously, getting a sell out down the venue is financially rewarding and just a great achievement if you think to yourself, regardless of the money side of things, you haven't lost anything, it's just all these people come down to see an event that we put on, that's just fantastic. Just to see some of the fights inside the cage; the first event, we had Michael Bisping and obviously look where he is now... we had Abdul Mohamed, Leigh Remedios, Paul Daley in there. You sit back and you watch that and think, "They are fighting on the event that I run, all these people are here to watch it." I don't think you can get a buzz like that, even though it's stressful and you do run around and you don't get to see all the event, the whole thing's a buzz really, as long as it all goes to plan!'

For Andy Lillis, meeting a crop of new friends and acquaintances adds to the thrill of putting on a well attended show. 'One of the best things about being involved has been meeting a person by the name of Ian Dean [Cage Warriors match-maker and human mma encyclopedia], that man will always be a legend as far as MMA in the UK goes; he has taught me everything I know and if one day I can be as respected as he is by the fighters and promoters that we deal with then my mission has been accomplished. His passion, love and commitment for the development of this sport are second to none and I am proud to have him as part of our team.'

Making in-roads on behalf of the sport and putting on good shows seem to be a commonly-held motivating factor for the men behind the scenes, as Paul Murphy confirmed. 'We don't get a lot of financial gain out of it. In fact, all we've done is lose money, predominantly. We've had a very small bit of profit, but put it this way, you wouldn't get a holiday out of it!' he laughed. 'At this moment in time, we're trying to put on great fights which has obviously cost us more. Rewards would be praise, rewards would be seeing our own team, we have our own team obviously, and it would be seeing our team do well, develop, grow, it's great when you've got one of your fighters like Tengiz [Tedoradze] who has out-grown your show really and he fights for you as more of a favour to the show than anything else.'

On the subject of smaller shows, Murphy insists that there is no substitute for quality, when putting on a live event. 'I think there's quite a lot springing up in the North East [of England] and there are a lot of money-grabbers there. I've been to one of the shows and they are not even a snip at ours, they can't compete on the production value of it. There is one guy who has been there consistently, started about the same time as me and we get on very well, do a lot of work together – that's Peter McQueen. I know he finds it difficult with the amount of shows up North, but he's a consistent trooper. He's still providing good value. The other guys; what they are doing is they are bringing in foreign fighters for a snip and putting on shows that way - but, it won't last.'

The Ultimate Fighting Championship

Aside from upstart promotions looking to make a fast buck in the fight game, the UK has also seen the Ultimate Fighting Championship make a renewed commitment to the UK market, even going so far as to stage the 'UFC v Pride' light-heavyweight showdown between then champion, Quinton 'Rampage' Jackson and Grand Prix tournament winner, Dan Henderson.

The organisation has since held its first all-British clash, between Paul Kelly and Paul Taylor; however, Paul Murphy would like to see more. 'What I'd like them to do is allow more British fighters in. I'd like that aspect to come through, but they've shown that they're not interested in working with anybody. No, they just want everybody out of the way I think. That's the impression I got, however I did go down to London to meet up with Marshall Zelaznik, who is running it from the UK point of view and I was most impressed by his humbleness and obviously, the professionalism of the whole outfit is beyond belief.'

Will the UFC's involvement in the UK be of benefit to the local promotions?

'I think it's a double-edged sword,' Murphy answered, 'it elevates the sport, makes it more mainstream, they've got the TV capability, so it does highlight it. However, they've also got the capability to shut a lot of people down. So, like I say, it's a double-edged sword. It's a bit of a frightening scenario at this moment in time, only time will tell.'

Murphy, however, is not the only promoter to have felt UFC-related fear in recent months, as Paul James explained, 'I have actually been contacted by the UFC; they did actually send me legal letters with reference to the "Ultimate Cage Fighting". We were advertising "Ultimate Cage Fighting" but obviously, they brought a legal suit against us, nothing too serious, just saying that we had to change it otherwise they will prosecute us. You know, I don't want to step on anyone's toes. I don't want to fall out with the UFC.

'I've actually got very good relations with the UFC UK,' James clarified, 'I speak to Marshall there on a regular basis, so I don't want to fall out with them so we have adapted our marketing to "Extreme Cage Fighting", rather than Ultimate Cage Fighting because, you know, irrespective of whatever the legal stance is, we don't want to start falling out with people like the UFC. I don't think the UFC see me as too much of a threat at the moment which I think is a nice thing. I don't think the UFC would want to work with any UK promotions, I don't think there's any need for them to. They are obviously running the UK's biggest shows, there's no doubt about it, they are an absolute phenomenon, that's what we all aspire to be like really.'

When it comes to the affect the UFC had had on the UK scene, Cage Warriors promoter, Andy Lillis is confident that he could write his own book on the subject. 'The UFC are the leaders in mma and rightfully so, they have brought mma into the households of many a fan worldwide, all the household names are UFC fighters. UK fighters now have an aim, they dream about one day getting into the UFC Octagon and reaching the top of their career, every serious fighter has the same aim, to grace the UFC Octagon. Cage Warriors pride themselves in developing fighters for that platform. We pride ourselves in the amount of fighters that have developed their skills on our show then moved onto the UFC.

'We will never tie a fighter up with a bullshit contract which will stop them from progressing in their career', he added, 'The UFC coming to the UK has been a God send, we need them here to show the UK public that this sport is here to stay and it is not "human cock fighting." It has got MMA the exposure that UK promotions cannot do, and we can all survive off the back of the UFC and progress. I enjoy working with the UFC they are a great bunch of guys. People say to me "How come you let Dan Hardy go to the UFC, he was the Cage Warriors star?" Simple, because that is where he deserves to be and if I was a fighter that is where I would want to be, end of. Who am I to stop fighters reaching the Premier Division?' Lillis asked rhetorically.

'The UFC are in my eyes the best thing that has happened to UK MMA since I got involved, and I hope they are here to stay. Elite XC came to the UK and what have they done? Nothing at all, except in my eyes turn a good solid UK promotion into a circus', he quipped, unable to resist the temptation of taking a swipe at his rival Cage Rage promotion, 'The UFC have come here and turned the none believers into believers and fans of our wonderful sport.'

CHAPTER NINE
FINISHING TECHNIQUES
KNOCKOUTS

The trials and tribulations of a promoter are quite remarkable; however, one factor which will always count in their favour is that mma is the most exciting sport on the planet and, quite possibly, the most exciting sport possible. After years of training, fighters can pick up an incredible array of techniques which have the potential to bring an end to the contest in a matter of seconds and, as numerous mma highlight reels on Youtube will confirm, these exhilarating weapons are put to use in almost every contest.

The following sections discuss just a few of the many techniques which make mma such an incredible spectacle, beginning with a quick insight into the infinite complexities of stand up fighting presented by Tony Quigley – a trainer at the Wolfslair Martial Arts Academy who has a deep understanding of both the science and the rough end of the striking arts.

In his long training career, the former Karate champion and professional boxer has assisted stars such as Antonio 'Junior' Silva, Cheick Kongo and Mike Bisping with their striking preparations, sharing the wealth of his vast experience to give them an edge over their opponent. 'A lot of clinching goes on in professional boxing,' he began, 'hitting and holding, that's very much like dirty boxing, clinching, hitting and holding against the cage, dirty tricks from professional boxing that you're not supposed to teach, but it's allowed in mma. There are certain boxing techniques that can work in kicking range and certain techniques that can't.'

Drawing on his traditional martial arts knowledge, Quigley explained that there are techniques from across a broad spectrum of styles which can be used to great effect in mma. 'There's the punching charge from karate which Vitor Belfort used against Wanderlai Silva, that's a karate technique that and also there's the stepping, changing stances because in martial arts you train both sides equally, in boxing you don't tend to do that. I've tried to bring that into this so they can push that.'

Eddie Bravo once famously labelled mma without the ground game as 'bad kickboxing', but Quigley and a wave of new striking trainers are now adding new layers to their mma specific striking techniques, blending the best aspects of different styles for maximum efficiency. 'I like to try and work a lot of angles because I find MMA is very direct, it's very straight line. So I try to emphasise side-stepping, spinning off rather than going back in a straight line because sooner or later, you'll hit the cage and that's where you don't want to be.

'Boxers are the best punchers, you've got exceptions in the martial arts world, but basically, to throw the best punch you've got to be in a boxing stance. I encourage them to go from the Thai, or martial arts stance when they are on the outside - in kicking range - and as soon as they come into punching range to revert to a boxing stance to maximise their punching power. Then you've got the best of both.'

All too aware that a mma opponent has numerous options, Quigley gives his students the best chances of getting their techniques off by preparing them for every eventuality. 'I'll have them sprawling, I'll have them getting up fast from the sprawl to strike. I'll have them clinching... they are not boxers, they're not doing boxing, but they want boxing skills, put together with all the other skills. With the sprawling, they are not just thinking boxing, they are thinking, "I could be taken down here" and I want to keep that fresh in their mind as they put together their techniques.'

ROUTE ONE
THE BIG RIGHT HAND

I n a fight, the most natural thing for the untrained combatant to do is to close his right fist and hit his assailant, or opponent, as hard as he can; it's the very first action which springs to mind for the majority of people. Safely within the confines of sporting endeavour, the punch is such a potent weapon that, for some fighters, it forms a platform for their whole stand up style, with such diverse names as Igor Vovchanchyn and Urijah Faber being known to gear their entire game plan towards landing a fight-ending right hard.

There are many ways of throwing an effective right hand; from a pure right hook, as delivered by Phil Baroni at Cage Rage 27, as he knocked out the over-matched Brit, Scott Jansen; to the brutal right uppercut and hammerfist delivered by the Belarusian Pitball, Andre Arlovski on Vladimir Matyushenko at UFC 44. However, this chapter is going to concentrate on the traditional straight right hand, as thrown by a heavyweight – and a featherweight.

The Heavyweight

One of the strongest right hands in the business belongs to former UFC heavyweight champion, Tim 'The Maine-iac' Sylvia. His feared right hand has brought the adopted Iowan numerous successes throughout his career, stretching back to Sylvia's break out event held in Hawaii. 'I hurt a lot of guys in the Superbrawl Tournament with the right hand, but Cabbage [Wesley Correira] I hurt, but obviously, later in my career, Ricco Rodriguez, I knocked him out with a right; Gan McGee, knocked him out with a right, Andre Arlovski, knocked out with a right, Tra Telligman, hurt with a right. I hurt all my guys with the right, it's just being able to land it flush when you're going to be able to get the knock out from it.'

The 6'8" tattooed fighter paused to explain how he found his way into the cage on an apparent mission to wreck any and all-comers with his punishing stand up. 'I was training in Maine, Marcus Davis and I were training together. We were just training at a local Gold's gym, just a couple of hours a week and I was training at the PAL boxing gym a couple of days a week. I just enjoyed the training and started doing some grappling tournaments.'

After some success, Sylvia moved swiftly on to the world of mixed martial arts. His first fight was scheduled for a single 7-minute round, allowing only open hand strikes, but as Tim explained, he can bring an abrupt end to the fight without even closing his fists. 'I went in there and knocked the guy out in 17 seconds with an open hand! I thought "Wow, I kind of like this!", but, I had a hard time finding fights because I was 6'8", 240lbs and nobody would fight me.'

However, Sylvia was lucky enough to meet future mentor, Pat Miletich whilst attending a UFC event as a spectator with a group of friends. Miletich invited the giant of a man to train with him at his world famous school and the talented and outspoken coach soon began training up a fighter that would go on to take the UFC by storm and become one of the most concussive punchers the sport has yet seen. 'I went back, sold everything I owed and a month later I was out in Iowa.'

Sylvia was not given an easy time, as the new, slightly unfit heavyweight in the gym. 'It was very overwhelming but I loved it!' Tim said enthusiastically, 'It was tough, it was hard work, but I'm used to it, being from Maine and all, I absolutely loved it. My first year there was real tough; I was getting beat up all the time and struggling, trying to make ends meet and stuff like that, but then fights started happening and I was fortunate enough to have a good break!'

This break came in the shape of the 16-man Superbrawl tournament, in April, 2002. 'I remember knocking out four guys, Mike Whitehead being the first one and the last one. He came in and he lost to me, just a quick TKO in the first round. Somebody got hurt so they asked him, "Hey, do you want to fight again?" He said yes, so he fought Ben Rothwell and beat him, worked his way back up through and ended up meeting me in the finals.'

After beating Whitehead on the Friday night, Sylvia returned the following night to use his right to great effect as he smashed his way to victory in a tournament, raising the eyebrows of the UFC talent scouts. 'The first fight was Roy Ballard, I knocked him out with a flying knee, next fight was Jason Lambert and I TKO'd him in the second round just due to strikes and Mike Whitehead was a TKO again in the last fight. Cabbage wouldn't fight me in the finals', Tim said regretfully, 'He pulled out and said he was injured, somebody had replaced him so they said, "Don't worry about it Cabbage, we'll just have you fight Tim Sylvia in the UFC."'

Leaping on this opportunity to make waves in the world's biggest mma organisation, Sylvia put on the performance of his life as he debuted against Correira, landing every strike in the book in one of the organisation's most famous brawls. The Maine-iac smashed and battered his Hawaiian opponent from one side of the cage to the other; amazingly, Cabbage was able to take on a huge amount of punishment, occasionally firing back with quick flurries of lefts and rights.

'It was just a fun, fun fight.' Sylvia said, 'It's not too many times you get a guy out there who is going to walk around the ring and let you back him down and punch him as many times as you can! It was a fun fight; he threw a little bit of hands in the beginning and stuff, but nothing too serious. He had a flurry and I just kind of covered up and let him flurry and then I was like, "OK, it's my turn!", and I just put it on him. I think if they had given me 30 more seconds I would have knocked him out cold. But BJ Penn in his corner saw how bad he was taking a beating, so he stopped the fight by throwing in the towel.

'It never went through my mind that I wouldn't be able to put him away,' he added, 'I just knew that Cabbage was a tough, tough guy and I was just trying to keep staying on him and finish it, but I remember thinking 'This guy is tough' I hit him with everything that I've got, but I hadn't really got hold of his head and started throwing the big knees yet.'

This display of dominance somehow did not distract the incumbent UFC champion of the time, Ricco Rodriguez from his wayward lifestyle; he barely seemed to make any serious preparations at all in advance of his defence against the Miletich-trained fighter and would soon become the first high-profile victim of his heavy right hand. Asked if he felt Rodriguez underestimated him as a fighter, Tim was quite sure, 'I absolutely believe that he underestimated me! He didn't take the fight so serious, yeah. He didn't go to Big Bear, he didn't train with Tito, he was like, "Ah, I'm the champion now, I'm the man, I'm fighting this bum named Tim Sylvia, I'm going to go out there, beat him up take him down and walk away with my belt."'

Once the fight at UFC 41 began, the submission specialist champion quickly discovered that he was unable to take Sylvia down and the huge slugger began to cut off the ring in an attempt to land his big, fight ending punches. Just over three minutes into the contest, a hard right hand from the Maine-iac rattled the champ's teeth and sent him crashing to the floor. 'I didn't know that he was finished immediately, that's why I jumped on him and tried to finish him. I jumped on him and tried to give him as many more as I could to finish the job.' Two more rights landed flush on the unconscious champion's jaw and, in a lucky escape for 'Suave', two more heavy shots from the marauding power-puncher narrowly missed his head.

Surprisingly, Sylvia claims that his initial punch was not the hardest, but definitely made his over-confident opponent pay with the following shots on the floor. 'I didn't think it was a big punch at all, he threw the kick and I countered it with a straight right. I go out there and try to throw punches in bunches. Not every punch I hit people with hurts them, just the ones that they don't see coming I hurt guys with. I didn't think that it was a big punch but when I got on the ground, I was coming down with full force with the first one.

In his first defence of the title at UFC 44, Sylvia took on a fighter that perhaps for the first time in his 18-fight career was taller than he was in Gan McGee, a fighter who had spent years training with former UFC Light-heavyweight champion, Chuck Liddell. However, Sylvia did not see the height and reach disadvantage as a significant disadvantage. 'I was just out there trying to land my strikes, you know. I threw a double jab and then I threw a straight right. I saw that it hurt him, so I cut the angle and threw another one, that's what dropped him and then I jumped on him and tried to finish the deal.'

I was getting frustrated and I thought, "OK, I'll just keep my jab going" and as soon as I got my jab going and kept my hands up, it all came together.' McGee dropped to the mat and the Maine-iac followed up with five more hard right hands which drove Gan's head into the canvas, leaving him out cold on the floor.

Even with all his power and experience, however, Sylvia still professes that if experienced opponents see even his hardest shots coming, they will more than likely be able to survive the blow and fight on. 'We're trained professionals, so if you see a punch coming you're able to put your chin down and bite down on your mouthpiece and protect it. You see if coming so you get ready for it. It's the one that you don't see, the ones that you can't get ready for that are going to knock you out, so I think that if I hit any professional heavyweight with my straight right and he saw it coming, I don't think I'm going to knock him out, no, I have to set up combinations and be a little tricky with it!'

After landing a plethora of hard right hands in his career thus far, Sylvia struggled to recall the hardest punch he has ever landed. 'I remember hitting Arlovski a lot with my right hand and I was like, "Wow, he's stuck around for that one." I hit Tra Telligman a lot with my right hand, good, hard straight rights and it didn't knock him out, so there's a few guys. Obvious, Cabbage, I hit with my straight right and it didn't knock him out. I hit Nogueira with it; actually, I hit Nogueira with a left hook and followed up with a straight right hand behind it and that dropped him, but I couldn't quite put him away either you know, he's a tough guy as well' Sylvia finished, with a typically humble note.

The Featherweight

Another fighter with a blistering right hand is Pancrase London fighter, Ashleigh Grimshaw. As a featherweight, he relies less on the weight of his punches, instead working on his speed and technique to deliver devastating result with his right hands. One such punch landed squarely on the jaw of Grimshaw's unfortunate FX3 opponent, Phil 'Billy' Harris.

'I felt confident all the way through, to be honest', Ashleigh said, as he reflected on the contest. 'I didn't throw anything at the start because I wanted to see what he had, so I was moving to keeping my distance and realised that as much as he said he'd been working his striking, you could see that he hadn't. He had no distance, he was throwing punches when I was well out of range - I didn't even have to move because he was hitting my closest hand, so I was like, alright, move around, move around…

'I just heard Jess [Liaudin] say, "Let your hands go!", so I dropped my level, dropped it a lot so that he brought his hands down and then; "BANG" – a right hand straight on the chin. I was working on my striking a lot with Harry [Selby] and Sham at the time, so I knew my distance was perfect. As soon as I stood, I knew I was going to hit him with it and I just let the hands go.'

Selby confirmed that Grimshaw's improving mobility and striking was the product of many hours in the gym, 'I had been working on Ash's footwork, using your jab and footwork to gauge both yours and the opponents distance. This had been building steadily for about a couple of months and we got his hips, footwork and shoulder rotation down to a T and as Ash is a powerful fighter it worked perfectly that night. "BANG", and Harris dropped like a sack of coal, "BANG BANG BANG", and it was all over.'

As Selby points out, although 'Billy' was unable to defend himself, Grimshaw was given no choice but to put an exclamation mark on his win. 'I dropped him and then looked to the ref, "Do you want me to continue?", and the ref didn't say anything and unfortunately, I had to hit him again', he laughed, 'I didn't want to! I really didn't want to because I knew he was out, completely. I looked at the ref, the ref didn't stop it.' Four shots followed in, 'I went - right cross, left and then banged in the right twice more. I've got it at home, I've watched it like, 10 million times', he added proudly.

'To throw the perfect right hand,' Grimshaw advised, 'just make sure you twist your hips. All it comes down to is twisting those hips and full extension. I always say, "Commit to the punch"; if you're going to throw it, commit to it, but don't cock it. In mma you can get away with it more, but if you start to fight some boxers, they are going to see you move and as soon as you've pulled back, they'll be like, "Take that" - "bam" and hit you with two shots.

'It's a rotation from your toes all the way up to your shoulder. A lot of people have got good hands, but not got big bulked up muscles. You don't have to hit someone hard to knock them out; that's the point, it takes three pounds per square inch of pressure on the jaw to knock someone out.'

SLUGGER'S CHOICE
THE LEFT HOOK

Behind the right hand, every good puncher has the option of throwing an equally devastating left hook; a very natural punch for many fighters which has long been seen as one of the most potent weapons in a boxer's arsenal. A versatile punch, it can be used to great affect in very close quarters or thrown at a looping angle to cause problems at a more traditional boxing distance.

The left hook has been used to dramatic affect under the Queensbury rules for years and has served as an instrumental weapon for some of boxing's most famous knock out artists, such as iconic heavyweight of the 60's and 70's, 'Smokin'' Joe Frazier who famously flattened Muhammad Ali with the punch. More recently, USA Olympic boxing team member, Jeff 'Left Hook' Lacy has seen such success with the punch that he has taken it on as his moniker.

However, now employed in mma by fighters wearing the far smaller 4oz gloves, when used properly, the left hook can bring a conclusion to a bout in a fraction of a second; as demonstrated with ruthless efficiency by two Americans; bleach-blond wrestler, Kevin Randleman and Arizona warrior, Curtis 'Bang 'em Out' Stout

The left hook which shocked the world

Not known as a technical stand up fighter in any way, Kevin Randleman does not boast a noticeably tight amateur boxing style and has hardly thrown a kick in his entire career. Instead, 'The Monster' is able to rely on the incredible power he is able to generate in both hands; and as a result, he is a danger to even the most technically gifted opponent as he swings for the fences in stand up exchanges.

'I always think I can knock anybody else if I can get my hand on their face once', the former Ohio college wrestling star confirmed, 'It's not power I don't think, but I'm a lot faster than most guys. I move in and out fast and I don't think people realise that until they get into the ring with me, that I'm faster coming forward and backward than they are.'

In the opening round of the 2004 Pride Heavyweight Grand Prix, Randleman used his range-shifting ability to score what one of the biggest upsets in the sport as ever seen. His victim that night, Mirko 'Cro Cop' Filipovic, is a former K-1 kickboxer and had been the bookmakers favourite to destroy Randleman inside the first round and was also seen by many as the heir-apparent to the now defunct Pride heavyweight crown

As the routinely cautious Croatian kept a close eye on his opponent, the tiniest mistake brought Randleman surging forward with a lightening-fast left hook. 'He just took a step forward... I faked like I was going to shoot, lowered my level and then just came up with the punch.'

Taken completely unaware by the explosion of energy hurtling towards him, Filipovic stumbled backwards to the mat, his defences in obvious disarray; yet, somehow was able to regain his senses on the mat. 'I felt his body just go' Randleman explained, 'I felt his body just dropping. As soon as I hit him he went to sleep, but he went to the ground and he was back!'

With a place in the next round of the Grand Prix almost within his grasp, Randleman charged in with a stream of vicious hammerfists which smeared the former Croatian Parliamentarian across the floor, prompting commentator Mauro Ranallo to launch into a high-volume monologue of exhilarated praise as he announced the unlikely victory of this ultimate underdog.

The Monster revealed that in preparation for the fight he joined the ranks of fighters who have flocked to train alongside the hard-punching stand up specialist, Chuck Liddell, and feels a debt of gratitude to the man who previously knocked him out inside the octagon at UFC 31. 'I'm going to give a lot of credit to him. Because he's a kickboxer himself, he told me exactly what to expect and how to defend it and it worked.'

Looking back on the finish, Kevin could hardly believe that the initial left was not enough to get the job done, but incredibly conceded that it was by no mean the hardest punch he has ever landed. 'No. Heck, no. No way. My right is way stronger than my left, I just never throw it. I've hit a lot of people with my right hand. But a lot of them are street fight right hands and practise right hands.'

'Bang 'em out' terrorizes the Cage Rage middleweight division

Every so often in the sport of mixed martial arts, a fighter can show such proficiency in the use of one technique and use it to such effect that the entire division sits up and takes notice. Exactly that happened on the London-based Cage Rage promotion in 2005 as Curtis Stout dismantled three straight opponents with the punch, knocking them senseless with his mighty left hook, earning himself an army of fans in the UK and his sincerely appropriate nickname, 'Bang 'em out'.

Though both his wrestling and jiu-jitsu skills are on a par with most fighters, Stout considers himself a striker first and foremost, with a natural aptitude for throwing a heavy left hand. 'I always loved boxing and the left hook has always been my favourite punch' he said, 'Even when I was training in the gym I would never have to throw it really, really hard, it was just like a little flick that catches people and it's always the punch that you don't see that knocks you out.'

Curtis grabbed the attention of the Wembley Conference Centre crowd at Cage Rage 13 when he scored one of the most famous knock outs in recent mma history, his stunning and equally gruesome finish of UK fighter, Sol Gilbert. Looking back on the roughest night of his entire career, Sol conceded that after a couple of sharp wins, stepping up to face the American banger represented a genuine step up in competition; however, the Brighton fighter did not feel out of place in the cage with Stout. 'In the first round, he took me down,' Gilbert said, 'but I was comfortable, I was looking for keylocks, I was very active on my back, didn't manage to get anything, but I got up and I felt fresh. I come back and I was like, "What's he got?" You know what I mean? He ain't gonna stand with me and even when I was on my back I wasn't in any trouble.'

However, this new-found confidence was short-lived as he dipped the level of his guard, giving Curtis the only chance he needed to bring the fight to a swift conclusion. 'It was just like instinct, you know?' Curtis added, 'I saw him drop the hand and just threw. It wasn't even a powerful left hook, I just think it was so fast and right on the button that it knocked him out.'

This was no partial knock out where the victim retains some sense of his faculties; Sol was instantly knocked unconscious and fell dead weight towards the nearby cage post. In line with the worst possible scenario, Gilbert's head landed on the base of the post, violently forcing his chin to his chest, before he head flopped back to the canvas - his deadened eyes staring up to the ceiling.

A shockwave of dismay spread around the arena as the paramedics rushed into the cage. 'I was just in disbelief' Curtis said, his tone perfectly summarizing a moment of complete panic. 'When it happened, it almost felt like slow motion, but once he landed I was hoping he was alright and that was it.'

Certainly from my own vantage point, behind the very post in question, there seemed every chance that Gilbert has suffered a severe injury – or worse – and several tense moments followed as he was brought back to his senses by the medical staff. Once conscious, however, Gilbert's journey back to health had only just begun. 'It gave me a prolapsed disk, knocked my vertebrae over and knocked out five of my ribs. It gave me paralysis down my left arm for six months, I had a bulging disk... yeah, I was fucked up.'

Incredibly, and as a testament to Gilbert as a person and an athlete, the head coach of the Zero Tolerance Fight Skool has remained remarkably cheerful about the knock out, one which will be watched on highlight reels for years to come.

'It was one of the best fucking knock outs in mma' Gilbert said: 'That was a real good knock out for him. For me, what it proves is that no matter where you are in the fight, however confident you are feeling, it only takes one second, you know what I mean, to get knocked the fuck out – and that's exactly what happened.'

'Bang 'em out' was in complete agreement, 'I'm glad he's ok, but it just affirms my belief that I've got probably one of the best left hooks in the sport. I thought that was probably one of the best knock outs in any combat sport.'

Next in line for a taste of the Arizona fighter's left hook was Chute Boxe representative, Nilson de Castro; a veteran of the Brazilian No-Holds-Barred circuit and an expert in Muay Thai. Stout remains convinced that Castro was taking him lightly, 'I just think he thought I was a joke, he just really didn't take me too seriously. He was playing around a bit', Stout said, having clearly taken some offence at the Brazilian's nonchalance.

Castro took up a strange-looking stance, holding his hands very wide apart, as if convinced that his reflexes were so good they would make a prime Roy Jones Junior green with envy. Curtis was not impressed and immediately went after his opponent; 'I threw the inside leg kick, it made his body square up and I went over the top with a left hook.'

The punch whistled past Castro's virtually non-existent defences and crashed hard into his temple. 'The left hook I threw at him, it was right on the temple but it wasn't hard at all. It was just like it caught him off guard. He stumbled back and I knew I had to jump on him and try to take him out!' Three of the most brutal left hooks the sport has ever seen landed directly on Castro's jaw, leaving him completely incapacitated with a small river of blood flowing from his mouth. 'I thought he was hurt too!' Curtis laughed as he looked back, 'I felt bad after that! Because when I jumped on him, I pounded on him with my left and he was completely out.'

The final chapter in this trio of unforgettable knock outs came in Stout's very next contest as he took on, pound-for-pound, one of the best strikers in the UK, Mark 'The Wizard' Weir. Known for his elastic legs and kicking ability, Stout was keen to implement his own game plan when they met at Cage Rage 11. 'I always respected Mark Weir as a fighter; I figured that I was stronger than him and I had to watch out for his high kick, you know. I knew that if I bullied him around and hit him with the left then he would go down and he did.'

From Weir's point of view, however, it was no bully that he faced in the cage that night, rather, a solid technician with hours of specific training behind him. 'I've got a combination I practise,' the Gloucester Tae Kwon Do expert began, 'at the start of the fight I do a lot of heavy round kicks, even if they put their hands up to defend it shakes them. I remember throwing a round kick and it really went through his guard, it shook him and as he stepped back, he threw a hook, he must have been working on that combination.'

In a painfully recurrent theme, the blow was as sharp as a lumberjack's axe as it cut Weir down, 'I remember thinking "Right, I've got to hang on here", but I just remember him coming in with more shots, one after the other. That was definitely a hard punch. I remember still feeling dazed as I was walking back to the changing room. It was just one of those punches where it takes a while to recover, I don't think that I could have recovered while I'm still in the round getting hit. It was a heavy, heavy hit, well timed. Definitely one of the hardest punches… I think it probably is the hardest, come to think of it.'

Amazingly, of all the devastating hooks Stout landed in his incredible run on the Cage Rage promotion, the shot which stands out in his mind as being the most powerful did not bring a conclusion to the fight; as the heavy-handed American explained. 'My whole time over in Cage Rage, the only guy I hit extremely hard with a left hook was [legendary Japanese punching bag, Daijiro] Matsui. Unfortunately I didn't put him out, but when I hit Matsui, I swear that's the hardest I've hit anybody. When I punched him, it felt like electricity going through my hand. It was really hard to put that guy out.' He finished, laughing at the understatement of what he had just said.

KILLER INSTINCT

A fighter can train his techniques all day long, he can train to hit harder and throw more complicated combinations, he can take on board numerous sweeps, submissions and counters. However, on occasion, what he really needs is a killer instinct; an awareness of when his opponent is at his weakest, coupled with the mental ability to follow with an explosion of focussed action at precisely the right time.

For many fans of the UFC, one mention of 'Killer instinct' and the first thing which springs to mind is Phil Baroni's performance at UFC 39 against Dave Menne. After losing his UFC middleweight crown, Menne was given the rare opportunity to choose his next opponent, almost as if to ease him back into competition; sadly for him, he took the ill-fated decision of calling out Baroni at precisely the wrong time.

UFC 39: Phil Baroni vs. Dave Menne

'I remember the fight before,' Baroni began, 'he'd lost to Bustamante who was the champion and he had an opportunity to pick who he wanted to fight and he chose me and I took that personal. I wanted to punish him for choosing me after having the opportunity to choose anyone he wanted, but he chose me for his comeback fight. Also, I wanted to prove that I was one of the best fighters in the world – he was the former champion, I wanted to prove I was on that level.'

What happened next has a place in UFC history as perhaps one of the quickest, most effective and one-sided beating the organisation is ever likely to witness. Baroni tore across the cage and almost immediately staggered his disjointedly tattooed opponent with a hefty overhand right. Menne was shocked and out of sorts, yet before he had a chance to recover his senses, the living embodiment of malicious finishing power charged towards him with, throwing a whirlwind of left and right hands directly at his jaw.

'It was instinct, it was just instinct', Baroni recalled as he considered the reason why he stormed into his staggered opponent, holding nothing back from the ten unanswered punches which put Menne to sleep only 18 seconds into the contest. 'It wasn't a decision exactly, I followed him up and I kept throwing till the referee got between us, that's when he slumped to the canvas.'

The Finishing Machine Paul 'Semtex' Daley

Paul Daley is another fighter who prides himself on his ability to hammer out an unsettled opponent in double-quick time. Reminiscing about his most impressive victory to date, when he over-powered and smashed the highly regarded striker, Duane Ludwig, Daley insisted his opponent was still dangerous after what appeared to be a fight-ending punch early in the second round.

'He had still something about him,' the Nottingham fighter recalled, 'he was a bit disorientated but he still had something about him, but I hit him with two heavy shots, a lot of people said it was stopped early, but those two shots that landed were heavy shots. You know as a fighter when you land a heavy shot – and the ref did the right thing, I landed two heavy shots and that bout was stopped.'

Pausing to consider his rare finishing ability, Daley thought back to his acquisition of this important skill. 'It was trained, but now it's instinct, if you know what I mean. It was trained, I would stand over opponents in early fights and amateurs, but now, it's my instinct just to finish the fight because mma is such an unpredictable game and if you don't finish it when you have the opportunity, you know, second round you could find yourself being choked out, so if I get an opportunity to finish, I'm going to take it. That guy could get back up and fucking knock you out; it's that kind of sport, so whenever I get the opportunity now, I'm going to finish it.'

To the untrained eye, a volley of finishing blows delivered to a downed opponent can appear an unsightly formality; however, downed or not, a good opponent is dangerous to the very end and as such, Daley stressed the importance of either retaining a good base to avoid being swept or simply banging in hard punches.

'There are certain techniques and positions you can put yourself in standing over somebody who is on his back,' Daley explained, 'but usually, after landing a hard shot, I just tend to fall into whatever position comes. Whether it's mount, taking their back, side control, I just secure that position. I'm trained to strike from wherever I am, so it doesn't matter whatever position I fall into or wherever I am, as long as I can throw my shots, I'm cool.'

Apart from his devastating performance stateside against Ludwig, 'Semtex' appears most proud of perhaps his best domestic showing, against Mark Weir. 'That was pretty cool to watch, I like the way that fight ended, that was nice. I fell straight in mount and every shot from mount just pinged off his head; that was probably my best finish from on the ground.'

Sami 'The Hun' Berik unleashes a storm

Another fighter who has consistently shown himself to possess a devastating ability to seize on the slightest of chances is Zen Machine and all-purpose modern day warrior, Sami 'The Hun' Berik. Though his ordinary-looking, journeyman's record makes every attempt to hide some staggering victories, for those who have seen Berik at his marauding best, the experience is not easily forgotten.

When he senses victory, it is as if he involuntarily unloads his entire stock of energy in a brief, but unbelievably intense outpouring of hurtful hammerfists and punches. 'It's like changing gears in a car,' Berik explained in typically mystic fashion, 'you don't think about it, you just feel when it's time to do it. I go more with, rather than thinking about doing things, I just do what's right when it feels right to do it. All I do is mould my urgency, so to speak. I don't use anger, urgency is different; like if you were to bring a cup of water to an old lady, you put urgency into it, not anger.'

Among his most precious scalps is that of UFC veteran, Dave Lee, a fighter that pretty much everyone picked to blow straight through the fearless Londoner. However, just when you think you can predict what is coming next from Berik, he hits you with a surprise. 'Dave was fishing for an armbar or something on his back. After I hit him with a few punches I wasn't thinking about cardio or nothing, I was just thinking, "Finish it off! Just keep the momentum going!" Once he was on his back and I was punching him, I linked that momentum onto another punch, so I knew it was going to cost him more to try and block it or keep going for an armbar. I was just leaning forward and concentrating on keeping the momentum going and raining down the punches.'

Berik pointed out that his instinctive punching attacks often open up submission possibilities, an area of his finishing ability that he is constantly seeking to refine, and on one occasion memorably led to the downfall of talented opponent, John O'Mally. 'I really like that one because as soon as he gave his back I just swooped in for the rear naked, he was expecting me to hit or something, he even lifted his neck up as well, panting for breath. At the time, he didn't expect me to come out with a submission, so that was good just for the linkage.'

Almost offering an apology for one of his most precious fighting assets, the Hun set out how he hopes to add yet more pieces his game in the future. 'In my fights, OK, I do blast and there are bits where I'm using quite a lot of aggression, but in the long run I'd like to be refined a bit more. I might throw these filthy, landing guard breakers and switch to an armbar or something, that's what I want to link it to, eventually. So it's not just repeated "Bash, bash, oh, that's another fight won from that", sort of thing, but improving in context each time.'

'PUT YOUR FOOT ON HIS FACE'
HIGH KICKS

In the early days of no holds barred competition there seemed to be a clear winner in the battle of the styles as seemingly invincible Brazilian jiu-jitsu practitioners set about wrecking the challenges offered by every other style. The initial Ultimate Fighting Championships and vale tudo contests around the world bore witness to the apparent supremacy of the grappling arts. For many observers at the time, it did not appear remotely possible that one of the fighters representing the striking arts would ever be able to achieve the pinnacle of his craft by scoring a clean knock out with a perfect high kick.

Therefore, in the nascent years of the sport, high kicks were dismissed as being flashy and impractical. Instead of polishing these effective strikes for competition, martial artists from across the spectrum fell over themselves to learn these new jiu-jitsu techniques which had taken the fighting world by storm. However, just at the very peak of grappler dominance, former Kung Fu fighter, Maurice Smith paved the way for a new generation of strikers who could force the grapplers to engage in their realm of expertise.

Extreme Fighting 3:
Maurice Smith vs. Marcus 'Conan' Silveira

Smith began his mma career in the pioneering Pancrase organisation in a bid to make a living, rather than become one of the most respected striking coaches in the sport of mma. 'At that time, my ground game wasn't there,' he said of his early fights with the likes of Ken Shamrock and Bas Rutten, 'I didn't have a ground game at that point. They offered me good money and it was helping to build their company. I hadn't had any experience in grappling at that point and even if I had learnt it for a month, six months, or a year, I still wouldn't have been on the level those guys were at. So it was more of a business deal and it turned out to be a great thing.'

However, after training his ground game for a sustained period, Smith started to become more confident in his new found skills and, contrary to popular opinion at the time, he gave his striking skills a good chance of coming to the fore in his bout with the intimidating Carlson Gracie representative, Marcus 'Conan' Silveira on John Peritti's Extreme Fighting promotion. 'I'd started working with Ken and Frank [Shamrock] – more Frank than Ken, but I started asking them questions, "What's so big about the mount... what's so big about this, what's so big about that...", and Frank made it simple, they are only that big, if you don't know what's going to happen. So I started to learn the basics of what to look out for and I became pretty comfortable on the ground.

'By the time I fought Conan,' he continued, 'I had a better understanding of how to reverse, for me the biggest part about that fight wasn't that I knocked him out, but the fact that I was able to reverse him at something that's he's good at and I did. I wasn't worried when I got mounted. I wasn't worried about any of that stuff, I'd trained for about a month straight in the Shamrock's gym, the Lion's Den, and it paid off.'

It seemed incredible that the fighter most famous for landing one of the most devastating kicks in the sport would be more interested in a change of position on the floor, but putting his new abilities into practise was central to the implementation of his stand up strategy later on in the fight. 'The focus was to get his hands to go down by hitting him with the low kicks a lot, thinking that the high kick opportunity would present itself and it did. I was kicking him and kicking him and just thought, "OK, now is the time to do it", but the primary thing was just low kick, low kick and high kick.'

The thudding slap of Smith's low kicks soon got the attention of Conan, a fighter who – at the time - had very limited stand up training. 'There were a couple of hard kicks,' he said, 'I knew that he didn't like it and after a while he started responding to me, I went with the low kick again and he put his hands down and I finally went for a high kick.'

The switch from low to high took Silveira completely by surprise and the kick landed as sweetly as the former K-1 fighter could have hoped. 'It was the crook of the shin, but it hit his neck, not his head - it happened to me in my last fight with Ernesto [Hoost] and Peter [Aerts]. It stops the blood flow to your brain, I think. If somebody gets kicked in the neck, they are OK to the most part, it's not really a shot to the head as in to the skull, but more the blood flow gets interrupted for a short time and you go out.'

Explaining the split-second unconsciousness caused by the blow, Smith added an interesting surprise, 'Your body just stops. It's kind of bad, when I got knocked out by Peter, same kick to the neck, my short term memory was not very good. But compared to punches and kicks to the head, it was actually quite pleasant to be honest with you.'

After the blow landed to Conan's neck, Maurice looked away for a second as if to consider there was no chance that the Brazilian could continue, before seeing that he was still on his feet and rushing in to finish his rattled foe. 'I'd seen he was already out, but then the referee prevented me from going after him. I think that kick, I felt it was enough to stop the fight but he didn't stop it as quick as I thought he would, so I went in to finish him off and he stopped the fight. I knew it was a good shot, that's why I turned away.'

As one of the first to land under mma rules, the kick, in many ways, represented a turning point for striking in the sport. However, for Smith, landing strikes is bread-and-butter basics; his main source of pride from the fight came from the success he had on the floor, as a nascent submission fighter in the cage with a BJJ black belt.

'That kick was not so much of a concern. Being able to punch or kick is par for the course for me. I wouldn't be as big a deal for me as it would be to shoot in on somebody or something like that – or in the case of Gonzaga versus Cro Cop, where the wrestler beats the kickboxer with striking. For me to punch somebody out who's a grappler isn't the biggest accomplishment. The most important thing to me was the reversal; that was a big deal, not the punches or kicks. The exciting part of the fight for me was being able to reverse a guy in his game. It means that I can beat a guy in his game or compete in his area of expertise. So the KO, if you check me reaction on the video, it's like it's no big deal, no great thing, it's just a fight to me.'

Pride 10: Gilbert Yvel vs. Gary Goodridge

Another iconic knock out from the relatively early days of the sport took place at Pride 10 in Japan as the legendary Dutch bad boy Gilbert Yvel demonstrated his unbelievable kicking ability as he blew past the tough Canadian heavyweight, Gary Goodridge in only 10 seconds. 'We were checking Gary Goodridge's fights out and saw him getting knocked out bad by Igor Vovchanchin.' Gilbert began, 'Every time, he got hit from his right side - so my left side. We were training only for left kicks and a left punch.'

At the start of the fight, Goodridge appeared unaware of the danger he faced as he as he crept towards his foe. 'Gary was so close to me,' Gilbert said, recalling the nervous energy he felt when he realised his opponent was open for a heavy kick, 'I thought, "He is so close, I can hit him any time if I want to", so first I switch to my right standing and my trainer yelled, "No, no! Keep standing with your left foot back!"'

Wisely taking his advice, Yvel switched back and launched his high kick with devastating effect. 'He was so close, I threw the left high kick and I think he never really saw it coming', the Dutchman said of the kick, which caught Goodridge high on the temple, folding his neck as it slammed into his Canadian opponent's shaved head. 'It wasn't the hardest kick I have ever landed,' Yvel confided, 'but it was hard - and the right thing to do at the right moment.'

King of the Cage UK:
Martin Kampmann vs. Brendan Seguin

From one of the most watched high kicks in front a sold out super-stadium in Japan, we move on to another equally brutal knock out which only a couple of hundred fans were able to witness in the flesh. Due to a string of unforeseen difficulties, the first and only King of the Cage event to be held in the UK suffered from a terrible lack of support, but in fact provided an excellent evening of entertainment, topped off by the incredible knock out of American fighter, Brendan Seguin, by the UFC-bound Danish fighter, Martin Kampmann.

A life long martial artist, Kampmann looked back on one of the most outstanding fights of his early career. 'It was a good fight. It was a good win and it was good for the highlight reel as well too. I knocked him out with a left high kick!' He said excitedly. 'He kept circling to the left every time I was chasing him down, so I stepped over and threw that left kick - I don't kick that much, but I like to mix it up with the hands. I used to kick more when I was doing kickboxing, but now in MMA it's a lot more risky when you're throwing a kick, but on that occasion, he walked into it.'

Moments previously, Seguin had laughed off the Dane's attacks, but the laughter turned to snoring, as Kampmann tucked him into bed with one of the hardest high kicks ever witnessed in a UK arena – and one which sent a shocking clap around the entire auditorium. 'I hit him with, I don't know the word for it in English but, the top of the foot. It didn't contact with the shin because he was too far away, but it connected well and I got a lot of his jaw. That's a knockout high kick for sure.'

Seguin lay unconscious for several worrying moments, before making a full recovery and receiving a warm ovation from the tight knit crowd. 'I was worried, of course,' Kampmann said of the tense moments. 'I'm a fighter, but I don't want my opponent to get hurt. Right that second you're probably thinking more about the win, but afterwards you hope your opponent's OK. I don't want to injure somebody, you know?'

Cage Rage 20: Tom Blackledge vs. Tom Howard

Wolfslair fighter, Tom Blackledge is better known for his jiu-jitsu than his kicking ability, yet the versatile fighter has shown some very precise kicks in his career, not least in his incredible Cage Rage 20 performance against American pro-wrestler-turned-mma-fighter, Tom Howard.

'I've always been very confident with my kicks,' Blackledge began, 'I had a knock out over John Nicholson many years ago in Grapple and Strike, but with Dave [Jackson, Thai boxing trainer at the Wolfslair,] it's really made the difference between having a powerful kick and having a very powerful kick. Little things that make a big change I suppose, he's a very good coach, as all our coaches are.'

Howard had taken a ribbing on the internet forums in the run up to the contest; posters mocked his background in sports entertainment and mercilessly ridiculed his 0-5 losing record. However, the tattooed American showed a flash of talent early in the contest, 'I got him with a lateral drop [take down] and he got straight back up, for a big guy he was pretty quick at getting back up.' Howard sprang back to his feet, but straight into a rear-bodylock by the home town fighter. 'The funny thing is, when I got that position I was going to suplex him, but I'd injured my hand in training, but my thumb was damaged and he was defending well.'

Unable to execute the throw, Blackledge saw his chance to finish the fight immediately with a brutal high kick. 'He scrambled, pushing off my hand and I thought, I wouldn't be able to suplex him and if I tried I'd probably put him on top of me, so I thought, "I'll just throw the kick", and as I threw it I thought about Yves Edwards and Josh Thompson.

'I'll throw it anyway and see if I can catch him with it', Blackledge decided, 'as soon as I threw, I knew I was going to catch him', Tom said confidently, 'I was always good at kicking and when I started training with Dave, Dave brought kicks to a totally different level. I know if I kick somebody… they'll not take more than a couple of kicks off me.' Indeed it only took one kick to bring an end to the fight, a mere 40 seconds into the contest.

Blackledge pushed his opponent away and whipped his right shin directly into his opponent's face, instantly turning out the lights, calling an end to the American's night, whilst simultaneously opening a huge gash on Howard's face. 'It was on his forehead, he got 33 staples I think across his head; he walked into the after show party later on – because there's no animosity between any of the fighters, you don't want to continue it after the fight - well, I don't anyway! And I felt quite bad for the guy so when he came into the after show party at half three in the morning, four o'clock, he walked over and I was with Mark Epstein at the time, there's were a few of us, Dave and I think Mark Kerr was there, we was talking and he walked over and said hello and I was like, "Oh shit!", with that many staples in his head he looked like Frankenstein or something.

UFC 49: Yves Edwards vs. Josh 'The Punk' Thompson

The kick which inspired the UK heavyweight's show of flexibility took place at UFC 49 as Yves Edwards defended his then 26-9-1 record against the upstart, well rounded newcomer, Josh 'The Punk' Thompson. Pushing an opponent across the cage to deliver a strong high kick is business as usual for the Thug-Jitsu fighter. 'That's just something that I really do all the time,' Yves said, 'not necessarily jump up and kick people in the head, it's just that a lot of times, I've found that a lot of times when guys separate from being tied up their hands seem to get really lax and come down.

'Some guys have really quick reflexes and they can bring their hands up,' Yves warned, 'but I figured I was behind him, so he's not going to really see it. If he does, he's going to throw his hands as fast as he can, but at that point, I said to myself, "He may block this, but I don't care if he does, I'm putting everything behind this kick and if I don't knock him out, I'm going to break his arm."'

As a lightweight fighter, the power of the kick was unlikely equal to that thrown by Blackledge, but the effect was just as conclusive, as the instant knock out struck a parallel with Maurice Smith's previously mentioned KO, 'I think the fortunate thing for his jaw was that I didn't hit him in his face and mouth; I caught him just under the chin, in the neck. It was one of those knock outs that doesn't put you to sleep, it just makes your whole body not react to what you're telling it to do. It felt really smooth, it felt really soft, it really felt like kicking a Thai pad.'

Asked if it was one of the hardest strikes he has ever landed in his career, Edwards was unclear but proudly confirmed that it was definitely one that he will remember for the rest of his days. 'I think it was one of the hardest, maybe that and a few knees I've landed in the past; that's got to be in there, if it's not number one, then it's very close to the top!'

Expert kicker and Outlaw

Another fighter who has an affectionately memorized list of fight ending kicks and knees he has landed in competition is Dan 'The Outlaw' Hardy, who has put his Tae Kwon Do background to good use in the cage. 'A lot of people struggle with high kicks because they are just not used to the explosive movement, getting the foot off the floor and because I've had years of that' Hardy began, 'Competing from when I was six, it's just a natural movement for me, I've got the flexibility and I've got the speed and explosiveness. It's just like throwing a jab for me, throwing a high kick.'

'It's just practise really it's the same with everything. You need to concentrate on being relaxed, if you tense up, it's going to slow the kick down and you're not going to get as high with it as well. Just practise. Have somebody watching you, or record yourself doing it, keep checking it and keep altering it and find the best way to do it. You'll find eventually that your body will find a natural movement and it will be a comfortable movement for you and you won't have to think about it anymore. It's second nature to me now, I don't have to think about it', the Nottingham fighter said.

However, unlike Gilbert Yvel who undertakes meticulous preparations in order to throw the kick at the correct time, Hardy feels comfortable taking his opportunities as they are presented. 'There are times when I look at my opponent and I can see an opening for it, but like when I fought Diego Gonzales I had no intention of stopping him with a head kick, but it was a head kick which cut him. It was just there and I think I must have spotted it with my subconscious and just threw the kick and it did the damage. It's not really ever something that I really train for; I just spot it and throw it when it's there. Occasionally, I'll build a game plan around it, but usually when I do that I don't ever land it', he said with laugh of acceptance.

After receiving the blow on Cage Warriors Strike Force 5, Gonzales suffered an appalling cut which required several stitches, leaving the young Swede a permanent reminder of his decisive second fight with Hardy. However, as the Rough House fighter revealed, he has landed harder kicks in a career stretching back to 2004 'I think the most unlucky opponent I've ever fought was Aaron Barrow. When I fought him, it was a couple of years ago in December', he began, referring back to another on the Midlands promotion.

'I'd just got back from American Top Team, so everyone was thinking that I was going to take the guy down and submit him because I'd been working my jiu-jitsu. He ran across the cage at me and I kicked him on the side of the head and knocked him out in 13 seconds. Nobody expected that. I'm a fighter, I like to warm up a bit and dismantle my opponent over a couple of rounds; nobody was expecting a knock out that fast. He ran across the cage to throw the left hook, he dropped his right hand from his chin and I saw it fast enough to get my foot up there and make contact.

'It was a heavy kick,' he emphasised, 'if you watch the video, you can actually see his feet lift off the floor a tiny bit. I caught him under the chin on the side of the neck and it lifted him off his feet a tiny bit and he looked like a rag-doll as soon as I hit him and he fell in a heap on the floor. Grant Waterman was the referee and I looked at him and Grant just looked back at me so I thought, "Well, I'd better give him a few more shots" – I jumped on him, gave him a few more punches. He was alright a minute or so later, but when he got back to the changing room he had no idea what had happened.'

Adding to a point masterfully demonstrated by Cung Le in his March 2008 destruction of Frank Shamrock, Hardy showed in his fight with perennial UK contender, Lee Doski that you do not necessarily have to land a hard kick on a target zone to do enough damage to end the fight. 'Unfortunately for Lee, I threw a kick, it was actually a body kick, a right leg. He managed to block it, but broke his arm at the same time. It's just one of those situations, when you've got somebody who knows how to kick, you don't really want to be blocking it; you don't want to be in the way of it at all! You can get a lot more power in a kick than in a punch, especially a body kick as well.'

The obvious question for the Outlaw, therefore, became; 'Have any opponents so far been able to stand up to your kicks?'

'Not really, no.' he answered, without a hint of vanity, 'I landed a lot of high kicks on Sami Berik, I caught him over and over again with the high kick, because of the disagreement I had with Sami before the fight, I promised him the full 15 minutes of the fight - he said he was going to be able to knock me out. Every time I threw a high kick, I didn't put 100% power into it. Other than that, usually when I land a high kick cleanly they fall over, asleep.'

At the time of writing Hardy is yet to make his UFC debut, however, I would not be at all surprised if, by the time of publication, the Nottingham fighter has put his shin through the face of an unfortunate opponent inside the Octagon.

KNEES IN THE THAI CLINCH

The unforgiving sport of Thai boxing allows a striker to demonstrate his full repertoire of attacks inside its competitive ring; under traditional rules punches, kicks, knees and elbows are all permitted techniques. Perhaps as a reflection on the effectiveness of the technique, in Thai boxing competition, more points are awarded for the effective use of knee strikes than any other weapon at the fighter's disposal.

Tightening up an incredibly effective 'Thai clinch', an experienced fighter will clasp his hands around his opponent's head and effectively take control of his whole body as a result. This position has been brought back to prominence in recent years with fighters such as Anderson Silva blasting their way through opponents, with apparent ease, causing damage to legs, body and head - in Silva's case, smashing teeth and noses in the process.

UFC 46: Frank Mir vs. Wes Simms

In a fight where clean knees landing to the head with full effect were the order of the day, Frank Mir employed the strike with ruthless efficiency in his bout with Wes 'The Project' Simms at UFC 46. A contest that he would be expected to win blindfolded nowadays, Mir struggled terribly in the opening round with his towering, but mostly inept Hammer House opponent, and even had trouble controlling the fight on the ground. By the middle of the second round, Mir was tiring quickly and appeared desperately vulnerable on his feet. Suddenly and completely against the run of the fight, the Las Vegan took control of his opponent's head with both hands and lifted his right knee straight to his opponent's jaw, swiftly followed by his left knee which crashed home with equal accuracy. 'It was good because I was beginning to fatigue and was having a hard time on the ground applying a submission on him, so it worked perfectly, I clinched and brought his head down into the knee.'

Although he had just slammed both knees into his opponent's skull with full force, Frank did not even acknowledge the connection that was made in landing the near fight-finishing shots. 'I don't really feel anything in the fights' Mir continued, 'I can feel my lungs, I can feel my legs, but I've never really felt my hands on someone's face and any time I knee people I don't really know what the impact feels like. I think, mentally, you acknowledge it's happening but you don't really feel anything. I feel everything in practise, if someone kicks me in the leg, I'm like "Fuck, that hurt!", but in the fight, I don't know what happens in you, but it seems that your brain cuts off a lot of bullshit.'

After the impact, Simms lurched backwards in a state of bewildered semi-consciousness, desperately trying to clear away the cobwebs; however, his Las Vegan opponent punctuated the knee strikes with a pair of solid hooks to seal the deal. 'I think that when we train, we train a lot of combinations – and one combination that I always train after I throw a knee is to finish off a person with hands to get back out safely. When I was punching him I really don't think I was trying to knock him out, it was just I was trying to protect myself.' As the old timers say, the best form of defence is attack, a point well served by the image of Simms on his back, counting the arena lights.

UFC 83: Mike 'The Count' Bisping vs. 'Chainsaw' Charles McCarthy

For the knee strike to be an effective weapon in the cage, however, it does not necessarily have to land flush on an opponent's jaw; a stream of knees can serve to damage, disorientate and dishearten an opponent to such an extent that he becomes a sitting duck, waiting to taken out. Britain's most famous mma fighter, Mike 'The Count' Bisping demonstrated this point at UFC 83 with a shocking display relentless aggression against 'Chainsaw' Charles McCarthy.

Within the opening seconds, Bisping closed the distance and landed a hard knee on his American opponent, who began laughing and stuck out his jaw, taunting his younger foe. 'He started talking to me and pulling stupid faces and being silly' Mike remembered with a sour note: 'That was obviously a sign of frustration if you ask me. He was trying to goad me and take me off my game plan. I thought, "You might be smiling and grinning now, but we're only one minute into the fight. You're not going to be grinning in another two or three minutes", as you saw that was the case.'

Bisping was able to shut down McCarthy for much of the fight and, when the jiu-jitsu fighter eventually became a static target, the Britishman ripped into him, showing a vicious streak a mile wide. Looking back on the blistering onslaught, Mike added that there was a personal element to the contest. 'He completely disrespected me as a fighter in the pre-fight interviews. He said I had no stand up, no jiu-jitsu and no wrestling, he said I was "the most average fighter in the UFC". That's a very, very personal insult considering I dedicate my life to mixed martial arts and to say that, I've got to be honest, it really pissed me off and I thought, you know, I'll prove a point.'

Though Bisping was able to prove his point for much of the bout, he had to fight his way out of a potential submission hold on the floor to do so. 'Obviously, I knew that's where he wanted me. I was a little bit annoyed that I'd let myself get there in the first place, but you know, I knew the defence to the armbar, I knew what I had to do and I did it textbook, just like I did in training. I'd drilled it a thousand times in training and thank God it worked perfectly. In that position, it's just about remaining calm and keeping your composure under pressure and using your technique. You can't just thrash around and try and squirm out of it, you've got to you correct technique, fortunately I did.'

As the fight resumed in a standing position, McCarthy's frailty in that area became clear as he was forced to absorb a terrific series of knees supplemented perfectly by well-placed bodyshots and uppercuts. 'I've been working my body shots a lot. I think bodyshots are an underused thing in mma, especially with the small gloves on, you can do some real good damage with bodyshots. I got to throw a few in that time, mix up it up with the knees, he was covering up well from the knees you see, he was taking a lot of them on the forearms, but I could see that he was open to bodyshots so I switched to the body and he might have dropped his hands down for the knee. That was the idea.'

Bisping continued to apply the pressure, twisting his body as he launched knee after knee on his cowering opponent, 'My knees were very sore for about three weeks after that because I kneed his elbows on some of them. But I kept throwing the knees in, I knew he was covering up, but I knew it was only a matter of time before one or two got through. Obviously, you can't take too many knees, all you need is one good one and you're going down, so it probably wasn't the wisest, the best strategy from his side. So I thought, "Just keep persisting here, keep throwing the knees, throw the odd bodyshot in, mix it up so I don't get too predictable and then he'll go down."

'I know I threw about 23 knees consecutively, one after the other, some of them were taken on the arms, some of them went through to his head. I think he probably took more on his arms that he did his face. I know there was one good one at the end, that's when he dropped like a sack of spuds; that was the big one that did the job.'

McCarthy covered up as best he could to defend himself from the ensuing blows, but the damage had been done and the referee called a halt to the bout very quickly after the end of the first round. 'I knew that was the end of the fight right there,' Mike said, of the remaining seconds he spent punching away at his downed opponent in a relentless attempt to finish the fight.

'He had no offence at all there, he was just curling up in a ball and waiting for the fight to stop or the round to end, so I was just ground-and-pounding him, being careful, just in case, you know, I didn't want to put myself in a bad position, so he could roll to a kneebar or anything like that. I was picking my shots, kneeing him to the body, punching him in the head, but like I say, he was curled up in a ball so there wasn't much of a target, but I did hit him with some good shots there. I did say, "Come on, ref!" I think I actually swore and said, "Fuckin' hell, ref!"

'As I was hitting him because I thought, "Come on, he's not doing anything here, curled up in a ball being punched and kneed isn't intelligent defence." I thought the fight should have been stopped, the round finished and he wasn't fit to continue anyway.'

After taking out his pent up aggression on his previously impolite opponent, Bisping could not help but make the statement verbally, just to leave the battered McCarthy under no illusions as to who was the better man on the night. 'When I finished, if you watch the tape back, I walk over to him and I said, "I'm not so average now, am I?" Now some people might not say that's too sportsmanlike, after I've just knocked him out, but you know, he slandered my skills completely, so I wanted to say, "Not so average now", and obviously I proved that.'

WEC 31: Jeff 'The Big Frog' Curran vs 'The California Kid' Urijah Faber

The fight game is evolving extremely quickly as trainers and competitors constantly develop new techniques, finding new ways to implement old techniques, or adjust any traditional skills for use in modern mma scenarios. A perfect example of this inventive approach is an apparently new way of applying a knee strike which has recently surfaced as a way to counter the single-leg takedown. This flashy, but effective manoeuvre was demonstrated by Urijah Faber in his match up with Jeff Curran.

In the second round, Curran shot in for a single leg takedown, Faber resisted the attempt, hopping on his free leg and pulling his hips away from his opponent, the Big Frog, however, held on tight to the single leg. If a competent wrestler gets a good grip on his opponent's leg, there is every chance he will be able to take the fight to the floor, Curran knew this and worked hard to force his foe to the mat. However, as Faber continued to hop on his free leg, keeping himself free from his opponent's grasp, he saw the perfect opportunity to launch his grounded foot off the canvas and fire a knee to his opponent's head with all his might. He leapt in the air, landing the strike perfectly, sending his foe crashing to the mat and wide open for a guillotine submission.

'I've practised things that are kind of similar to that,' Faber said, 'but not in the exact circumstance, it was just the spur of the moment. I feel I've come to the point in my game now where I can do just about anything that I want and not really worry about getting in danger. It's a good feeling man, I've come a long way and I'm always real aggressive and so being able to let it all hang out is real nice for me.'

EliteXC 'Street Certified':
Yves Edwards vs. James Edson Berto

Yves Edwards has since demonstrated his proficiency with the technique by landing a similar fight ending knee against James Edson Berto. 'That knee is something I play with a lot in the gym, you know, when guys are working, trying to get the single [leg takedown] in on me, if I can get the whizzer in and push on the head, I kinda pop up and try to land the knee but you can't really do that in the gym, you can't really hit your training partners with something like that. So I play with it a little bit, I was in the fight and I figured, "Hey, this might work!"' He exclaimed in an understatement on an explosive strike which had severe consequences for the 'Little Tiger'.

'I was pretty excited about trying it, my corner was telling me to throw it, I figured the round was about to be over, so I threw it up there and it landed pretty clean, it felt good and it finished the fight for me.' Sure enough the contact was hard and concussive, folding Berto up like a concertina as he fell to the floor in a heap.

WILD FLYING KNEES

The flying knee takes the knee strike, quite literally, to a different height as a fighter leaps in, throwing all his power behind one or both knees. More conservative mma practitioners often deem the technique to be too flashy, risky or impractical for effective use in competition. In equal measure, many striking specialists in the modern era, such as Gilbert Yvel, appear to be cashing in on their notable advantage with knee strikes by throwing them at every opportunity in an attempt to cause damage quickly, putting opponents at an early disadvantage.

Not many fighters throw the jump knee with such enthusiasm, or wanton abandon as Yvel and are content to throw the strike so frequently and without concern, occasionally trying it after a feigned shot or mixing it in to punching combinations. For Gilbert, however, the strike has in the past served him as a staple offensive manoeuvre, leaping in the air to drive home his heavy knees on several occasions during what can often be comparatively short-lived contests.

Gilbert Yvel, Master of the Flying Knee

Boasting a true command of the knee strikes and kicks of all description, Yvel outlined the backdrop to his striking-heavy skill set. 'I started doing kickboxing in the local gym where I used to live,' Gilbert began, referring to his early training as a 15 year old. 'At that point, it was just like the toughest guy from the village was the teacher and at that point, it was basically, kicking each other's ass!' he said laughing as his first days of training. It was not until he reached the Dutch capital that his confidence began to soar. 'When I moved to Amsterdam that was when I told everybody I was going to be the world champion.'

Once in the unofficial capital of European Muay Thai, Gilbert soon found that his rough application of bone-crunching art led him naturally to the more limited rule set of mma. 'I saw the kickboxing on TV first, like the K-1 actions, then I thought this is what I want to do. Then they showed the free fight, mma and the cage fight on TV. At first my opinion was like, this is not for me, but my teacher thought I was strong enough to do mma.' Within three months, the hard-punching kickboxer was plying his trade in the Dutch branch of the Rings organisation.

Taking on grapplers for the first time, Yvel was wary of the fight going to the floor; as a result, landing a deceptive jump knee thrown with all of his power was instinctively a good way of striking effectively, as his opponents look to take him down. 'It's just what I did all the time, not really practising, it's what I did – it's hard to replicate the movement because I throw it with all my power right into you and the thing is, sometimes I threw the left knee first, sometimes I threw the right knee first. It was very difficult to catch, so it's just a good thing to destroy somebody.'

Looking back on memories of numerous heavy knee strikes, Yvel remembered the first time he threw a jump knee in competition, starting a career-long love affair with the technique, 'The trainer I used to train with, Lucien Carbine, was really good with his knees, just a straight knee, without jumping. I was in a fight on the biggest show in Holland, I was destroying this guy and I got a good idea of trying the knees with jumping. It worked very good, so I always keep on doing it. If something works, why switch it, why do something else? It became a little bit of a trademark, jumping with the knees and if you hit somebody, it's fucked up!' he said, marvelling at the strike's effectiveness, with a note of remorse for his former victims.

Unfortunately for Gilbert, K-1 kickboxing champion, Semmy Schilt was one fighter who managed to escape from his countryman's leaping knee attacks, 'I beat him more with punches, because Semmy was too tall. If I threw a jumping knee at him, it would just hit his belly button, you know?' he said, racking his memory for other fighters who had fallen victim to his aerial assaults. 'Let me think… I got so many guys with the knees. Todd Medina, it wasn't really a jumping knee, but I switched in the air and he was knocked out for like 10 minutes. I've knocked so many people down with the knees that I don't even remember! Oh man, I've had over 60 fights!'

2Hot2Handle 2:
Gilbert Yvel vs. Carlos Barreto

In the end, one of the most damaging jump knees in the history of mma leapt out of Yvel's memory. 'Carlos Barreto!' He barked, 'That was the best knock out because he was sleeping!' Thinking back to the fight in March 2001 on Holland's 2Hot2Handle promotion, Gilbert added some background to the contest. 'I remember I was fighting Vitor Belfort in Pride; I lost, my first real loss and Barreto was standing by the corner, shouting shit. So I thought, "OK, fucker, let's see when I fight you."'

Bravely taking a fight in the Dutchman's local promotion, Barreto was entering the lion's den; however, the vale tudo veteran did not look at all nervous at the start of the fight as he shot in for a double leg take down which looked more like an American football tackle. Before long, the lanky Brazilian was in mount position, raining down blows on Yvel, before - in what was a decision influenced by the home town crowd - the referee called for a stand up, bringing the fight back to standing to the Brazilian's considerable disadvantage..

This one brief taste of the ground (and Barreto's bitter punches) was all Gilbert was prepared to tolerate and he ripped into his opponent, swinging heavy punches with bad intentions in an attempt to finish the fight. 'The next moment, I threw a right hook and he went down. It was not like a real hard punch,' Gilbert recalled, 'but he never saw it coming, so he went down and the referee stopped the fight and he was like, "I'm not knocked out, I can fight another round."'

Barreto was all over the place; it was a clearly one of those moments when a fighter's determination and confidence blinds them to the fact that their plight is hopeless, and they wander towards certain disaster like a once talented, but sincerely punch-drunk boxer, looking for one last crack at the title.

'They are letting it go?" Announcer, Eddie Bravo said in amazement.

'They are going to restart!' Co-commentator, Steven Quadros added with an equally bewildered tone. 'Unbelievable!'

From Yvel's point of view, the fight was there for the taking. 'You could still see that he was how do you say wobbly? Wibbly? Wobbly on his feet' Gilbert laughed, taking a stab at one of the more ridiculous sounding words in the English dictionary. 'So it was my moment to jump in with the double-knee.' Yvel could not have timed the strike better if he had all evening to get it right; he sprang forward, twisting his hips in mid-air and dragging his body from side to side as he banged in a pair of brutal knees in quick succession.

'I hit him two times,' Gilbert said excitedly, 'The first one on his chin and the second one on his body. He went down!' The Dutchman landed a hard right hand for good measure and attempted a soccer kick as the referee stepped in to save Yvel's fallen opponent; Barretto, however, lay unconscious on the mat, his legs folded under him in a grotesquely unnatural pose for several seconds before his cornermen and paramedics were able to reach him, and eventually resuscitate the stubborn Brazilian.

THE LEAPING HEAD STOMP

When a fighter wearing mma gloves punches his opponent in the face as hard as he can, there is no doubt that he is going to cause some kind of damage. Soft tissue can easily be cut or bruised; while the nose, the jaw, teeth and eye-sockets can all be broken by a hard, perfectly timed punch to the face. However, in the extremely unlikely scenario that a hard punch were to actually kill an mma fighter, observers could say with some justification that the death was a terribly unfortunate accident, as it is quite reasonable to expect, as a puncher, that your opponent is unlikely to suffer any long lasting damage.

If, however, a fighter were to launch a leaping two footed attack on a downed opponent, with the express intent of landing flush on his opponent's head with a downwards stomping motion, it does not seem quite so fair to expect that he will not suffer a serious injury, or worse. A leaping stomp is about as dangerous an attack as a human can possibly launch in a hand-to-hand combat.

Even still, the technique was legitimate in the Pride Fighting Championships from the Japanese organisation's 13th show until its unfortunate demise in 2007, and could be used without restriction, alongside the more traditional striking techniques of punching and kicking. In a clear attempt to follow the Japanese based show, Cage Rage sensationally relaxed its rules on stomping and kicking to the head of a downed opponent at Cage Rage 13 by introducing the 'Open Guard' rule.

Under this controversial and, thankfully, now defunct rule, if a downed fighter were more than one metre away from the cage, and in a position to defend himself, the referee would shout 'Open guard', and raise his hand. This call would inform the standing fighter that he could now legitimately kick his downed opponent to the head, or execute any kind of stomping attack to a legal target area. Under this rule, a nightmarish, yet all too real possibility loomed large; that a serious, long term injury was on its way.

Cage Rage 13: Ozzie Haluk vs. Brad 'One Punch' Pickett

Then Cage Rage promoter, Andy Geer informed me at the time that each of the fighters booked for the first show where the rule was to be unveiled were unconcerned about the possible consequences to their health and were looking forward to the event. Brad Pickett, for one, was less than concerned when the rule was brought in, ahead of his clash with Ozzie Haluk. 'I didn't really think much of it, thinking "No-one's ever going to really use it, realistically, are they?" That was what was going through my head. You think, "Man, it's a very dangerous move", but it's very unlikely that you're ever going to hit with that move, unless the guy's really tired. Especially if they are going to call 'Open guard' it's not like in Pride where you can do it all the time. With Open guard, the referee says "You can do it now…" so people know you're going to do it. I wasn't worried in general about it being used on myself – and I didn't think I'd ever use it either… and then I did."

Pickett overcame numerous takedown attempts from his determined opponent and mid way through the second round Haluk's pace had slowed to a crawl. Pickett saw his opportunity and demonstrated some impressive athletic ability as he leapt over Haluk's defending legs to deliver a full-on, double-footed head stomp.

Asked how he feels to have the dubious honour of being the first person to use the dangerous technique within the rules, Brad laughed, 'I never really thought of it like that… part of Cage Rage history I guess! When you're in a fight, you fight with bad intentions anyway – I'm a nice guy outside the cage, but when you're in the cage, you're looking to hurt the opponent or cause pain. I didn't fear for his health or anything like that… it's not like it's a sharp object – the feet – it's not like an elbow or something like that which would cut you open. I didn't think it would hurt him badly.'

Although it is highly unlikely that Cage Rage, or any other organisations outside of Japan will ever resurrect any kind of rule which allows stomping to the head of a downed opponent, just after the fight, Brad remained sure that including the Open guard rule was not as dangerous as it appears and makes for a far more entertaining fight.

'It definitely does make it more exciting, because it stops guys rolling to their backs and laying there. If someone calls "Open guard", they're going to get stamped on so it's a bit more exciting without people trying to lie down and pull guard. It's good for the crowd, it can look very eye-pleasing, it's very flashy; but it can look quite violent, when it's not really that bad.'

Well known UK referee, Marc Goddard confirmed his assessment. 'I think they thought about it quite well, they employed it when a fighters head was a metre away from the cage, so he wasn't going to get trapped up there with no chance of moving his head. I think it worked quite well, but I'm going to say that because I'm from inside the sport, I can see it for what it is, obviously people on the outside looking in and they see someone jumping up in the air and trying to kick him on the head when he's on his back, they are going to have a different view to it than me, aren't they?'

KNOCK OUT UPKICK

If, like Ozzy Haluk in the previous section, a fighter is on his back with his opponent standing over him, there is no doubt that he is in a tricky situation. The standing fighter is the one making the choices; he might decide to make a concerted effort to pass the guard, putting his opponent in a tight spot, or he might simply hack away at his legs with low kicks, gradually wearing down his opponent's explosive capabilities. However, if the standing fighter makes the mistake of coming too close, there is every chance that his precarious positioning will make him pay dearly by firing off a stinging upkick to the face.

The first time that this technique was demonstrated to a wide audience came way back in 1996 when Renzo Gracie took on the Russian Sambo master, Oleg Taktarov, on the ill-fated, Martial Arts Reality Superfight promotion. At the time, the Gracie family was miles ahead of the competition when it came to grappling technique; however, Taktarov was no mug on the ground himself, so when the opportunity came to pressurize his downed opponent, the burly Russian stood over Gracie, his threat looming like a dark cloud on a close horizon.

However, armed with the collective jiu-jitsu experience of many brothers, uncles and cousins, Renzo appeared perfectly unbothered by his predicament. The more that Taktarov gained in confidence, the closer he edged towards his downed opponent until he came that quarter of a step too close. Out of nowhere, Renzo launched a hard upkick which landed directly in the middle of Oleg's exposed forehead, causing him to stumble back to the floor in complete disarray. The elated Gracie sprung to his feet and delivered a devastating right hand to seal the deal, hardly missing a step as he ran past his opponent and leapt onto the cage wall in joyful celebration.

The precedent had been set and fighters quickly began to develop ways of keeping themselves out of danger as they carefully crept into an opponent's standing guard. However, as these techniques for a standing fighter to attack a grounded opponent began to become almost commonplace, some of the more high wire mma fighters began throwing caution to the wind, fearlessly launching themselves at their downed opponent in the hope of landing a fight-changing, or even fight-ending, punch.

Cage Rage 25: Tom 'Kong' Watson vs. Pierre 'The Professional' Guillet

As this new leaping attack began to gain prominence, it appeared a matter of time before the lesson Renzo Gracie taught the sport way back in 1996, would again raise its head. That it did in dramatic style at Cage Rage 25 when Tom Watson took on Pierre Guillet. 'I just went out there with a plan of being more aggressive and didn't really worry if he took me down,' Watson recalled, 'I knew he was going to take me down. When he was in my guard it looked like he was quite worried about submissions so, he was staying back which was giving me room either to stand up, or upkick to the face,' he laughed, as he unveiled the nastier of the two options at his disposal.

'It's funny,' Kong continued, 'you practise things for different fights and I remember practising that a lot before I fought Professor X [Xavier Foupa Pokam], it didn't pay off for almost another year but I remember when he was stood above me, he did a dummy first of all and I pushed away his hips. I think he thought the legs were cleared so that's when he launched.'

Guillet leapt into the air and dived straight down to deliver the hardest leaping right hand he could muster and seemed to hold absolutely nothing back. To his infinite credit, Kong reacted immediately and sent a piston–like upkick to meet his airborne opponent and caught him under the jaw with full force.

'As soon as it landed I knew he was out' Watson said, 'I just felt my heel hit him on the jaw. I'm not sure how he cut his eye; maybe that was an old cut, so perhaps that was to do with when he fell down. I remember my heel hit his jaw and it was just like a limp body coming down – sounds a bit graphic!'

Even though Pierre appeared to be out cold, fighters can often recover from a concussive blow in a matter seconds, so Watson took no chances and sat up to land a series of punches until the referee dived in to stop the contest. 'It's funny because it's only like a second, but it feels like ten, I thought "Grant will stop this", but you can't afford not to put in a few punches or whatever, because obviously I couldn't have waited a second, he might have got back up.

'I predicted a first round KO,' Kong laughed, 'but that was even better, it was great!'

CHAPTER TEN
FINISHING TECHNIQUES
SUBMISSIONS

After years of struggling to make ends meet and teaching jiu-jitsu to a faithful band of students in his garage, Rorion Gracie made one of the most influential moves in the history of martial arts by setting up the Ultimate Fighting Championship. The idea was to use the show to demonstrate the effectiveness his family's art; Rorion, therefore chose his younger brother, Royce, to represent the truly technical nature of Gracie Jiu-Jitsu.

With the notable exception of Kimo Leopoldo, who caused Royce all manner of trouble in their UFC encounter, the skinny Brazilian cruised past all of his physically more capable opponents, putting on some mesmerising performances in the process. Brushing past the challenges of early mma hardmen, Ken Shamrock, Pat Smith and Dan Severn, Royce showed the world the stunning efficiency of his grappling art.

All to aware of how potent his jiu-jitsu was after a string of challenge matches in his garage, Rorion had no concerns in the run up, remaining assured that his brother would come through victorious. 'Unless the person throws a perfect punch, if you stay far enough away, he can't touch you and when they move closer to close the distance, you can get a hold of them. I've seen that happen for 50 years of my life, back in Brazil, you know what I mean. I have seen that over and over.'

However, whilst Royce was the first family member to demonstrate their art to a wide audience, as he explained, Rorion also did his part to defend the family name throughout the 70's in both bare-knuckle challenge matches and the most polite of sparring sessions.

'I don't like the idea of beating people up. I think it's much more humane, much more intelligent to demonstrate the technique and prevail by choking the guy out or making him submit by an armlock or a choke or something like that – or simply by pinning them to the point where they can't get out and they struggle and exhaust themselves and say, "I give up", that's the idea, it's to make the guy understand that you don't have to beat him up.'

One of the best grapplers in the modern world of mma is Frank Mir, who has been training karate since he was a child. At the age of 20, he began training jiu-jitsu in his home town of Las Vegas with BJJ black belt, Ricardo Pires. Under the tutelage of the Brazilian, Frank quickly discovered that he had a genuine talent for applying pressure to opponent's joints and arteries.

It makes perfect sense to the former UFC heavyweight champion, because in previous fights he had discovered some opponents are capable of withstanding heavy strikes. 'Some people are very good at disguising pain,' Mir said, explaining his preference for the grappling arts, 'but whenever I submit people and I feel their bones crushing, I know that no matter what, that I'm inflicting pain. I've choked out a lot more people than I've ever knocked out, so I'm just more comfortable if I end the fight with a choke, I'm more confident in that than a knock out.'

A powerful striker who scores a knock out after swinging for the fences can be accused of landing a 'lucky punch', his efforts falling into a lesser category of victory. Whether or not this interpretation is correct, there is no such thing as a 'lucky' submission hold, each is the product of a concerted application.

Mir demonstrated his mastery of damaging submission holds at UFC 34 against Roberto Traven. 'Jiu-Jitsu-wise, he knows more about jiu-jitsu than I do. If we both put a gi on and went at it, he would have probably choked me out. It was just that it was a fight, so the fact that I punched him in the face and then armbarred him, helped with the armbar. It wasn't that I was that slick at jiu-jitsu, it was just that anyone who gets caught in the face and stunned, they change. He probably never trained to receive punches on the ground viciously.'

Referring to the armbar finish, Mir continued regretfully, 'He went to the hospital; I think I fractured his arm. I don't mean to go through with submissions, if I feel someone tapping, I'll sit there and I'll pause. I don't apply more pressure, I don't take pressure off either and I wait for the referee to stop the fight. If I don't feel you tapping, I'm going to apply more pressure, but I'll never break anybody's limb if they're tapping, that's pretty dishonourable.'

However, explaining his submission selection whilst grappling, Mir explained that he only goes for submissions which have the potential to cause damage. 'I see some people who train submissions that hurt and it will make guys in the gym tap, but they don't inflict damage. I think that's a mistake in mindset because, you know, a professional fighter, a guy who's going to step in the ring, really doesn't care about how much a certain move hurts, so I train only moves that are capable of inflicting damage because then if he taps, fine; but if he doesn't, I've accomplished something. If you just cause pain, like a neck crank, it doesn't do anything; all you do is waste your energy. It's not that I train to go ahead and in the gym break bones, it's just I only go for moves that are capable of injuring someone.'

A well trained submissions fighter can threaten to finish the fight from more or less any position, whilst there are too many submissions to list, the following eight sections are dedicated to a selection of submission holds often seen used to devastating effect in mixed martial arts competition.

HYPER-EXTENSION CITY
THE STRAIGHT ARMBAR

The straight armbar is a staple submission hold for practitioners of the grappling arts from across the world, and is quite possibly the most versatile armlock in current use under mma rules. The origins of the hold can be traced back hundreds of years, yet only in the last couple of decades, the armlock has shown its true potential in a no-rules fighting environment, as the Gracie family and their disciples so aptly demonstrated in the early days of the sport.

The modern game of mma reflects the effectiveness of the submission; it can applied from numerous positions and once on, it is extremely difficult to escape. Attempts to resist tapping can be at best uncomfortable and, at worst, extremely damaging. Indeed, several fighters competing to this day complain that they cannot fully extend one arm or another as a result of the submission. However, as you will gather from this section, there is a long list of fighters willing to take that risk.

UFC Japan:
Frank Shamrock vs. Kevin Jackson

One of the fight world's most famous victories came in December 1997 at UFC Japan: Ultimate Japan as a young Frank Shamrock shook off the nerves to take on the aggressive and extremely well decorated wrestler, Kevin Jackson. 'I was scared of course, everybody's scared at the time, but I truly believed that I had the better system, the better game, the better understanding of the game and I truly believed that I was going to get him quick and expose him. My fears were just, don't trip and fall, don't make a fool of yourself, don't hurt yourself, but I always truly believed that I was going to beat him handily.'

'Handily' is an excellent way to describe his victory, in a contest which lasted only 16 seconds. Jackson went into the fight undefeated, having smashed and choked his way through his first three straight opponents. He won an Olympic gold medal is the discipline of freestyle wrestling five years previously and many observers of the time thought that the powerful grappler would smash through Shamrock. However, as a pure wrestler he had nowhere near the submission knowledge of his well-rounded opponent and it showed. As the Olympian bundled his opponent to the floor, Shamrock adjusted his weight and slipping his leg around Jackson's head to straighten out a perfect armbar to seal victory.

An elated Frank Shamrock walked around the octagon in celebration;

however, it turns out to be a bitter sweet victory, as he explained. 'To be honest with you, it was kind of anti-climatic because I had trained so hard and I had prepared myself so much for it and to have it end so quickly was kind of a let down for me. I was kind of bummed; I could even say that I was almost depressed, because I had worked it out to be such a big, painful and hard event. I attribute that to my coaches, my wrestling coach at the time had wrestled Kevin Jackson in the Olympic trials and NCAA wrestling, so he knew about his style, he knew about his body type, so when I was armbarring my coach in 10 seconds, I'll probably give Jackson about 20.'

UFC 48: Frank Mir vs. Tim Sylvia

A more recent, but equally memorable armbar win in the organisation came in June 2004 as, the subject of the introduction, Frank Mir famously destroyed Tim Sylvia's arm en route to victory at UFC 48. The Las Vegan did not appear to have Sylvia in any trouble as the first 30 seconds on the fight drifted by, but as Mir explains, things can change very quickly in mma. 'I remember that I didn't think the armbar was on tight, but I still extended my hips, just basically holding on. He looked like he was going to slam me, so I was going to transition to a triangle, but as soon as he lifted me off the ground, I felt something popping on my hip, whatever I had across my hip, cracking. So I didn't know exactly what was breaking, I just knew something was breaking, so I just held on and applied more pressure.'

Thankfully for Sylvia, referee Herb Dean was on hand to stop the contest, 'I actually heard it before I saw it.' The official recalled of the hideous compound fracture, 'I remember hearing a strange noise and not really knowing what it was, it was just a random noise, you know what I mean? It could have been anything, maybe something that had nothing to do with the fight. I heard it and then I saw his arm bulge at the forearm. I saw his arm break at the forearm, once, then twice. It was a very dry sound,' Dean continued, 'almost like breaking a very dry twig, or a sound that sounded similar to tape being ripped off something really fast.'

Mir, almost unbelievably, did not hear the sound of bones snapping in his grasp as he tighten his grip on the 'Maine-iac''s arm. 'I'm not sure if I really heard it pop, but it's like anything else, the vibration against your leg... I don't know if my mind was playing tricks, I thought I heard it, but I definitely felt it, felt like I stepped on a bag of chips.'

Something had clearly gone wrong, so Dean instinctively stepped in to bring and end to the contest. 'Both of them were concerned as to why I was stopping the fight when Tim Sylvia hadn't tapped out.' Dean recalled, 'Tim Sylvia started to protest, going on and on saying that he wanted to re-start the fight and Frank Mir said that he heard the guy's arm pop, I don't think he realized the damage… when you say "Popped", I think you're talking about a hyper-extended joint, I don't think that he was talking about "I've actually just broken this man's forearm… in three places." I think it took a little bit of time for it to settle in that so much damage had been done.'

Even though he was convinced that some kind of injury had been done to Sylvia's arm, the reaction of the fans and the Miletich corner left Mir wondering if they were about to restart the fight. 'It had me doubting though, I really thought I broke his arm. I went back to my corner and my corner was like "Did it break?", I'm like "I'm positive!"' Facing the very real prospect that the fight may resume, Mir adjusted his tactics accordingly. 'I remember just looking at him and thinking, "Shit! Maybe I just dislocated his arm? I don't know, I heard something popping, something broke!' They were like, "I doesn't look like it broke", so I was like "Fuck, I guess we're still fighting!" I thought I would throw a really hard kick to his head and see what would happen if he blocked it.'

In a potentially career-saving judgment call, however, Herb Dean stopped the contest to a chorus of boos from the audience. 'Of course, I remember being booed, I remember… everyone… [UFC President] Dana White, the Miletich corner were trying to climb over the fence. They were booing, they weren't happy about that at all.' However, from the moment he made the call, Dean was quite sure of his judgment, although he feared this fact might have been hidden from the public. 'I thought it was the right choice, but Sylvia seemed to be ok and that he was able to pull the wool over everyone's eyes and say that he was ok and maybe hide when he got to the hospital. Then we would never know. That was my worse case scenario, my best case scenario is what happened, people saw the arm break and then realized that I stopped the fight for a good reason.'

The feeling of vindication came as quite a relief to a referee who has seen his fair share of criticism. 'I feel that I did a good job. They tried to get me to start the fight again, but I refused. When I look back on it, there were a lot of pressures to do other things. I think I made a decision that was really good for both of the athletes and the sport and that's why I pat myself on the back a little bit. I was just doing what I thought was right. I was hoping that the video would vindicate me. I thought I made the right choice, but I didn't think I would be back refereeing at that level again.'

If a fighter suffers a broken bone in a submission hold, the fight is called off immediately; however, if an armbar causes one fighter's elbow joint to hyper-extend, the referee will often leave the affected fighter in charge of his own destiny, with the professional fully aware that he faces the risk of receiving significant ligament damage if that should be the path that he should chose to tread.

FX3: Fight Night 3:
Wesley Felix vs. John 'The Hitman' Hathaway

Pancrase London fighter, Wes Felix is one such fighter who made a conscious choice to continue in such a dangerous predicament as he went up in weight to face a monster of the UK welterweight division, John Hathaway. 'My original opponent dropped out a couple of weeks prior,' Felix explained, 'I don't think there's anything worse than training for a fight that doesn't get to happen, plus I had seen John win at ZT Fight Night, and clearly remembered saying to Ash[leigh Grimshaw] "I wish I was a welterweight so I could fight that guy", because he was very impressive. So when FX3 offered me the fight, well, it'd have been rude not to, although Ash, Dean [Jones] and Jess [Liaudin] all suggested it was unwise of me to take the fight.'

A genuine talent, and by far the naturally bigger fighter, Hathaway forced his way into control on the floor very quickly, before catching hold of his opponent's left arm and straightening it out. 'At that point, I'd got the arm, I got it straight and I pretty much thought, "Wicked, I've won!"' Hathaway explained, 'Then he wasn't tapping, so I put it in more. He still wasn't tapping so I put it in even more and it went and I thought, "Please stop the fight!" almost, it was horrible! I don't know whether it was a loud noise, or if I could just feel it just because the arm was actually touching me. It was like a crunch, or a crack, whether it was loud, I don't know; but I could feel it and I'm sure Wes could feel it as well. It was a horrible thing to happen. I went in pure shock, you know, trying to tell Grant that it had actually broken. I was just literally looking for the ref to stop it.'

His opponent, however, was in no mood to capitulate and stubbornly fought on, refusing to quit even as his arm bent backwards at an incredible angle. 'Once it was on and I heard "the sound of a thousand twigs snapping"', Felix laughed, 'I didn't see the point in tapping, but there are reasons for this; I wanted to get as much time in the cage as possible, it was only an arm bar, I'm right handed. I'm a "glass-half-full" kind of guy, when you're in class, sparring with someone who is more skilled than you, stronger than you, you can still get a win or two - an actual fight is no different. Plus, if I'd managed to somehow win, the story of how I won a fight in the next weight category up, with one arm broken, would have kept many a listener entertained forty or fifty years from now.

'This was something you don't normally read about.' Felix continued, 'It seems that the actual "break" is the last thing to happen. First your muscle gets damaged, then the tendons, then the ligaments, and finally the actual joint. When you watch the dvd, you can clearly see that I was debating the whole "How bad is this injury?" issue. It looks like I go to tap, then change my mind, then hear some more snapping, cue more pain, go to tap, then

Former undefeated UFC Middleweight Champion Frank Shamrock

Vitor 'The Phenom' Belfort and the near unbeatable current UFC Middleweight Champion Anderson 'The Spider' Silva.

Paul Reed finds himself on the business-end of a rear naked choke, applied by French Jiu-Jitsu ace Emmanuel Fernandez.

Controversial Hawaiian bad boy and former Royce Gracie foe, Kimo Leopoldo looks ready for action in the cage.

UFC veteran and MMA ambassador Dan Severn bashes Dave 'Death Wish' Legeno on the floor.

Jason Young lands a beautiful jump knee en route to his decisive points victory over Francis Heagney to claim the vacant Cage Rage British Lightweight title

Ashleigh Grimshaw lands one of his trademark heavy right hands as he challenged Robbie Olivier for the promotion's British Featherweight title at Cage Rage 27

One of the most dominant champions in MMA history - Wanderlei Silva

Vitor 'The Phenom' Belfort attempts a high kick on Italian Ivan Serati.

Kevin 'The Monster' Randleman chases after Mirko 'Cro Cop' Filipovic after landing the most astonishing left hook of his entire career.

Przemyslaw Mysiala stretches Italian fighter, Matteo Piran's tendons to the limit with a beautiful straight armbar.

'The New York Bad Ass' Phil Baroni, one of the most emotional and hard-punching fighters in the sport.

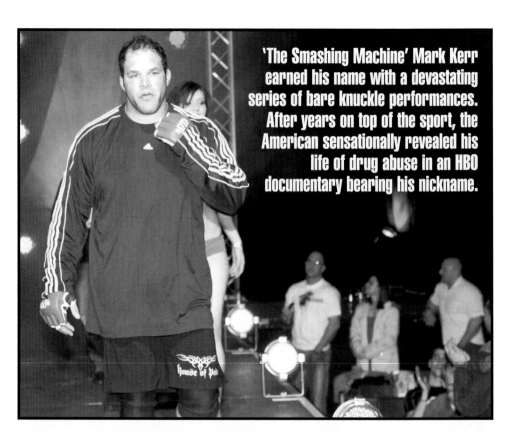

'The Smashing Machine' Mark Kerr earned his name with a devastating series of bare knuckle performances. After years on top of the sport, the American sensationally revealed his life of drug abuse in an HBO documentary bearing his nickname.

Mark 'Manslaughter' O'Toole catches Lola Bamgbala in an agonising armbar.

Cage Rage promoter Dave O'Donnell gets into the party atmosphere at the pre-fight weigh-ins

Legendary MMA veteran Frank Shamrock battles it out with Renzo Gracie

A blood splattered Michael Bisping, UK's number one UFC fighter claims yet another victory

'I'm sure I could have bashed him' Jimmy Page with the world's hardest man, Fedor Emelianenko

UFC Middleweight Champion Anderson Silva lands a hard knee on Miletich trained fighter, Tony 'The Freak' Fryland

The godfather of MMA Royce Gracie

Piere Guillet launches a flying punch, only to land, jaw first, on the sharply rising heel of Tom 'Kong' Watson

UFC and MMA legend Ken Shamrock enters the cage

Heavyweight brawlers, Stav Economou (left) and Piotr Kusmierz land simultaneous punches in their memorable Cage Rage 27 shoot out.

'New York Bad Ass' Phil Baroni stands over Scott Jansen - the latest addition to the American's highlight reel after he landed a perfect right hook.

One of the most influential figures in the early days of the sport, David 'Tank' Abbott arrives in London to fight Gary 'Smiler' Turner on only 48 hours notice.

Japanese submission-madman, Masakazu Imanari catches Tsunami Gym fighter, Robbie Olivier with a flying armbar after only 27 seconds.

Norwegian fighter, Simeon Thorensen triangles Clifford Hall from mount position, supplementing the chokehold with a stream of vicious elbows.

**London Shootfighter, Tony Pasos trips the bewildered
Lithuanian, Mamarizaev Jahongir**

change my mind.'

Felix's arm folded back to an unnerving degree, but he was somehow able to mask his pain, a point that was not lost on Hathaway, 'I felt the arm go, but he didn't make a sound, he even smiled after he got out of it!' This all came as a genuine shock to Hathaway who openly admitted to being unnerved by his opponent's show of guile, 'I was only 18 at the time, it's not the nicest thing to happen!' he laughed.

After the first round, Felix returned to his corner in the full knowledge that his arm was in a bad way, but as he explains, a pre-fight plan with his cornermen saw him step back in to fight on in the second round. 'I definitely knew it was going to be sore for a few days.' Felix joked, 'We'd already had a million conversations about stuff like this, and come to the conclusion that when it comes to submissions, a sore arm is not really a legitimate reason to pull a fighter who wants to and is able to continue. I didn't have another fight lined up in the immediate future, so I could have as much time off to "nurse my sore arm", as I liked. It's only a big deal if you think it is.'

The Pancrase London fighter soon noticed, however, that his arm was nowhere near as strong or responsive as it had been earlier. 'It was a little slower and weaker than usual, but after I got mounted, and John had one of my arms pinned I didn't really get an opportunity to escape.' He said, referring to his eventual, and virtually inevitable, stoppage loss in the second round. 'The x-ray showed a fractured radius. I didn't get an ultra-sound, but I reckon the major damage was to ligaments and tendons. One or two acupunctures, and a couple of weeks later and I could train on it again. It seems that if you train well, and keep the surrounding muscle as strong as possible, then this kind of injury doesn't normally catch up with you till you're older.'

Cage Rage Contenders & FX3:
Jason 'Bad Ass' Barrett vs
Nigel 'The Pitbull' Whitear

Another fighter prepared to take on serious injury to put on a show is the preacher, entertainer and fighter, Jason Barrett, a solid Thai fighter who gave his all in the heated rematch with Reading fighter, Nigel Whitear. As it happens, the fast-paced first match up on Cage Rage Contenders 2 which set up the contest is a story in itself, taken up by Jason Barrett.

'The game was to throw low kicks. I was throwing the low kicks. It was probably about three-and-a-half minutes into round one, I gave him a low kick and I just remember him buckling, he just stopped. I remember thinking, "It's over, innit?"', he laughed, 'and at that point, go for the kill.'

Opponent, Nigel Whitear had similar memories of the explosive encounter, 'The first round was quite intense by both of us. He absolutely blitzed me with leg kicks, absolutely annihilated my front leg with leg kicks, I remember that clearly. I also remember he had no ground game whatsoever. He had no strength on the floor at all.

'I hit him with a left hook,' Whitear recounted, 'I remember clearly, I could see he was dazed but for some reason, instead of just charging in I held back, that was a big mistake. But, he said that in his interview as well, he said he was going to Disneyland and he didn't want to go. I've got the utmost respect for Jason, totally, 100%; he's a good guy, he's a strong character.'

'I didn't think he'd get off in a standing exchange with me,' Barrett admitted in response, 'but funnily enough, he was actually getting the better of me in a couple of exchanges. I've taken some big shots, but the closest I've ever been to being knocked out was against Nigel Whitear in that first fight. He punched me in the mouth and I just remember thinking "Fuck in hell", excuse my language. I just remember thinking "Whoa!"'

'When we got to the end of the first round, I was absolutely knackered.' Barrett continued in repentant fashion, 'I'd only trained for two weeks and I was exhausted. I remember leaning on the cage and my cornermen were going to me, "Are you alright, I will fucking throw that towel in if you tell me, can you see properly?" I'm like, "I'm cool, I'm cool, I'm cool", but I was thinking, "Yeah, throw the towel in, I'm knackered, mate."

'I just remember looking across the cage at Whitear and he looked worse than me, he was leaning on the cage. I could see he was shaking his head saying no to Sol [Gilbert] about something and seeing that energised me. I just thought, "Fuck! Right! Bring it on mate!", and I just went for the kill. I really did.'

The fight ended in controversial fashion as it appeared that Jason took a deliberate punch at his opponent when the fight had been called to a temporary halt, by referee, Grant Waterman. Whitear took over the narration, 'To be honest, not pulling any punches, it pissed me right off how the fight ended and at the end of the day we were both told to stand up. We were both gassed, don't get me wrong, as we were told to stand up, Jason's turned to me and smashed me in the jaw. Obviously, in his defence, he's there to fight, but in my defence the referee had touched us both and told us to stand up. So my jaw was all relaxed and, in all fairness, I couldn't continue afterwards. In my eyes, it should have been a no-contest really.'

As you might expect, Barrett remembers the outcome differently, 'He was on top of me and I rolled him over, I didn't actually realise that Grant had said "Stop fighting," Grant was going to stand it up. I rolled him over and I hit him and Grant grabbed me and I looked up to say "What?", he told me to get up, so I got up and walked over to my corner and I could just see Nigel lying there, shaking his head, saying he's had enough. I knew it was over, but it was already over from the beginning of the round.'

Hungry for revenge, Whitear went to great lengths in preparation for the rematch on the Berkshire-based, Free Fight Federation [FX3], 'I went away and trained my arse off at the Miletich team in America for two-and-a-half weeks! It's the best camp I've ever been to. You've got Drew McFedries who is the most technical pad-worker I have ever seen; Pat Miletich is a legend himself, Robbie Lawler, Tim Sylvia and everyone else, it was awesome.... The only person I didn't like out there was Matt Hughes, thought he was an arrogant prick, but there you go. I don't like him at all, he knows that.'

'I knew I was going to win,' the Pitbull continued, 'I said I was going to break his arm, but I didn't know I was actually going to do it. My exact words were "I'm taking something home to put on the mantelpiece to show him that he can't fuck me over twice." Those were my exact words, there was a little bit of bad blood there, it wasn't personally to Jason, it was more of the point of fact that I think the referee should have called it a no contest, so there was a point to prove in this.'

Nigel was forced to absorb a series of stinging elbows on the floor, but as Barret over-reached, 'The Pitball' immediately grasped hold of his opponent's arm. 'The first armbar was the one that done the damage, that was when it cracked like mad. I tried saying to Jason, "Your arm's buggered mate. What are you doing? Just tap."

'He was like, "No, no, no', and I said fair play to him.

'It was horrific. I've never heard anything like it. You know when you used to snap twigs when you were at the park or at school? The way is just goes crack; it was a slightly duller sounding version of that, more of a twanging snap than it was a cracking snap, it was horrible, I didn't like it. Obviously, at the time I'm going to do whatever it takes to make him tap, for me to win the fight. I'm not out to ruin anyone's career or anything like that, but it was not nice.'

As luck would have it, Barrett professes to have a high tolerance of pain. 'I pulled one of my teeth out before that was giving me a bit of jip. I literally dragged it out of my mouth at home. So I've got quite a high tolerance for pain. He had me and I thought, "Ooh, this doesn't feel right." I did hear it clicking and Nigel' shouted himself, "Jason, don't be stupid! It's broken."

'Leon said to me, Jason, do you want to give up? It looks like you're caught, and I was like, "No way!" I was pulling on it, thinking I could get out of it. I pulled it free and just remember that my arm had a mind of its own. It was just dangling! Not responding! - Then he grabbed it again!'

Whitear, who had previously been so concerned for his opponent's safety explained why he had no problem with going after the injured arm, 'He hit me with the same damaged arm and that wound me right up then! So that was when I got the omaplata. It did nothing,' Whitear insisted, 'I just got him with it in the end and twisted what was left of his elbow.'

'This time he rolled me and he actually had me down.' The 'Bad Ass' recalled, 'He had it properly and he was shouting "Don't be stupid!", he was shouting that at me and I thought, "Yeah, he has got me you know", but my pride was just saying "No!!!"'

Whitear was not impressed and tightened his grip on the arm still further. 'I wanted to pull it off, I honestly wanted to pull it off because I felt like I was doing him a favour by getting him to tap the first time, and when he didn't, that's just arrogance and stupidity. Tap today, fight tomorrow, you know, so I thought, if you want your career ended, I'll oblige!'

Thankfully, Barrett was back in the cage within a few months, but at the time, his arm injury appeared to be very serious. 'When my corner ran in and looked, it was their response,' Barrett said, 'I saw Deano [Durrant]'s face, he was closing his eyes and covering his face saying, "That is disgusting!"'

'I remember thinking, "This shit must be bad. It must be really bad." Why didn't I just tap? It started to swell pretty much immediately, but when you've got your adrenaline going through your body still, you're not really feeling it, but on the way home in the car, I was saying to my girlfriend, 'Ah, I got beat' and as the adrenaline is leaving your body, then you start feeling it!' he added, pissing himself laughing with a sense of bizarre joy once again. 'You don't feel the pain instantly, you really don't.'

Cage Rage 8:
Sol 'Zero Tolerance' Gilbert vs.
Jean-Francois Lenogue

After a series of horrible injuries, I thought it might be best to finish this section with a somewhat light-hearted tale, in comparison to the previous three; after all, contrary to the impression you may have received, not all armbars lead to injurious consequences.

Zero Tolerance Fight Skool head coach, Sol Gilbert has a heavy background in boxing, but as he proved against French fighter Jean-Francois Lenogue, he has picked up some significant ground skills since his mma debut. 'It was really just a matter of him trying to take me down.' Sol recalled, 'I thought he was going to stand. I watched his fight with Damien Riccio which was a three round war, effectively, from a 50/50 position against the cage. A lot of knees a lot of strikes, I thought that was what I was going to be in for; as it was, he just kept looking for the takedown all the time. I'd been training at London Shoot for about six months then, so my wrestling was getting a little bit better, but it wasn't at a level where I was switching it on from boxing to takedown defence mode.'

'Every time he took me down I had to try and create space to either stand back up, or try to go for a submission.' Gilbert continued, 'One thing I did remember was when he took me down one time, I had an overhook on his left side and kept control of him but he was really, really tight and I couldn't get distance to get a kick out or to get a submission, so I started taunting him and stuff, you know. Every time he's hitting me, I'm laughing, blowing him a few kisses and starting to rile him. I was like, "Hey, hey, Frenchie, Frenchie…"'

Gilbert's light-hearted display of xenophobia had the desired effect, 'He looked up and me and I said, "Come on, man, you're punching like a girl!", and with that he just come up and started striking!' Lenogue was furious and bellowed with frustration as he brought down a series of hard hammerfists, which the Brighton fighter was largely able to defend as he squirmed around on his back. 'I've got quite a good defence from that sort of stuff, like Curtis Stout for a whole round I managed to negate his stuff and I got up as fresh as a daisy.'

As the ineffective shots poured down, Sol picked his spot and executed a picture perfect armbar as the Frenchman struggled to break free. 'I just managed to cut the angle, get the armbar and finish it from there. I had both of them; it was almost like a double armbar. There was no way I was ever letting go of that, I heard it click and everything. He was alright afterwards, but I actually thought that something might have broken on him. It was my first fight on Cage Rage going up from smaller shows so there was a lot of anticipation. It was a good fight, it was a fun fight, you know.'

Joint-Pop Shoulderlock
The Kimura

The kimura shoulderlock is named after Japanese legend, Masahiko Kimura, a man widely considered as the best judoka of all time who competed in the sport throughout the first half of the twentieth century. Kimura famously broke Helio Gracie's arm with the hold now named after him in a submission grappling match held in 1955. It is a hold with a heritage; however, it also continues to spring out from unexpected angles in competition, as modern mma fighters continue to find yet more fresh applications for the submission.

In the late 90's, the skilful application of the hold came back to haunt the Gracie family as the latently suicidal Japanese showman, Kazushi Sakuraba committed near sacrilege at the time as he turned his back on Renzo Gracie, secure in the knowledge that his kimura grip would pay dividends. The former pro-wrestler cashed in, dislocating Gracie's elbow with the submission and simultaneously dispelling the myth that turning your back is necessarily a fatal mistake.

Since then, the submission has taken on an even wider role and is consistently used by today's fighters to sweep their way out of trouble or set up another complicated submission attack. However, one thing remains clear from mountains of uncomfortable Youtube viewing; the kimura itself is still an extremely potent and potentially limb-snapping submission hold.

UFC 74: Frank Mir vs. Antoni Hardonk

A talented submission fighter with the ability to apply a tight, virtually inescapable kimura is Frank Mir. Talking the talk as regularly as clockwork about his determination to apply only the more damaging holds in the sport, Mir knows his way round a kimura rather well. 'I like transitioning for the kimura from cross side. I think a lot of times from the bottom, from like half guard, sometimes it takes a little more power when the guys defend, but when you're on the side of them it's a little easier, especially when your weight is bearing down and pinning the guy.'

Mir most recently put his kimura to work in the octagon as he submitted the rising Dutch heavyweight, Antoni Hardonk; 'That guy's shoulder is pretty flexible.' He recalled, 'I put his hand all the way back to the mat! I didn't feel him tapping, but then later on I realised that it was because his hand was between my legs and he was tapping me on the back, it was kind of a weird angle and I didn't notice the tap.'

Pride 32: The Real Deal:
Phil 'New York Bad Ass' Baroni vs.
Yosuke Nishijima

Not noticing the tap is one thing, but when your opponent simply refuses to submit, that is something altogether quite different. Phil Baroni was put in this difficult position when he flew in to take on local favourite, former cruiserweight boxer, Yosuke Nishijima at Pride 32. A former undefeated boxer and kickboxer himself, carrying power in both hands, Baroni was fancied to take a risk and stand with the razor-sharp Japanese striker; however, Phil played an intelligent game, taking the fight to the floor within the opening seconds of the fight and transitioning smoothly to side mount.

Once in position, Baroni took control of his opponent's wrist and without rushing his work, steadily worked his way into a strong finishing position, cranking the arm as he went. 'I remember his elbow dislocating for a second. I motioned to the referee and when the referee stopped it, it went back in place, like Renzo's elbow did against Sakuraba. It was a similar type thing you know only double as bad, I'm sure he's had some problems ever since then.'

Famed for his brash in-ring persona and a healthy disregard for his opponent's well-being within the competitive arena, I asked the New Yorker whether he had any qualms with wrecking an opponent's arm if they refused to tap. 'You don't want to injure anyone permanently, because we're all fighters, we're all competing, trying to make a living and stuff like that – but if they ain't going to tap out, I ain't going to let go of the hold either. I leave it in their hands, you know?'

HIGH-PERCENTAGE ARMBAR
THE KEYLOCK

The keylock is one of the simplest, but also the most effective submission holds in the arsenal of any grappling expert. This bent armlock draws an opponent's elbow tightly into his ribcage, whilst forcing the back of his hand away from his body, causing tremendous pressure on the elbow. Fighters often defend with their free hand by pulling their trapped hand down, in relation to their body; however, if a defending fighter misjudges the effectiveness of his defence, he can easily fall victim to the keylock's full joint-popping power.

More often than not, the submission is applied from side mount, a position of dominance; this makes it a low risk option, doubling as a crafty set up, as an opponent's escape attempt is fraught with danger. Whilst the hold has earned an unfair reputation for being a strength-based submission, the mechanics of applying the technique are complicated; the slightest change in position can mean the difference between wasting a great deal of energy, and quickly forcing your opponent to tap in no uncertain terms. Few fighters understand the subtle points of technique which make the keylock such a potent weapon better than American multiple Pride and UFC veteran, Heath Herring.

The 'Texas Crazy Horse' counts the keylock among his effective, but under-rated submission holds. 'I think for big guys, especially heavyweights, the keylock, or what the Brazilians call, the 'Americana' is a good move', said Herring, who has challenged for both the UFC and Pride heavyweight titles in his long career. 'It's a low risk move', he continued, 'You're in side control. Even if you don't get it, you don't lose position. You can hold it and there's not a whole lot the guy can do on the bottom at that point. I like low risk submissions, if I'm going to go for something, I want to go for it and if I don't get it, I don't want it to change the outcome of the fight - or change the position that I'm in. I don't want to give up my position to go for a submission, so to speak.'

Pride 12: Enson Inoue vs.
Heath 'The Texas Crazy Horse' Herring

Herring has used the keylock to great effectiveness, tapping out Denis Sobolev in only 22 seconds at Pride 13. However, the Texan warrior's most memorable application of the hold came in his previous bout with respected Japanese jiu-jitsu master, Enson Inoue. Looking back on some of the many bouts of his long career, many memories become hazy, not so when it comes to his fight with Inoue. 'I've had 60 fights and they kind of all run together sometimes!' he laughed, 'but, I really remember that fight because a lot of people ask me about it, because I think we were talking at that point.

'I knew him I little bit and I really respected him as a really good ground coach, things like that. For me, the fight is more of a sport than anything, I go out there and I want to win – I really don't have any animosity to my opponent. I don't pump myself up before the fight thinking how much I hate the guy and I want to kill him, that's just not me. That's just not how I prepare myself to go in and compete. I know a lot of fighters where that's a big thing, I guess they feel like they have to really hate the person and try and hit him for whatever reason.'

However, as Herring took control of the Inoue's right arm and twisted it to the point where many an opponent would tap out, the Texan's determination not to cause unnecessary damage to his opponent left him with somewhat of a conundrum. He could either snap his opponent's limb, abruptly sending him into a lengthy recuperation programme, or he could release the hold and search for another method of victory. As it turned out, Herring mercifully chose the latter option.

'If I catch anybody', he explained, 'and I have them clean in a hold, for me there's no reason to cause any unnecessary damage. I felt at that point that I had him and I felt that it was pretty tight and I really didn't see the need to tear the ligaments in his arm and I was trying to tell him, "Hey Enson, tap out!" If I remember correctly, he said "Do what you've got to do, bro."' Thankfully for the Japanese submission's expert, Herring released the hold, only to bludgeon him to defeat with knees on the floor only five minutes into the contest.

The Texas School of Jiu-Jitsu

There is no doubt that Herring has a crafty knack for applying the hold; yet for him, this proficiency and finishers instinct comes from experience and natural ability, rather than through any detailed submissions knowledge. In fact, Heath even professes not to be a technical wizard; however, when he takes control of his opponent's wrist, he seems able to find a way of coming out with the submission win. Asked what his tips are for applying the perfect keylock, Heath laughed.

'To be honest with you, I'm kind of a bad guy to ask on that, because I'm not a technician. There's a lot of guys who grew up doing jiu-jitsu, I think I'm one of the only fighters not to hold a belt in any discipline or anything like that. I kind of jokingly refer to my style as "Texas Jiu-Jitsu", I go out and I kind of fight my own way and my own style that adapts best for me. I understand a lot of the things I do, a lot of people say they are just horrible, I give up my back and I do a lot of things that traditional coaches say is bad, but just sort of challenge them. If they don't like what I'm doing, then why is it working for me? That's kind of my whole thing!'

HIGH-PERCENTAGE CHOKE
THE REAR NAKED CHOKE

The rear naked choke, or mata leao (Lion killer) is simultaneously one of the most basic submissions holds in the game and one of the most devastating; if you are caught in the choke in practise and hold off tapping by as little as just half a second, you could easily find yourself coming round a few moments later, surrounded by concerned training partners.

It is hard to mention the rear naked choke without reference to Royce Gracie, who famously choked his way to victory over Dutch mentalist, Gerard Gordeau to claim victory in the opening Ultimate Fighting Championship tournament back in 1993. The technique is still as effective in the modern game of mma as it was back at the beginning, though today's mma fighters tend to be far better equipped to hold off the submission and, as a result, no longer regard it as the danger that it was during the 'clash of styles' match ups of the mid to late 90's.

Drew Fickett - The Throat Specialist

However, that is not to say that fighters in the modern era are routinely able to defend the submission, as confirmed by a quick look at the record of American submission fighter, Drew Fickett. 'I don't know, I've had 40 fights and I have finished, maybe like, 25 with the rear naked choke. That's just a guess, but I'd say probably about that.'

'I grew up with wrestling, Greco-Roman and freestyle wrestling,' Fickett explained, 'in order to get the takedown, sometimes you've got to get behind someone so they are belly down and you've got their back, basically. When I started doing jiu-jitsu and submission grappling it just came naturally.'

When Fickett takes his opponent's back, sinking the rear naked choke is the first thing on his mind. 'It's like the highest percentage move you can really do, because once you have the back, even if you don't have the choke, you're not in a bad position. Whereas if you are on your back and you go for a triangle or an armbar and you don't get it, a lot of the time you end up without anything, losing position and end up on your back, which isn't a good place to be in a fight.'

In order to avoid falling victim to a ground-and-pound attack on the floor, fighters scramble to stay off their back. However, Fickett points out, when he sinks his hooks from rear mount, pinning his heels into the opponent's waist area, they are equally vulnerable to strikes, a set up that he uses to throw people off their game. 'Occasionally it will loosen them up, it will distract them from what's really important and that's the hand-fighting. The biggest thing is securing the technique of the choke, but with the gloves it's really a crutch. They can grab the glove, they've got a bigger hand to work with; you've got to kind of weave it through. The only thing to be able to neutralise that is being able to use strikes. Strike them, hurt them a little bit, enough to make them think about that and then you slip in the choke. My biggest thing with finishing with a choke is just taking your time and when you have it, you've got to rip it like a dog on heat.'

When under fire in rear mount, a defensively minded fighter will pin his chin to his chest to avoid the blows, also making it far more difficult to sink the choke. Fickett doesn't see this as a great problem, offering this tip to the attacking fighter. 'I'd say I'd usually take the jaw with it. I'd crank the neck, it's not going to submit them, but it's going to get to the point where the leverage is going to be too much for his neck and jaw. It's going to lift up the chin and then the arm slips under the jaw, into the throat.'

At the pre-fight press conference for Cage Rage 24, Fickett was bouncing off the walls, telling the assembled press that he was in London purely for the purposes of choking his British opponent, Mark Weir. Fulfilling his prophecy in handy fashion, the Arizona fighter caught Weir in the rear naked choke after three minutes 55 seconds of the first round.

'It's a mindset,' Fickett explained of his pre-fight confidence, 'I'm down to bang, I'm down to fight mma but like I said, taking the back and choking someone is the highest percentage finish in grappling fighting that you can possibly do - so when it comes down to it when you knock someone down, instead of trying to finish them and hurt them, I'm going to take their back and choke them because they are more vulnerable to it. 'Just like if someone is beating me on my feet,' he continued, 'I'm not going to stand with that guy, like Mark, I'm not going to try and trade with him, that would just be stupid. So I'm going to try and get him to the ground somehow, that's my world and that's where I usually come out on top.'

During the wild four minute fight, Fickett was forced to eat some hard shots; however, fully aware of their fighter's ability to scramble to his favoured option, the American's corner remained calm throughout the brief moments of concern. 'Obviously, you can see from that fight that I made the mistake of giving him that space. I didn't really have anybody to train with that was such a specimen, tall and have the leverage that he did – and I made the mistake of giving him the space to punch. No matter what you do, you never want to do that. But if you are on your back and someone is striking you effectively, you've gotta think head movement, you always think movement. If you just sit there and play the grappling game, you're going to get bombed because he's trying to hit you. Whereas if you have good movement on your back and the other guy is really trying to hurt you, most times if you are moving well he's not really going to hit you and he's going to expend a lot more energy than you until eventually, you are going to have that moment where there's an opening to submit him.'

ULTRA-TECHNICAL
THE GUILLOTINE CHOKE

Since Pat Smith virtually picked up Johnny Rhodes with a standing guillotine choke way back in time at UFC 2, the whole world has known the danger of giving up your neck, even to a submission artist with rudimentary skills. Applied by holding your opponent's head under one arm and pressing his temple to your lower ribs or hip, the choker slips his forearm under his opponent's chin, clasps his hands together and raises the 'blade' of his forearm until the pressure on the throat is such that the victim has to choose between submitting or sleeping.

With his vicious flying knees and all-action kickboxing game, Alistair Overeem may not be the first submission artist that springs to mind in association with the guillotine choke; however, the Dutchman has seen more than his fair share of success with the hold, 'I've been doing this choke my entire career,' Overeem said, so as to dispel a rumour to the contrary. 'I have like 10 or 15 wins with it. There are many guys I submitted.'

Pride: Total Elimination 2005:
Alistair Overeem vs. Victor Belfort
The first super-high profile name that Dutch fighter snared in his ruinous guillotine was Brazilian jiu-jitsu fighter, Vitor Belfort – a win which came on the big stage of the Pride middleweight Grand Prix 2005. Referring to his Brazilian adversary, Overeem began, 'We fought two times, the first time was in the light-heavyweight Grand Prix in 2005 and the second time was on Strikeforce. I won both times.'

It was the first meeting of the two at Total Elimination, however, which sticks in his mind. 'I won by submission, that was the first time that a Dutch guy submitted a jiu-jitsu black belt from Brazil. What can I say about the first fight? I trained my ass off and we trained a very good strategy against Vitor, and in the fight you could see the strategy working out perfectly, cutting off the ring, I was putting pressure on him. Building up slowly, but looking out for the counter because Vitor is a counter-puncher, he's really sharp on that, so I eventually cut him off and, piece by piece, took him apart.'

Overeem implemented his strategy brilliantly; however, catching his opponent with a chokehold was not necessarily part of his grand design. 'Basically, I was not looking for the guillotine, I was just looking to dominate the fight and hurt him. Every second, just keeping on the pressure and hurting him. I punched him; that was like a direct hit. He was stumbling on his feet, so I went in for the kill; he dropped back to the guard as he always did and I followed with some hammerfists.' In desperation, Belfort went for an armbar; however Overeem was able to escape and a moment later, the Dutchman saw his chance. 'He went for elbow-knees and then he was ready for the guillotine and I just slid it in there and it was on perfectly. Of course, I'm happy about the win, but he is just one of the names that I have beaten.'

Critical Countdown 2005:
Alistair Overeem vs. 'Ice Cold' Igor Vovchanchyn

In his very next fight, Overeem once again stunned the crowd into silence at the Critical Countdown show later in the year as he submitted yet another fighter famed for his near watertight submission defence, Russian knock out artist, 'Ice Cold' Igor Vovchanchyn. In this fight, however, the guillotine choke came of no surprise, as Overeem explained. 'We started in his game, Vovchanchyn being a striker wanted to bang it out, he was strong and good in the conditioning, so we just went in there, same sort of thing, keep the pressure on Igor, he's going to come in hard with punches, just keep the pressure on him.'

Overeem forced his way into the clinch with a pair of knees to the body and tripped his opponent to the mat. 'I went for the takedown and we knew he was the type of fighter that wanted to escape, so we trained on that and he attempted to escape a certain way.' Like Belfort, Vovchanchyn fought to regain his feet by first moving to his elbows and knees, leaving himself wide open for the waiting Dutchman. 'We saw him coming and he went right into my trap and that was the guillotine choke.'

The Drew Fickett Choke Clinic

Another gifted submission artist with a knack for catching hold of a tight guillotine choke is artery-restrictor extraordinaire, Drew Fickett. 'I've kind of been playing with it of late,' he confirmed, 'I just think that any submissions that you practise and try to do, it's all about transitions, that's why I can go into these fights and be like, "I'm going to choke him!" They can defend the back as much as they want, but I have so many different transitions and so many different times when I can hit that move that no matter how someone trains for it, they are never really going to be ready for every single technique that I have.'

With an eye constantly on the possibility of catching a quick choke, Fickett sees most opportunities coming off his opponent's takedown attempts. 'When someone's shooting in, it's a really optimum time. It usually works better at the beginning of a fight though because on a lot of guillotine moves, once both fighters get sweaty and wet, the heads slips out. It's better to hit it at the beginning of the fight, it will still work at the end, but it's a lot more effective during the beginning of the fight for sure.'

158

Traditionally, if an opponent is able to pass one of his arms into his opponent's guillotine hold, he is considered to be in less danger; however, many submission fighters have been claiming for years that choking a fighter with an arm in is just as simple. Fickett takes a clear side in the debate. 'I prefer to have the arm in actually. It's just about different leverage points of using the guillotine. If you just try to squeeze the head, that's not really going to work. I would prefer to have the arm in because there's more to hold onto and then there's a few transitions off that guillotine, rather than just having the head, I mean, just having the head is pretty rough, it's pretty hard to finish. But if you get the head right close to your hips, turn your body the right way, don't just try to squeeze with the muscle, you actually use your whole body to hit the guillotine, it's pretty effective with the arm in.'

At a lot of local shows, you do tend to see fighters grabbing hold of the guillotine and pulling on the hold for all they are worth. Overeem concurred with his American colleague; going all out to finish with arm strength alone is a recipe for disaster. 'That's one thing for sure,' Overeem advised, 'don't use any power. If you use a lot of power, you are going to get tired and if the opponent is a clever guy, like the Brazilians are pretty clever, they know that when you are using power that you are going to get tired. So you have to use it without force, without power and be technically, 100%. If you do it many times, like I have done the guillotine a couple of thousand times, then you get this feeling and you know that it will work. You just feel it like, "Now I got you!" You have to practise it on technique anyway, do it many times.'

One point of the technique that Fickett made every effort to stress is the need to turn to your side when attempting to finish with a guillotine. 'It's everything, if you've ever seen Joe Stevenson fight, you'll notice Joe has one of the best guillotines in the business and you'll notice that when he does it, his whole body is almost doing a crunch towards the guy with all the leverage on his neck and head. He'll turn, at least onto one shoulder blade. If you're flat on your back, you're just squeezing with bicep muscles; a tough guy is never going to tap to that.'

Thinking back to a recent success of his own with the guillotine, Fickett explained that he has no fear of going to his back with the hold, but stressed that for less experienced fighters it can easily lead to trouble. 'I ended up taking the guy to the ground and from mount I ended up getting a head and arm, I felt like I had it locked in pretty good, so from mount I pulled guard and pulled his head close to my hip, twisted and turned and choked him out cold. But, I would say pulling guard is risky, I would say it's an advanced technique and I definitely teach my younger fighters that it's definitely more risky than it is effective. If the guillotine is tight, it doesn't matter, but if it isn't tight, then you have to watch out.'

IT'S ALL ABOUT THE ANGLE
THE TRIANGLE

Dan Severn no had idea what can of hold he had just submitted to when he tapped out to a triangle choke from the master of patience and technique, Royce Gracie in UFC 4. Traditionally applied from the guard, the hold is used by the downed fighter to constantly threaten the top player; however, it can also be applied from the mount by a very highly skilled submission fighter.

Brazilian jiu-jitsu specialist, Dean Lister has his own particular way of finishing with the triangle which has seen him grasping victory from an unexpected position. 'There's a special angle that I have that I like to use for a triangle. It's a little bit different, I'd say it's better, because that's my best way. There's all sorts of ways that people can resist triangles, but I have a way of putting a triangle on that's very difficult to escape and [Akira] Shoji discovered that, [at Pride Bushido 6] that night. It's very difficult to escape my triangle.'

Dean Lister: 'The Twist'

In what appeared to be a strange angle from which to finish with a triangle, Lister trapped his Japanese opponent's arm on the ring floor, in contrast to traditional jiu-jitsu thinking which suggests pulling an opponent's arm across his body. 'It's a special angle, it's a special twist that I do.' The American submissions man explained, 'It's not necessarily pulling the head down, I don't worry about that, I worry about the angle. If you pull the head down, you're choking a little bit – and this is what a lot of the legendary coaches teach by the way, so I respect what they say, but I just have my own way of doing it, it works really well and it does not involve pulling the head down.

'It involves a special angle, it involves a twist. It's very hard to teach it, but it's something that I do really well. I have good restrictor strength versus being really explosive; I'm really strong, the strength in my legs and my arms, it's more for me a matter of, once I get it on, I'm going to wait and in time, he's going to tap, I'm not going to worry. I'm not in a hurry, I know he's going to tap soon, so I just apply the pressure and wait for him to tap.'

In an important tip for trapping an opponent in a triangle, Lister emphasised the necessity of breaking his posture. 'If the guy is posturing up really well that means that he's already defeated your position. It means that you made a mistake. You can't let someone get that space, if you let them get that space they can do whatever they want really. You need to pull them down, but if you pull them down they are going to react in some way, they are going to react by putting their hands on the ground, or they are going to put their hands on your chest, or they are going to try and punch you.

'Who knows what they are going to try and do,' the San Diego fighter added, 'but there's only a certain amount of things that they can do, so you need to pull them down. If you can't pull them down then they have the posture and they are probably going to win and you're not going to triangle them, so that's as simple as it is really. Pull the guy down; if he's getting away from you, you're not doing the right thing that needs to be done.'

'The Bogeyman' is all too aware that, even with his vast technical skills, he and other grapplers are still vulnerable to strikes on the floor. In the changing game of mma, where ground-and-pound continues to become an increasingly significant factor in the outcome of many fights, Dean is not confident that the future does not hold a great deal to be cheerful about for guard players looking for a triangle from in increasingly unfashionable position.

'I think you're always going to have a few that can do it; but also, look at Mirko ["Cro Cop" Filipovic], the guy is always looking to kick you with the left foot in the face. You're not going to have too many of those. Generally speaking, you're going to see more knock outs from punches, but there's some people who are exceptions, kicks are an important part of the game, and so is submissions, so is the bottom game.

'But I will be honest and say that it's going to be harder and harder for guys to win from the bottom – more difficult, but that's my opinion, that's just because people on top are going to start understanding that they have to keep posture, if they can keep posture, it's pretty simple, it's not easy, but it's a simple thing to do. So if they can keep posture, they are going to have a much easier time. I think the guy on the bottom is generally going to be trying to stand up a lot more than they were in the past.'

BONE-RATTLERS
THE SLAM

When wrestlers go to sleep at night, they dream about picking their opponents up, high into the air and spearing them into the floor; there really is no better way to let your opponent know that you have the wrestling angle of your game covered than by taking them off their feet in such dramatic fashion.

If the fight goes to the floor, landing on top of your opponent is nearly always preferable; but scoring with a spine-rattling slam, or suplex, not only puts an exclamation mark on your dominance, but can often provide the perfect opportunity to land a hard punch or pass your opponent's guard as he fights to replace the air in his lungs.

Due to the protective flooring used by most promotions to protect their fighters from unnecessary injury, a hard slam is unlikely to bring an end to the contest. However, in some very rare cases, this visually exciting technique can not only end the fight, but also bring a premature end to a combatant's career, as was the case when Frank Shamrock delivered one of the sport's most devastating slams on Igor Zinoviev at UFC 16.

UFC 16: Frank Shamrock vs. Igor Zinoviev

'I saw a huge hole in his style early on', Shamrock recalled, 'and that hole was, every time somebody shot in on him, he'd throw his hips back, but he would also grab the head and I saw technical opportunities to scoop him up and throw him on his head and I practised that move every day for about a month. I'd have scores of guys, boxers and kickboxers lining up and punching me and I'd do the same thing, over and over, so when I lifted him it was completely effortless.'

It makes sense to point out that repeatedly slamming your training partners is not going to make you a popular figure at the gym; Frank laughed, however, dismissing the possibility that anyone was injured during his preparations. 'We practised that on a big crash mat,' he explained, 'because when you take a bump like that on your head and shoulder, the weight of your body just breaks your bones - and that's what happened with Zinoviev.'

Previous to the fight, Zinoviev has shown flashes of brilliance in his fights with Harold German and 'The Zen Machine' Mario Sperry. In fact, the Russian did such a good job of escaping from the Sperry's clutches, a hitherto unheard of accomplishment, that commentator, John Peretti labelled him 'Houdini', and by smashing the Brazilian to defeat, Zinoviev thrust himself into the mix as one of the men to beat in the division.

162

In characteristic fashion, however, Shamrock had not read the script; as his opponent moved in, Frank dropped his level and in one fluid motion caught hold of his opponent's body, lifted him, turned and speared his opponent into the mat, causing irreparable damage to the Russian's spine. 'Before we fought, he had never lost a fight in Sambo, kickboxing or mma – and it ended his career.'

'Houdini' lay motionless after the slam, causing a wave of panic to spread throughout the arena, washing away any pre-fight celebrations that Shamrock had planned. 'I was terribly worried, I felt terrible because the last thing I want to do is hurt somebody and then I was really young and I had very mixed feelings about hurting people in general, it was something I didn't want to do. So it really affected me,' the younger of the famous Shamrock brothers confessed, 'I had to go and see him in the hospital.'

In about as happy an ending as you could hope for in such an awful scenario, while Zinoviev has not competed since that fight, he holds no grudges about the accident which could so easily have paralysed him. 'What's funny is that 10 years later we were having dinner together for the IFL. I turned to him and apologised and he just laughed with this big, deep colourful laugh and he said, "Frank, you know, I never cared, it's a fight it's what happens."'

PrideFC: Critical Countdown 2004:
Kevin Randleman vs. Fedor Emelianenko

A far more recent and perhaps even more famous example of a fighter slamming an opponent to the mat came at Pride Critical Countdown 2004 in the form of a beautiful suplex executed by Kevin Randleman on another incredible Russian war machine, Fedor Emelianenko.

'I've been suplexing people since I was ten years old.' Randleman said, providing some background on perhaps the sickest slam in mma history. 'I wrestled when I was ten. I was a three time division one finalist and a two time NCAA national wrestling champion. When it comes to wrestling, I know what I'm doing – I take my advice before anyone else's on wrestling, but when it comes to jiu-jitsu, I ask you for your advice before I take mine!' added the tough veteran with a burst of laughter.

Randleman confounded his critics at the start of the bout by shooting in for a takedown on his burly opponent; 'The Monster' lifted Emelianenko vertically in the air, but a pragmatic, but illegal, grab of the ropes by the crafty Russian significantly reduced the impact. Fedor scrambled back to his feet, but in his haste to escape, he made the crucial error of giving up his back to the Ohio suplex-machine, who immediately seized on his chance by taking hold of a tight waistlock and whipping Emelianenko into the air in a fluid explosion of focussed energy.

'Fedor Emelienko is a very fast and fluid fighter', Randleman recalled, 'You can make yourself feel dead weight, Cro Cop felt like dead weight the whole time I fought him. Fedor, I couldn't even feel his weight because he was flowing so I didn't feel how strong he was because he wasn't trying to make dead weight.'

In the split second that the Russian was in the air, his body twisted slightly, sending him careering towards the mat nigh-on head first. 'When I lifted him up, he was already flowing and it just happened that way and when we went in the air, I didn't realise how much force I used when I jumped up in the air, plus, he turned upside down in my arms, he just flipped upside down.'

The landing looked horrific; the majority of Emelianenko's weight appeared to come down directly on the back of his neck, forcing his body to buckle unnaturally. Though the Sambo master was able to absorb some of the impact with his shoulder, to observers watching on television around the world, it remained highly improbable that the Russian could have escaped without serious injury.

'We're fighters. We practise these scenarios all the time.' Randleman retorted, 'Guys do the same thing to me that I did to Fedor in practise. So it was a natural thing to happen, all I did was lift him up and drop down on him. What I did I see kids do everyday; I see my nephews do it all the time in practise and just fucking around in the back yard. It just seemed a lot worse than it was, I do that to people all the time in practise, trust me. Though, I kinda wanted to take a look and see if his eyes were closed, because he wasn't moving!' Randleman said, obviously concerned to some degree by his opponent's predicament.

Amazingly, not only was Emelianenko unhurt, but he soon gathered the wherewithal to reverse position and slap on a ruggedly applied, but nonetheless tendon-stretching kimura to seal the incredible turnaround win. 'My legs were in the ring ropes, no excuse! He's just a strong man, he's very good, he beat me and justifiably so, he's still been unbeaten. But my feet get in the ring ropes and I could switch around, going to the 69 position. As I tried to get my feet out, he saw that there was no pressure on him so he flipped over right away. He's a smart man and he's a warrior.'

TENDON DANGER

THE HEEL HOOK

Aheel hook is a twisting anklelock which affects both the ankle and, more significantly, the knee and it is without doubt recognised as the most damaging lower body submission in the sport of mma. If an opponent manages to get hold of your ankle using the correct technique, failure to escape or tap out immediately could result in some serious knee damage in a matter of seconds – it is for this reason that any responsible coach will warn his pupils time and time again about the dangers of applying this most devastating of techniques.

Leglocks are no joke

Often referred to as a master of leglocks, Jess 'The Joker' Liaudin laughs off the praise, pointing out that he is no master, he simply knows what he is doing in a world full of mma fighters who, in his opinion, really should be seeking further leglock instruction. Having travelled the world and trained with some of the very best leglockers in the business, Liaudin is quietly confident that he is in a position to feel comfortable regarding his heel hook techniques.

'I worked with Fred Rado who has a background in Sambo.' Liaudin explained, 'So most of the leglocks I've got were originally from Sambo. Then afterwards, because I was a big fan of the Japanese mma scene, I was watching Pancrase and Shooto and a lot of those fighters were doing it. When I got to Japan and began training there, I improved a lot of my positioning to apply it a lot better.'

Famous for sharing knowledge, Liaudin broke down the secrets to applying the perfect heel hook, 'It's just a few things that people have to know; putting the wrist in the right direction, a lot of times when people go for a leglock it's a desperate move, so people will lean back, try and reach for the leg, but I think you have to take a leglock like you would take an armbar or a triangle. You have to set it up properly,' the Frenchman continued, 'put yourself in a really strong position where you can secure your opponent and then put your hand in the right place so you can apply the leverage.'

However, going for a heel hook is a risky business, if it all goes wrong you might find yourself in a tight spot, absorbing punishment at an uncomfortable rate. As Liaudin explains, it is important to attempt the submission at an appropriate juncture in the fight. 'A lot of people go for a heel hook when it's the last 30 seconds of the round or something like that, they won't take the risk to go on their back and get pounded if the guy manages to escape. There's a few ways to lock your opponent, some are better than others, but if the guy

165

is also an experienced fighter who knows leglocks, he will know how to escape those positions. I won't necessarily go for a leglock in the beginning of the fight,' the UFC veteran said thoughtfully, 'I'd mainly go for it in the last 30 seconds, or perhaps if I'm in a defensive position.'

Whilst experienced fighters are often able to shake off heel hook attempts, the vast majority of fighters are less savvy when it comes to the submission. 'That's why in here,' he said referring to the Pancrase London gym, 'we train leglocks and that's why I think, we have been successful in using them in fighting.' Liaudin smiled, 'But I always make of point of telling people not to be silly, because it's just a few millimetres and your knee goes from being ok, to just popped. Everybody's different. Some people have got very flexible ankles, some others you just need to touch it and he taps straight away, it's all about training your brain to be very wary and knowing how to do it.'

Looking back on some of the notable successes that he has enjoyed with the heel hook, Liaudin cast his mind back to straight heel hook he used as defence in his fight with Shain Tovell 'He tried to punch me, so I flipped my leg just over his hip and just went for a standard, normal heelhook. Now, that's a technique which is quite well known and quite easy to defend, not many people get caught like that, but that was like 6 years ago, so at the time, not many people knew how to do them over here in the UK.'

Snap, Crackle and Pop

A couple of years later, it seemed that Liaudin was still miles ahead in terms of leglocking ability as he submitted the otherwise extremely crafty, Poole Jiu-Jitsu fighter Andy Walker – this time, with an inside heel hook, 'I initially went for a kneebar, messed it up, went for a heelhook and I just gave it up, instead of going for the heel hook, I flipped his leg to the other side for an inside heelhook, knowing that it was a lot more powerful.'

'I heard it crack a couple of times.' Liaudin winced as he remembered Walker's stubborn resistance, 'Sometimes it cracks, but it's just when your knee changes position, I think the worst one was probably Ross Mason [at Cage Rage 19]. I didn't hear it crack or anything like that, but I spinned it quite well and his knee was messed up for quite some time. The worst of the worst was actually at training when I got Ashleigh [Grimshaw] into it training the heelhook. I wasn't actually applying it, but he fell from stand up to the ground and he fell into it and his knee popped. That was four or five years ago and since then, he's always had problems with his knee because of that.'

'The most efficient one for fighting mma is the inside heel hook.' Liaudin added thoughtfully, 'The outside is often a lot harder to reach. Achilles locks are very hard to put on in a fight, especially when you're quite tired, they require quite a lot of strength. I think the most popular one and the most efficient one is the inside heel hook, so even if you go for a standard, normal one, you can secure his leg and flip it to the other side and get the inside heel hook on the other side.'

With only the slightest difference in pressure able to push a knee joint beyond the point of no return, if an opponent comes close to catching you in a heel hook, escape is always a better option than attacking with an ankle submission of your own. 'Usually when you see people caught in a leglock, instead of trying to escape, try to remove your opponent's leg and try to improve our position. Usually they try to counter with their own leglock; your leg is already in position, but instead of training to escape they will lean back and go for a submission, but by the time they do that they will obviously get caught and tapped already.

'If you look at the Masakazu Imanari – Jean Silva fight at Cage Rage 25, that's exactly what happened, Jean Silva got put into a leglock and instead of removing his leg and trying to stand back up, he went the other way and tried to grab his leg as well. And by the time you do that with a leglock expert, it's too late and that's how he got caught.'

To avoid a lengthy rehabilitation process, fighters may wish to hold onto this potentially ligament-saving advice from one of the world's more experienced heel hook experts. 'The worst thing you could try to do is try to counter with a leglock and try to catch him before he catches you. But if he is experienced, he will always try to get out, there's always a way to get out.'

TROUBLE FROM NOWHERE
THE TOEHOLD

I n comparison to other submissions, the toehold is quite often viewed as a cheap way out and held in low esteem. However, this view is usually held by people who aren't particularly good at them - in the right hands, the hold is a versatile blessing which can either be used to score an agonising submission win or simply to distract an opponent and keep him on the defensive. Seldom used in competition, the toehold is a vastly under-rated and damaging weapon which can be pulled off from an array of positions and in the most unlikely of circumstances.

UFC 41: Frank Mir vs. David 'Tank' Abbott

Cropping up once again, submissions magician, Frank Mir is one of a handful of fighters who has a deep understanding of the hold and showed his footlocking proficiency at UFC 41 when he used a toehold against notorious mma figure, David 'Tank' Abbott to send the brawler packing after his initial return to the octagon. Frank looked comfortable thorough the match and it turned out to be an easy night, despite Tank's infamous punching power.

'It's always nice to fight people who have got that name recognition that are really not that dangerous' the Las Vegan said bluntly, 'he kind of fell into that category. Obviously, if I stood in front of him and put my hands down, he could hurt me, but so could just about anybody who weighs over 200 pounds. So it's not that much of a skill to conquer, plus the fact that the technique level was so poor, made me feel comfortable. I'll fight a tough guy every day of the week. I don't really want to fight technical guys.'

When the fight hit the floor early in the first round, Tank landed on top and appeared ready to go to work with his spiteful ground assault. However, Mir was leagues ahead of the bar-room brawler in terms of grappling ability and soon began to twist his goateed opponent up like an overweight pretzel. 'I transitioned from an omaplata, I had a shoulderlock and when he tried to step over my head to escape, I grabbed his ankle and put on a figure four. It was a toehold, the reason it's called a toehold is because you're grabbing the end of the foot, but it actually applies pressure on the outside of the ankle. It's very painful; so far, when I've locked one up, everybody has pretty much tapped.'

Certainly, with his foot pointing at a gruesomely unnatural angle, Tank was forced to tap out in humiliation after only 46 seconds. "I heard a pop." Mir said over the microphone after the fight, "Tank didn't tap out of pain; he tapped because he had to. I sent him to the hospital."

"I got caught, shit happens", Tank fired back. "Next time I fight, somebody is going to be leaving on a stretcher and it ain't gonna be me! He said I was going to the hospital, I think I'm still standing here – you can see me in the bar later on…"

The Toehold seminar

However, Mir's movement on the ground and opportunistic use of the toehold had just separated the sportsman from the booze-hound. Enthused by the memory his effortless win, Mir revealed a couple of his toehold top tips, 'It's real easy to get to. Anytime you can put your hand on someone's foot, you can footlock them. The secret is just can you secure the hips and lock up the other leg. A lot of people just lock the legs that they are attacking which leaves the other person's leg free to kick you and push off. So anytime I lock someone up I try to secure their body or their other leg.'

However, in Frank's view the toehold should primarily come as a reaction to what your opponent is doing and a way of stifling their work rather than serving the role of a submission that he would specifically try to set up. 'I don't really go for them because a lot of times you put yourself in bad positions. I'm not going to go from cross-side for a footlock, or I'm not going to go from the top position and fall on my back. If you miss it, you could give a good position up, but I'll use a lot of footlocks, especially when people try to sweep me and stuff and they are using their feet in my hips. I might start attacking their foot because then usually they have got to stop what they are doing to protect their foot and I can stalemate the move, or get them and hurt their ankle.'

Underlining the effectiveness of the hold for a final time, Frank concluded, 'A lot of times, no matter what, guys have a hard time defending their legs. If you ever hear of a black belt getting tapped out by a blue belt, it's usually because he got caught in a footlock, it's easy to get caught in footlocks. They're hard to defend. I think you need to identify them early, if you mentally fall asleep during the match, you can easily get caught in one.'

CHAPTER ELEVEN
CRAZY SHIT

'The roots are there, it comes from Brazil; I'll never deny that - I've learned from the Brazilians, but the rubber guard in my system is something they can't teach.'
- Eddie Bravo

The early Ultimate Fighting Championships demonstrated beyond doubt that grappling can be used to great affect in No-Holds-Barred competition, particularly when used on traditional martial artists with little knowledge of jiu-jitsu. This public validation of submission techniques ensured that all fighters preparing for competition included jiu-jitsu in their training schedule and began adding this massive new dimension to their skill set.

Therefore, grappling specialists have been forced to find new strategies and techniques in order to stay ahead of the game, prompting a rapid evolution in the Brazilian jiu-jitsu which was so artfully demonstrated by members of the Gracie family during the 1990's. One of the first jiu-jitsu practitioners in the United States to kick-start this process was musician and martial arts enthusiast, Eddie Bravo.

After watching the second instalment of the UFC, Eddie was hooked - and on a mission, 'I was sold right there and I was looking for jiu-jitsu. I remember seeing a jiu-jitsu sign in LA somewhere. I went and it turned out it was Nin-jitsu, but they directed me towards the Machado's, "If it's the ground fighting you are looking for, the Gracie's cousins are out here in this part of town", and they directed me to the Machado's - I joined up and never left.'

'Jui-Jitsu was just so much more fun than other martial arts I had done.' Eddie said, recalling his first foray into the grappling world under the watchful eye of Regan and Jean-Jacques Machado. 'You could spar at 100%, when you tap someone out it's like a virtual reality video game, it's the funnest martial art ever. You're not kicking the air, punching the air; it's competition every night. It's addicting.'

Staying on a parallel with the majority of people who are deeply involved in martial arts, this entertaining new hobby quickly began taking on a more serious role in Bravo's life. 'Eventually, you know, I wanted to take it to the next level and test myself in competition, it was just a natural progression. I wanted to see if I was able to perform under pressure. I never planned on being a jiu-jitsu competitor for life; I was just testing myself to see whether I could pull some of this stuff off in a high pressure situation.'

The influence of no-gi grappling

Jiu-Jitsu was spreading across America like wildfire in the late 90's and, as a result, there was no shortage of grappling competitions to enter. However, whilst the mma fighters who inspired him to begin training fought without a gi, all of the grappling competitions of the time insisted that competitors wear the garment. 'That's all there was, there was no no-gi grappling in the 90's. There was no no-gi competitions, we barely were even able to grapple no-gi in class. It was all gi.'

It was around this time that Bravo began to see the gi as a hindrance to the jiu-jitsu practitioner in mma, as he explained, 'When I started watching UFC's in the 90's and no jiu-jitsu guys were sweeping, never really finishing or attacking off their back. It was a puzzle to me, when you go to jiu-jitsu competitions in schools there are always sweeps, there are always finishes from the guard but in mma there wasn't. So I thought it's got to be the handles, people aren't used to all the punches and they are not used to setting anything up without handles. That is when I realised that the gi causes problems for mma.'

Bravo swore that he would never rely on the gi if it were ever his turn to set foot in the cage, 'I knew fighting mma was always a back up plan if my music didn't make it, so I was always trying to prepare for an mma career just in case my music didn't hit it off, so I started really analysing the game and I thought that if I ever got to the point where I had to do mma, I didn't want to have to spend time revamping my jiu-jitsu, because I would have had to have spent time catching up with the wrestling and the kickboxing, so I decided to try and make my jiu-jitsu as mma-ready as possible. I started training with the gi, but pretending it was without the gi, I started developing overhooks, underhooks, head control, even with the gi because I knew that when the gi comes off, I wouldn't have any handles.'

This handy mma-readiness sideline appears not to have hindered Bravo's grappling career as, in 2003, he famously became the first American to submit a member of the Gracie family in competition when he tapped out Royler Gracie, a man widely acknowledged as one of the world's finest pure grapplers. An instant celebrity, Bravo kissed goodbye to the financial insecurities which came so close to forcing him into the cage, 'I could just teach jiu-jitsu, make a living and concentrate on my music. I still wanted to teach no-gi, just for my students, just in case they wanted to do mma so when I opened up my school, I went no-gi.'

'In class, on a Thursday night with Jean-Jacques, we would do no-gi and that was like the funnest night of the week. I thought when I opened my school I'd have fun nights every day. Forget the gi… for me, there was no reason. I didn't think it was going to be a big deal but Brazilians started coming up to me asking, "Why are you disrespecting the gi? You get your black belt with the gi and now you're teaching without the gi." I'm like, "It's just a piece of clothing. Who cares what I'm teaching in and why is it so offensive?" Everyone thought I was disrespecting the gi when I wasn't teaching with it.'

Bravo was keen to point out that he did not set out to offend the jiu-jitsu community by abandoning the gi, but given the nature of the criticism he received, Bravo still found it hard to take his detractors seriously. 'I wasn't putting on my gi, wasn't putting on my black belt, I didn't care about any of that. I like slapping on the black belt, don't get me wrong, it's pretty awesome, but I didn't want to roll around with a big assed Japanese super hero outfit. And the fact that many Brazilians are offended by what I have to say about the gi, that fact is pretty crazy, like someone would actually get offended if I said something about the gi. It's like me talking shit on a wrestling singlet and having wrestlers hating me, wrestlers would laugh too, 'Yeah, that's pretty goofy'. Can you really imagine wrestlers getting pissed off with me if I said, "No, I'm not going to wrestle in a singlet no more"? That would be ridiculous, but that is exactly what happened with the gi. They take it so seriously.'

The Rubber Guard

Bravo set out to develop an array of techniques which were specifically orientated for no-gi grappling. Comfortable with the idea of diverging from the traditional and well worn jiu-jitsu path, he was convinced that there were areas of the game which had previously been overlooked, as jiu-jitsu practitioners routinely went back to their tried and tested, gi handles game. 'There wasn't a day when it all started it's just the way my mind was, I was always trying to develop the best way to use jiu-jitsu in a no-gi situation, in an mma situation. I would watch Rickson and Renzo and watch how they played the guard in mma and it looked nothing like we would play guard in class. Spider guard, grabbing the sleeve, grabbing the collar – but you watch Rickson and Renzo, they were playing closed guard and they were headlocking the head, clinching to avoid punches. I was like, "If they are clinching and playing closed guard, that's what I'm going to do. I'm not going to play spider guard if Rickson isn't playing spider guard; he's playing closed guard and headlocking the head."'

This, however, was not enough for the ambitious grappling upstart, 'The problem was that they weren't doing anything in the closed guard, so I was like, "OK, we've got to play closed guard to avoid damage, to avoid punches and elbows, so now I've got to develop a way to attack from this closed, clinching guard", and it slowly developed into what it is today. My guard is 100% clinching, but moving in the clinch, defending punches while setting up submissions and sweeps. It's all from the clinch, all to avoid real damage.'

As previously mentioned, fighters from different corners of the globe are in agreement that when the fight hits the floor, the fighter on top is at an advantage and, therefore, fighting off your back should avoided whenever possible. From Bravo's point of view, if you're in a fight, there's always a chance you might be out-wrestled and find yourself in this position; therefore, it only makes sense to develop this area of your game to the best of your ability. With this end goal in view at all times, Bravo began to develop his most famous innovation; the rubber guard.

'I think it was Pride 2, I saw Renzo in the guard and he held his foot up.' Bravo explained, 'He wasn't doing anything, but he had like a really loose, loose mission control and he just held that position for a second, I think that he was just trying to catch his breath. Then he let it go and proceeded to do some other stuff, but I thought, "Wow, there's got to be something that you can do there." It just felt like there has to be something there. That was the key, holding the ankles up and I saw Renzo do it once and I just started developing the best way to hold the ankle up there, the best way to move, the best way to get yourself up. The rubber guard that you see me use in the Royler fight, that's just prehistoric, that's just the beginning's of the rubber guard, what it has evolved to now is a whole different animal.'

This animal, however, demands that you can bend your legs into some sincerely unnatural positions; unfortunately, not everyone in life has the flexibility of a professional ballerina. Critics of Bravo's rubber guard often point out that a high level of flexibility is needed to carry it off, and therefore, the style will not be effective for everybody as it can only be put into practise by the supplest of athletes. Bravo takes this point on board, but instead of offering condolences to his less flexible students, he offers solutions.

'You've got to get that flexibility together; it all depends on how much time you're willing to put into your stretching work.' he said bluntly, 'I've got guys coming into my class with shitty flexibility and it might take them three or four years to get the flexibility they need, it's because they're lazy they don't stretch as much as they should. Then I've got guys with pro football ethic, when you tell them what to do and they do it... I've had guys come in with the worst flexibility, like ex college football players and I tell them what to do and within a month they've got their flexibility together because they all work on it at home.'

'It's just like kicking to the head when you go into a kickboxing academy, if you can't kick to the head, you've got to work on your flexibility, no-one questions it', Bravo said, determined to dismantle what seemed for him to be the most frustrating of misapprehensions about his style. 'With jiu-jitsu and my guard and the flexibility that is required for the guard, it's a new kind of flexibility; it's like a yoga type of flexibility, a lot of people question it. "Oh, if I'm not that flexible now, there's no way I'm going to achieve that flexibility", and they are one million per cent wrong. I got guys coming in all the time with terrible flexibility, they work on it, they get their flexibility together and eventually, they'll be able to play rubber guard.'

The Lockdown

Another cornerstone of Bravo's system is 'The Lockdown', an unorthodox half guard position where the guard player's legs intertwine around the opponent's trapped leg, limiting his options and ability to move while also setting up numerous possibilities from the bottom. 'It's definitely been in judo for longer than I've been alive, that's for sure', Bravo laughed, but was unable to say for definite whether he came up with the position independently or if he was shown it by judo Legend, Gene Label.

'Gene Label used to come down to the Machado's back in '95 and show us some stuff. I think maybe I learnt it off Gene Label, but for sure, I'm not the first person to do it. It is possible that I came up with it on my own, but I know it's been done in judo for many, many years. As a matter of fact, the first guy that Rickson fought in Japan, the Japanese guy, he did the Lockdown to Rickson. That was the first time I'd seen it other than me, I was like, "Wow, he's doing the Lockdown!"'

Incorporating a myriad of traditional sweeps into his work on this position, Bravo has also added some genuine innovations, demonstrating that not only can you effectively sweep your way out of trouble on the bottom, but that there are numerous submission possibilities for the experienced guard player to pursue. There are, however, inherent limitations to the position. 'It's never going to be as dangerous as being on top. On top is always best, you know, but it's not always up to you whether you are on top or bottom, you could be rolling with a dude who took you down. It's definitely one of the inferior positions; you're on the bottom, you've only got one of his legs, but you can get that position to the point where you can make things happen from there. You can get sweeps from there...'

'Look at what Minotauro did with Tim Sylvia,' Bravo continued, his enthusiasm reaching a new peak, 'he couldn't take him down. He couldn't take Sylvia down and Sylvia was fucking him up standing, so he pulls half guard, sweeps and then gets on top. Minotauro's half guard, there are sweeps there that he's got. It's not the best position to be in and you don't want to be there, but you're going to be there whether you'd like to or not, so you might as well have as much offensive firepower as possible.'

Attacking from the top, Twister style.

As a fighter, being able to attack from a neutral or a defensive position is essential, however, to give yourself the best chance of coming out on top, it is important not to become too defensively minded and neglect aspects of your attacking game. Certainly, as Bravo has become known for playing rubber guard and looking for offensive possibilities from his back, he has also worked hard to develop his top game, in particular, his slant on a traditional position of strength, which he calls 'The Monkey Mount'.

'The rubber guard is high guard, playing offensive guard without the gi,' Bravo began, 'the Monkey Mount is the same thing. In gi jiu-jitsu people are playing the mount by grabbing the collar as an anchor and setting everything up by grabbing the collar. So for me, I was like, "That's not going to work, no-gi. That's not going to work mma." So I never spent too much time doing that, I had to work out what's the best we to play the mount, no-gi and it's very similar to the rubber guard, my mount is like the rubber guard on top. That's where "Monkey Mount" came from, very high, very offensive, head control, controlling the wrists. It's just an offensive way to play the mount without the gi.

'If you notice, there are so many black belts in jiu-jitsu whom, if they get the mount they don't have anything, all they do is start punching, they don't really have any true system for the mount or set ups. It's like, "I got the mount, there's no collar here, I'm used to the collar, if there was a collar then I would choke you but there's not, so I'm going to just keep throwing punches", which is great, but there's not really any submission set ups, or a system from the mount because they spend all their time grabbing the collar. They don't have the time to set up a true mount system – that's what I've done.'

As much as he disliked the name to begin with, the set of offensive tactics which Bravo is best known for revolves around a devastating spinelock, which, thanks to his jiu-jitsu trainers, has become known as 'The Twister', a name which has left an indelible mark on Bravo's brand of jiu-jitsu. 'It's an old wrestling move; in wrestling it's called the guillotine. It's an old, old wrestling move and I learnt it back in high school. Then when I joined jiu-jitsu and started doing it, the guillotine was already taken, the front headlock, so Regan and Jean-Jacques started calling it 'The Twister', every time I did it.

'They thought I made it up, every time I'm like, "Nah, nah, nah, it's called the guillotine, I learned it in wrestling." They didn't call it the guillotine because they already had a hold called the guillotine, so they started calling it the twister and eventually it stuck. I didn't like that name at first, I thought it sounded goofy, but I like it now, it stuck. If gogoplata stuck, then anything can stick!'

Enter, Shinya Aoki and his multi-coloured pants

Are these new 'innovations' really everything they are cracked up to be? Many grapplers from both the old school and in modern mma circles are far from convinced, in fact one of the world's top fighters, Josh 'The Babyfaced Assassin' Barnett has gone so far as to state on record that 'the less you know about the rubber guard, the better off you are', dedicating an instructional DVD to 'snapping the rubber guard'. However, some of the most heart-felt criticism of the style has come from traditional circles and in particular from one of the founding fathers of the sport, Royce Gracie.

In conversation at the salubrious Dagenham academy, just one school in his enormous empire of affiliated academies, Gracie was less than complimentary about Bravo's achievements, pointing out that the Californian has not produced any world champion grapplers, in stark comparison to the numerous world class fighters produced by the Gracie family over the years. For Royce, this awkward style that Bravo brings to the table is something only he can do, and not something which can easily be taught to others.

Rather than being offended, Bravo was upbeat about this criticism, 'You know what, I take that as a compliment. I've heard that from my own master, Jean-Jacques Machado feels the same way, that I can't teach it, it's like it's a personal style that I can't teach, but it's not true, it's just that my style takes a long time to learn. You could learn it in like three, four, five years; how long does it take to master Gracie Jiu-jitsu? It's going to take the same amount of time, but if you're not willing to work on your flexibility then you're like a guy who walks into a kickboxing academy and refuses to learn how to kick to the head. That's totally wrong, that's false – and that's not a theory that it's false, it's totally false. You go to my school and you see guys playing rubber guard, you see blue belts playing rubber guard and I have like five rubber guard masters. My school has been open for 5 years now and I have five rubber guard masters, guys who have stuck around and stuck with it, so it's not true at all. Look at Shinya Aoki, I taught him the style and he's doing great with it, so it's not true at all.'

'When I was in Japan, I showed him the rubber guard, it's the only reason he's been wearing pants, because I told him to wear the pants. The last time I was in Japan, Gong magazine wanted me to do an interview with them and the premise of the interview was "Two unorthodox grapplers exchange techniques". I show up at the place and meet Shinya Aoki, I didn't know who he was at the time; he wasn't very popular at all. I went first and showed him all my rubber guard theories; he was just totally blown away, he just fell right into it. He didn't speak English and after I was done, he said something and the camera crew and the writers started laughing. I was like "What did he say?" He said, "How am I supposed to follow that?" Then he showed me some cool stuff.'

Afterwards, the pair started talking and Aoki was very interested to hear more about Bravo's strategy and system. 'I told him, "if you really want to add firepower to your system, wear pants, take advantage of the fact that in Japan they allow you to wear pants." In the States, it's ridiculous; illegal. Totally ridiculous, banning pants is like promoting lay-and-pray, stalling, boring ground-and-pound decisions. I told him, "If you wear pants it will be more difficult for them to slip out of your stuff." It's going to be harder, which means more submissions, which means more action, which means less lay-and-pray. Who wouldn't be for that? Why would they ban that? Why are they taking away the firepower in the guard?'

The rule banning fighters from wearing trousers of any kind appeared a genuine sore point for Bravo, who continued to outline his case for gi pants to be a legitimate article of clothing for a mma fighter, denouncing the current rule. 'It's ridiculous, pants would only add to submissions, especially in the guard. If the UFC had ten fighters who had submission skills and they wore pants, there would be way more action, less lay-and-pray. You would have less new fans tuning in for the first time who get turned off by two greasy, sweaty guys rolling around on the ground doing nothing. When anyone turns on a UFC fight for the first time and saw Shinya Aoki, they wouldn't be turned off, they would think, "Oh my God, that guys got some crazy pants on and he's choking people out with his legs and his feet, it's amazing, I've never seen anything like it. Let's watch it again", instead of having two wrestlers all greased up on the ground, no-one is even able to pass the guard, zero offensive guard work because it's too slippery and too greasy. No-one wants to watch that – a hot oil wrestling match? Pants would clean that up.'

After talking over the American's theories Aoki was impressed and, in a move that would see the top-ranked fighter score a string of unusual submission wins, he took the American's advice on board. 'Shinya started wearing pants immediately; he started implementing the rubber guard immediately. When I do interviews with Japanese magazines, the first five questions are about Shinya Aoki's last performance and what he did right and what he did wrong with his rubber guard technique. It's well know in Japan that Shinya Aoki learnt his rubberguard from me.'

However, when Bravo advised his talented protégé to take up wearing gi pants, he could not have realised the crime of fashion that Aoki was about to unleash on the fight world, in the form of his multi-coloured day-glow tights. 'I think it's great because everyone's talking about the pants.' Bravo laughed, 'When people think of Shinya Aoki, they think of crazy guardwork and pants. It makes him stick out from the pack even more – not only are his pants making the guard 50 percent more dangerous for sure, he stands out and everyone thinks he's a character because he's wearing crazy pants. I think it's awesome! Now he's a major superstar, he's probably one of the most famous fighters in Japan now.'

Rorion Gracie: 'A lot of people like to say "Oh, I invented a new system!" - Bullshit.'

Another Gracie family member with a view on Bravo's work, and, by extension, any jiu-jitsu practitioners making developments in the field of jiu-jitsu is Rorion Gracie. When asked about the developments currently being made to his family's style of jiu-jitsu, Rorion issued a slightly backhanded compliment. 'Great. I think it's great, it's natural. jiu-jitsu is a very simple art, it's very efficient and if somebody wants to dedicate themselves and want to exploit and come up with new concepts, great for them, I think it's wonderful. But it all comes up from the same roots. Don't tell me you've invented your own style because that's not true', he said with almost an angry tone.

'A lot of people like to say "Oh, I invented a new system!", "submission wrestling", or "submission grappling"? - Bullshit. The whole thing came from Gracie Jiu-Jitsu. Before Gracie Jiu-Jitsu, these guys didn't exist. They know how to pass the guard, how to escape from the mount, how to escape from headlocks, the armlocks just the same as we do, they just like to put a different name to it to sound important. That's OK, it doesn't matter to me. I know where I stand and I know what my job is, I'm very excited about what I've done and I'd do everything again, it was worth every choke!'

'He says it's the same?' Bravo asked in response, 'Well, it's definitely not the same style, because no Brazilians can teach a rubber guard seminar. The roots are the same, if we're talking about roots, we can go back to ancient Japan and shit, if we're talking about roots. Yeah, it is jiu-jitsu and I got my black belt from Jean-Jacques Machado, but no-one was playing the kind of guard I was playing. The kind of guard I'm playing now, not Rorion, or Rickson, or Royce, or any of the Gracies... Renzo; they can't teach a rubber guard seminar. So it is different. The roots are there, it comes from Brazil; I'll never deny that – I've learned from the Brazilians, but the rubber guard in my system is something they can't teach.'

The Virus

Thanks to the internet, new training techniques and skills are passed around the martial arts world quicker than ever before. Anyone can go online and start downloading the latest instructional DVD in a matter of minutes and instantly get up to date with the most recent developments. Interestingly, however, whilst Bravo appears to have every confidence that at least aspects of his style will eventually become assimilated into mainstream jiu-jitsu, he does not believe that the process will be anywhere near as quick as the initial jiu-jitsu explosion in the martial arts world.

'When the Gracies did it, it was like an atom bomb, it just exploded. The UFC came out and there was just a big "KABOOM", Brazilian Jiu-Jitsu was born and just took over, and swept over the country in a fury. MMA is established now and jiu-jitsu is already a dominant force in the martial arts for the last 15 years – my style is spreading like a virus, not like an explosion. It's nice and slow and it's slowly infecting the martial arts population. A slow crawl; as opposed to a big explosion.'

That is not to say that fighters are not have success with his techniques at the moment; in addition to the work of Shinya Aoki, such established fighters as BJ Penn, Nick Diaz and even heavyweight TUF contestant, Brad Imes are starting to show glimpses of Bravo's future-style jiu-jitsu in the cage. Seeing fighters whom he has never met implementing his tactics and techniques is still a strange experience for Bravo, as he explains, 'It's very surreal, I can't tell you... people that don't know me personally, but know me and respect me as a martial artist. Especially in England, in England they are very, very respectful and they look at me in a light that I don't look at myself.

'I'm just a regular guy here in LA, trying to be a musician, who got good at martial arts. It's very strange for me, the praise that I'm getting. When I see people doing rubber guard – it's slowly popping up in shows here and there, it's very surreal to me, I just think I'm a regular guy trying to get laid, you know! It's very strange to have an affect on the world; the fastest growing sport on the planet - to have an affect on it? Very, very strange, very surreal, it makes me very proud and it motivates me to make sure that I kept going, keep innovating, keep on my path.'

Mash it up

Due to an audacious and meticulously created media image, Bravo is almost as well known for his use of cannabis as he is for his posture-breaking guard techniques. However, in contrast to the popular perception of a self-confessed 'pothead', he is extremely lucid in conversation, particularly when it comes to the legal status of his drug of choice. 'It's ridiculous; it all comes out of ignorance. Having pot lumped in with all those other drugs, coke and heroin and all that crap and having pot in there? It's like one of those IQ tests where you look at five things, and what doesn't belong here? Weed never killed anybody, ever. It's never given anybody lung cancer, as a matter of fact, if you look at the real research, it's very, very therapeutic and beneficial for your body and to have it banned in any way in sport or society, it all comes from ignorance. It all comes from serious brainwash and the 'Reefer madness' propaganda of the 1930's.'

Showing a real passion for the topic, Bravo continued with some genuine zeal, 'If you look into it and go to www.jackherer.com and you can find out the truth as to how and why marijuana was made illegal in 1937. It all comes down to economics because they had industrial reasons, you know, they really wanted to get rid of hemp, not marijuana. We got fooled into banning marijuana; no one even knew we were banning hemp for industrial purposes. It's a crazy, crazy story; the history of hemp is fascinating. There's a book called "The Emperor wears no clothes", by Jack Herer; you read that and you'll be blown the fuck away. The illegality of weed, it's all crap.'

In fact, rather than stunting his ability to take on board techniques, Bravo insists that weed has helped him to look at the ground game from a different perspective and counts numerous high profile figures as evidence to suggest he is not alone in receiving inspiration from the drug. 'It's a steroid of the imagination. It's no coincidence that all the classic rock songs from the 60's and 70's that are still rocking people around the world today, they were all written by people who had marijuana in their system. Look at all the great creative minds; William Shakespeare was a pothead, Bruce Lee ate hash, the Beatles, Bob Marley, all the great minds, all the creative minds. Even in sport, look at the greatest running back of all time in American football, Ricky Williams… total pothead. Over 50% of the NBA players smoke weed, they don't even test for weed in the

NBA because they know they can't, because they would have to suspend the whole league. The NBA is a league of potheads, so to ban it [in mma] is incredible. It shows you how brainwashed we are on this planet, we think we have free minds, but we're totally controlled by the media and the powers that be. We are not as free as we think we are.'

I bring you the future

Casting his mind to the future of mma, the grappling expert came up with a surprising slant on the areas of the sport where he expects the most influential developments to be made over the short-to-mid term. 'The state of grappling is in its infancy right now; I mean grapplers are still low level, overall. Everybody's wrestling is getting really good, it's getting really hard to take people down, but it seems that everyone is getting the striking down. There's a lot of great strikers out there right now. Guys who could compete in K-1, like Anderson Silva and all these wrestlers are starting to get their striking together.'

'The striking and the wrestling is looking really strong, really good.' Bravo continued, 'Seeing a guy like Cung Le, who's bringing back all those fancy kicks and fancy strikes that everybody thought were useless, I think he's changing people's ideas. I think that Cung Le and Lyoto Machida are definitely bring back the old karate kicks and stuff and they are definitely showing that you can add those fancy, flipping kicks and be effective with them. I mean, Cung Le landed 20 side kicks on Frank Shamrock, no-one ever landed side kicks; it would happen once every blue moon. I think that Cung Le and Lyoto Machida are going to help with the evolution of the striking of the sport and the grappling still has a long way to go, but it's getting there slowly.'

When it comes to his own competitive aspirations, what he sees as the low level of grappling skill currently being exhibited in the sport of mma is not a factor that could ever tempt him to step into the cage. 'I'm not going to do mma. I never wanted to do mma; mma was always the thing as a last resort. If I didn't make it in music, if it was a choice between doing mma and going back to the blue collar life, I would do mma. I don't like training all day, it's not my cup of tea; most of the grappling competitions that I did, I didn't train that hard. It was just something I just did for fun. But in order to be competitive now with all these wrestlers, you've got to dedicate your life to training, but my primary focus is on music, jiu-jitsu was a hobby that got out of control.

'I never had intentions of being this competitive guy that's always training and staying in shape, that's just not my style and now, there's so much pressure... I have an affiliate making money off of me. There's a lot of pressure, I can't just got out and compete and not be in tip top shape, so if I was going to compete, there would have to be a lot of money involved, for me to get into shape to compete, I can't just walk in there without being in tip top shape and have someone stalemate me, stuff me or even tap me! I'd have to be in incredible shape and for that to happen it would have to be a fight that would be worth it. So Royler Gracie, I'm trying to make that happen, he doesn't want the rematch. A rematch would be something that would be worth it for me to put my music career on hold for a couple of months and dedicate myself, submerge myself in training. A rematch to shut everybody up who said I got lucky. He's got most of the Gracie clan; they all think I got lucky. I would love to prove that I wasn't lucky and tap him again, that would be worth it.'

After talking enthusiastically about jiu-jitsu for over half an hour, it seemed impossible to imagine that Bravo could have a hobby that was closer to his heart; however, as he explained in parting, his passion for music is the reason why he gets out of bed in the morning. 'I grew up a metalhead, I was also a closet New Wave fan. I liked Metal, I like the Cure, Depeche Mode, I like hip hop, I like everything and the music I produce now, I'm producing three different bands right now. There's where I spend most of my time, producing my music. That's what I really do, my main focus has always been music and that's what I'm doing now. It's all happening now; the jiu-jitsu is blowing my music up!'

CHAPTER TWELVE
THE ART OF GROUND AND POUND

'You heard Joe Rogan saying that I needed to move to a good position, that is the best position, I'm sorry, but I know this - for my style anyway.'
- Paul Kelly

Ground-and-pound has a bad name. It is constantly referred to by critics of the sport as one of the principle reasons why mma is unacceptable to a vast section of the population, whilst even people from within the sport are sometimes caught complaining that a fighter 'only' won via ground-and-pound, as if to suggest that beating an opponent up on the floor is a lesser art.

The 'noble art' of boxing prizes the ability of fighters to deliver blows without themselves receiving punishment, it commends their ring control and the ability of a successful combatant to dictate both the range and pace of the exchange. A good ground-and-pounder will also be able to exert similar dominance and impose his preferred pace on the fight; instead, dishing out a beating on the mat from top position whilst staying out of range of his opponent's less effective retaliatory punches.

Ground-and-Pound, Machine-style

As he explains, striking on the floor comes very naturally to Ian 'The Machine' Freeman, 'You've either got it or you haven't. Ground and pound, I just knew where the openings were and once I realised how to create power, that is what I became known for "Heavy hands" as it were, the UFC used to put in their opening credits about me, they would say "Ian Freeman, know for being heavy handed", but that wasn't heavy handed standing, that was heavy-handed on the ground.'

'It's not rocket science,' Freeman continued as he outlined his strategy for turning an opponent over with strikes on the floor, 'but people who are not training day to day, using technique, they just start hitting the head and before you know where you are, you're hitting the hands, hitting the arms. It's just like boxing; you've got to open them up. You've got to open up with a few bodyshots, you've got to fake a few things. You've got to throw combinations in ground-and-pound just like you have to standing, people don't appreciate that, they think it's just a matter of getting on top of somebody and hitting them and it doesn't always work like that.'

Punching down on an opponent during a grappling exchange certainly does run the risk of being seen as one of the more brutal aspects of the sport, but as Ian explained, the art is much misunderstood, 'Ground and pound is only dangerous if the person that you're doing it against doesn't have a clue what's happening. Same with boxing, if you were playing tennis with someone, if the other person didn't know how to return the ball one person's going to look great and one person is going to look bad, it's the same as ground-and-pound. If one person knows about ground-and-pound and the other person doesn't, it's going to look a bit barbaric – that's why they have to be evenly matched up.'

During his long career, Freeman has pounded a list of tough opponents and he swears blind that bashing an opponent on the deck for a round can have a marked effect. 'The way I look at it, I use this analogy when I'm teaching ground-and-pound, it's like an energy bar that used to be on an Atari video game. Every time you hit them, their energy bar goes down to red and it's the same with ground and pound. We've both got energy bars, we're both green when we've started fighting, but every time I hit somebody with a clean shot to the head on the ground, their energy bar goes down to red and they get tired. Not only does it get them tired, it demoralises them. But if I threw 10 shots and 9 of them hit his arms, my energy bar would be going red and his would be staying green. That's why you've got to be cool, calm and collected, pick your shots, use combinations and make sure that out of every ten that you're throwing, you're getting about seven or eight that's connecting. Eventually, you'll win the fight.'

In addition to wearing an opponent down, fighters are increasingly incorporating ground-and-pound into their jiu-jitsu positioning, using strikes to open up opportunities to pass the guard and work from a more offensive position. 'It's very hard for somebody to keep their guard closed when you're pounding them in the head. Very, very hard.' Freeman said, with a due sense of justification, 'It's instinct, that if somebody is getting hit hard in the head, to open their legs and try and defend or try and push away or go for a submission, or do whatever. Very rarely do you see somebody with their legs totally closed while they are getting punched in the head. Maybe one or two shots here and there, but if you are throwing good combinations and putting pressure on, it always opens the guard and I can feel when somebody opens their guard behind me without looking at it, plenty of practise, and when you feel their guard open, that's when you get ready to pass.'

Causing Damage in the Guard

An American fighter known for his advanced ground-and pound is Heath

Herring, who impressively knocked Yoshiki Takahashi out cold at Pride Total Elimination 2004 after a sustained series of punches and hammerfists. After pounding the Japanese fighter unconscious after a sustained barrage of blows, Herring knows how dangerous it can be to play guard in mma. 'I kind of go against the grain with a lot of things, I know a lot of jiu-jitsu coaches think the guard is a good position for the guy on the bottom – I loath the guard, I don't want to be on my back with the guy on top of me at all!'

Conversely, Herring sees being on top in an opponent's guard as one of the safest positions in which to work your way to victory, 'I'll sit in the guard all day. If the guy wants to put me in his guard, I'll take it. I think that I can get the best of him if I'm on top. He'll be underneath me, I'm not really worried about armbars and triangles at that point and I think they need to be more worried about hammerfists and things like that from the top.

'I look at what works well for me, Herring continued, 'and I kinda take advantage of that, so if they want to pull guard, that's great. When me and Nogueira fought, he didn't really put me in his guard because I want to be there. If Nogueira wants to put me in his guard and hold me there, that's great, I'll play that game with him all day and I think he was smart enough to work out that it wouldn't work for him.'

Paul Kelly and the Secret of his Razor-Sharp Elbows

One of England's most famous fighters, UFC veteran, Paul Kelly could not have agreed more with Herring's assessment. 'My best position for ground and pound is in the guard.

It's strange. You heard Joe Rogan saying that I needed to move to a good position, that is the best position, I'm sorry, but I know this - for my style anyway. I drill ground and pound from the guard, I've got a good base and I'm pretty confident that I'm not going to get submitted.

'Throwing elbows from the mount is harder, you know?' the Wolfslair fighter continued, 'Elbowing somebody from the mount, you're sort of a lot more off balance, you don't have as good a base as you do from the guard... and side control, you've got no ground-and-pound really from side control, you're restricted to one arm, because your other arm is keeping you posted and keeping your base. If they are lying there, then I've got my hips to the floor in side control and I've got an arm tied up to keep the back flat, so all I can do if I'm lying across them is elbow them with one elbow - that doesn't suit me. He's got his hips and everything to knock my body and knock me off balance, so I don't get the same effect with my shots.'

Like Freeman, the Liverpudlian found that striking an opponent on the floor came very naturally, 'See me, I didn't really learn ground and pound off

185

of anyone, it just come natural to me and then watching the likes of David Loiseau. If you've ever watched him fight, he cuts a lot of people up with his elbows and there's a technique to ground and pound, which I've sort of learned myself, in terms of timing.'

Going ultra-technical and giving away a valuable trade secret, Kelly continued, 'Like if someone grabbed my wrist, instead of wasting the shot and trying to pull my arm out, I can use their wrist to help turn my arm in, it's hard to explain over the phone' he said, before managing an almost perfect job of it,

'If he's got hold of my wrists, he automatically turns my arm into the perfect position to cut someone open. If you stick your arm out and put your elbow into the elbowing position, when you're going to elbow someone – now turn the back of your hand towards your face, so your palm is facing outwards, now feel the point of your elbow. You so how much sharper it goes? It just sort of pushes that little bit of bone out and it doesn't take a lot to cut someone open, you know - if you get that point in the right place, or if you keep on hitting it because sometimes the skin needs to soften.

'If you look at my record, nearly all of my fights have ended up in TKOs because I've cut them with my elbow. Even if I have to soften it up with punches, I'll feel that then where it's softened and then I'll aim for that with my elbow. It might take two or three, but you know they are going to cut because it's impossible for them not to, do you know what I mean?'

The perfect interviewee, Kelly was on a roll as he approached the subject of Bruce Davis, an opponent that he mercilessly battered into defeat back in 2006 and has subsequently not competed in pro mma for the following two years. 'I softened Bruce up with loads of punches and as I was punching him and elbowing him, he wasn't cutting. I could feel the lumps in his skin ready to cut, and then it was like they all just cut at the same time and his face was a bit of a mess.

'That was through softening him up with punches, it was actually the smallest elbow which cut Bruce, it was a little one that I fell into with my left elbow. It must have travelled five or six inches at best, it didn't come from the ceiling or the other side of the cage, just little short snapping elbows, they are the ones which do all the damage, strangely enough.'

Adding another useful tip for an aspiring ground-and-pounder, Paul emphasised the importance of throwing combinations. 'Another thing, people sometimes elbow into their opponent's hands – if the other guy is guarding, there's no point in elbowing into his hands and forearms, so I try to work a combo into it and throw a left hook, right elbow or come up the middle with an elbow whichever way I can.

'It takes a lot of explaining, you wouldn't really think it with ground and pound, but there is really art to it. It's like throwing a right hand, anyone can throw a right hand, but if you are not taught how to do it, it doesn't land with the same effect, if you know what I mean. When I'm drilling elbows, I don't get to drill elbows on anyone's face, do I? So I just drill them on a bag all the time and think of working different combos into it.

'A lot of punches get mixed in with my ground-and-pound, only to open the gap up so I can stick my elbow in.' Kelly finished, finally revealing why he tries to catch all of his opponents with elbows whenever he possibly can, 'I've been caught with an elbow myself, you see, in training. I've been elbowed a few times in a fight but I've never been cut. I got caught with an elbow one time as I went to shoot in and I tell you what, he didn't even mean to elbow me and I really felt the affects of it. From that point really, I've tried my best to get stuck in.'

PRIDE GRAND PRIX 2000 SHOWCASE
KNEE STRIKES ON THE FLOOR

O n the 1st June 2000, the man known by many as the inventor of the term 'Ground-and-Pound' took his dominant and brutally effective style to new heights as he smashed his way to victory in the inaugural Pride Grand Prix in front of a packed house at the Tokyo Dome. In the opening fight of the night, Coleman showed the crowd what he had become known for in his bout with local favourite, Akira Shoji. The muscular American pinned the local favourite to the mat and battered his ribs for a full 15 minutes, leaving some terrible bruising as evidence of his style's effectiveness.

However, in the final against hard-punching Russian, Igor Vovchanchyn, the former NCAA wrestling champion demonstrated a whole new damaging aspect to his floor work as he took control of the contest and pounded 'Ice Cold' into submission on the floor with hard knees.

Looking back on the hard opening fight, Coleman began, 'The Akira Shoji fight is the only time ever, apart from against Dan 'The Beast' Severn, when I planned to stay on my feet. He's the only guy that I didn't plan on grounding-and-pounding, I thought I could beat him on my feet.' Quickly, however, Coleman reverted to his wrestling instincts, taking his Japanese opponent to the floor and unleashing an alarming barrage of punches on his exposed ribs.

'Well, Shoji, from what I understand, he writes out a will every time before he fights,' Coleman said with a smile, 'He definitely came there ready to die and I gave him some of my best shots ever and he took 'em all. I think as the years went on, I think that his heart softened a little bit, but back when I fought him, he had one of the biggest hearts in the business. He took everything I had and was ready for more, you could see when they raised my hand after the decision; even though it was about 95% a one-sided fight, in his mind, Akira Shoji was ready to go into some overtime.'

Due to a newly instated 'no time-limit' rule imposed on the tournament final, Coleman had some concerns going into the final, 'They didn't put that rule in until the day before at the rules meeting. It was supposed to be a 20-minute time limit in the finals, in my head, I'd done my work, that's the way I saw it ending up, with me and Igor in the finals and with the 20-minute time limit, I planned on taking him down and grounding-and-pounding him. Igor's never going to quit, I planned on pounding him until the referee stopped it.

'To be honest with you,' Coleman said, 'I wasn't too sure how I was going to end this fight because I don't have a lot of finishing holds; maybe I created one that day. I didn't visualise any way of finishing this fight, I wasn't sure how I could finish this guy off because he'd fought for over two hours in one night, so I knew it was going to be a long, long night.'

'The Hammer' was able to impose his will on the contest from the get-go and diligently worked his way through to the dominant North-South, or '69' position. Pinning his opponent to the floor Coleman switched gears and began to draw his legs back and unload a series of heavy knees to Igor's head. 'The contact felt great for me, the knee was feeling it. I was wondering, waiting to see if I was going to be able to knock him out with this, or if the ref was going to stop it or something, I just knew that I was so close to victory, I was just hoping that he wasn't going to squirm out of there – because I wanted out of there, with the belt. Fortunately, I got him stuck in the corner and I was able to knee him to the point where he had to surrender.'

Storming to victory in such impressive fashion, Coleman leapt in the air to begin what has fondly become known by mma fans all over the globe as the world's best victory celebration. 'World's best celebration' Coleman laughed, 'That's what I hear. It was just a complete loss of control over my emotions at that point, I think that I felt a little bit like superman and I felt like I could jump right out of the ring! I wanted to run to the fans, because I fight for the fans they are most important to me and I wanted to get to them as quick as possible.'

Coleman ran across the ring and propelled himself into the air before noticing a sizable drop between himself and the arena floor 'When I got in mid-air, I realised that I was going to come up a little bit short, but I think a made a good recovery though after that!' Just about managing to save himself from injury, the American turned himself back into the ring and came crashing to earth. Undeterred by this momentary set back, he sprung back to his feet and exited the ring to perform an excellent double-clothesline to roughly half of the spectators in the front row.

Pride 13: Mark Coleman vs. Allan Goes

More devastating success with knees on the floor followed in Coleman's very next bout at Pride 13 as he took on the tough Brazilian jiu-jitsu ace, Allan Goes, a fighter who bravely stepped in as a late replacement to fight out of his weight class and put on a show for the Japanese fans. 'I feel for Allan in that fight because sometimes in Japan, that was the first time that they really preferred that I won a fight and when they want you to win, they give you plenty of notice – I think Allan Goes took that on very short notice, I really don't think he wanted to be there, but once he was there, he thought he'd be entertaining, I guess that's not the way to entertain,' he said, referring to Goes' less-than-polished capoeira display, 'but he was there, so I guess he wanted to be as entertaining as possible, but let's keep capoeira a separate sport', he added with a smile.

In the fight, Coleman quickly brushed off the high-flying antics of his opponent and snared Goes in a tight front headlock. Forced to the ground, the Brazilian had nowhere to go, as Coleman explained, 'I think that he was in a lot worse a position than Igor was, he was face down. Igor was able to block a lot of my knees, if you go back and watch it, I think I had 16 knees, but with Allan Goes I had free reign, open shots to the head, so I felt a lot more solid contact when I hit him.'

After a pair of hard shots, Goes was in no position to continue and began to lean closer to the floor, slumped on the canvas under the force of Coleman's powerful knees. 'I knew he was hurt and I wanted the referee to stop it because I don't want to hurt no-one too bad.' Coleman pointed out. However, seconds after releasing his apparently unconscious foe, Goes sprang back to life and darted in on the American as he celebrated in the ring.

'I was just really excited, really happy and excited at that moment.' He said, remembering the point immediately before he realised that his beaten opponent had attached himself to him leg, 'I kind of realised that he probably didn't know what was going on, but the show is never over until you're back in the dressing room, so I continued to perform and show some entertainment. I didn't want to hurt him anymore at that point, but I still wanted to defend myself.'

THE DREADED CRUCIFIX

The Crucifix first raised its head as a potent attacking position in the modern game at UFC 8 when Gary Goodridge tied up both the arms of Paul Herrera and proceeded to land a series of vicious elbow strikes which caused multiple fractures to Herrera's jaw 13 seconds into the fight, ending his mma career. Though Goodridge demonstrated the control position beneath his opponent, ground-and-pound fighters such as Matt Hughes have since refined the crucifix to a near art form, claiming the position from side mount to control both arms in top position. Snaring Carlos Newton in the position, Hughes sent his trapped foe to a punishing defeat as a stream of hard, indefensible punches came crashing down on Newton's face.

Brad "Stream of Punches" Pickett

Since Hughes claimed this famous victory at UFC 38, the new generation of all-round fighters have eagerly taken on the crucifix as their ground position of choice; one such fighter is Brad 'One Punch' Pickett. As his nickname suggests, Pickett is primarily a stand up striker; however, as a malicious opportunist on the mat, the East Londoner never seems to pass up the opportunity to pound his opponents and has turned in some good performances using the crucifix. 'I've won 3 of my fights from that position. One was a submission with a straight armbar, and two TKO's from it. I quite like that position; I've worked it quite a bit.'

Trapping both arms of your opponent, yet leaving one hand free to strike, the offensive capabilities of taking the position are all too clear. As fighters scramble as hard as they can to stay out of harm's way on their back, catching the position in the first place can be a real battle. Pickett, therefore, has a couple of tricks up his sleeve to help him attain the dominant spot. 'What I do is strike them to the head anyway and then they try and block and when they block, you just push it and trap it with your knee. That's what I basically do.

'Sometimes I muscle it,' the former boxer continued, 'I pull the arm down to get my knee in. To trap it, you need to get your knee in, but a good grappler won't be caught so easily. When I'm rolling around with everyone here at Pancrase London, I catch everyone with it, I am yet to catch Ashleigh [Grimshaw] with it and I roll with him a lot. No-one catches me, but as I say, I'm so wary of the position myself, I'm not giving you my arm. If I am in it, I'm in it for a second or two and I'm spazzing out as I know I don't want to be resting there. Some people don't see the danger really sometimes until it's a bit too late.'

As an attacking fighter, the beauty of the position for Pickett is clear. 'It costs you nothing. If you get it, pin them down, it's hard to get out of. If you've ever been put in a crucifix, it's the most horrible position.' He's not wrong; I've been fortunate enough to experience the business end of a crucifix in mma sparring, and

191

even with a sympathetic training partner patting at your face with a generously padded fist, the psychological pressure which bears down on you is immense.

'In grappling, it's not a good position, it doesn't mean shit,' Pickett added, 'but in mma it's a perfect position, you've nullified both arms. They spend so much energy getting out of it – and if they get out of it and you're still in side control - then you just push on the arm and do it again. Mike Brown used to do it to me all the time at the American Top Team, that's why I picked it up; because I fucking hated being caught in it.'

No Defence other than Toughness

Another benefit to striking from the crucifix is that the downed fighter has a very hard time defending himself; as such even a series of seemingly innocuous blows can bring a halt to the contest. 'On of the guys I was fighting, JR Simms in Bodog got himself into a position where he couldn't defend himself and the ref intervened after seven or eight unanswered shots.' Pickett recalled, 'He weren't even trying to get out of the position. He was saying after the fight, "Ah you weren't knocking me out…" Yeah, it weren't about knocking him out but I still gave him black eyes.'

Looking back at his steam-rolling victory over Vaughn Harvey at Cage Rage Contenders 6 Pickett explained that even if an opponent is trying everything to buck you off, it is still possible to land some meaningful shots. 'He actually tapped from it, you know, I was banging him, you see him trying to get out of it and he's stuck and I hit him again, hitting him in the head. You give it everything to get out and you're still getting punched in the face. I think when he tapped the ref was going to stop it anyway. I had him caught in the position where you're taking repetitive blows to the face; it's not a good thing, especially for Vaughn Harvey as he's a bit of a looker. Me? I wouldn't give a shit!' Pickett said falling about laughing.

Against Harvey, Pickett was unable to put his elbows to use as Cage Rage outlaw their use on the floor, but the Londoner remained adamant that if he were able to use glancing elbows at will, he could have done some serious damage in no time at all. 'With elbows,' he said bluntly, 'if I get that position, it's over quick.'

Having taken control of the crucifix, accumulating damage with strikes is not the only option at your disposal as Pickett explained, 'Once you've trapped them, when they try to buck up, which they do, and lift their head, you can put your leg over it in a reverse triangle and once you get the reverse triangle, you're not going to tap them out, but they are just stuck there, you can hit them to the head easy or grab the straight armbar, but honestly, now in a fight, I don't think I'd ever go for a submission – I'd ground-and-pound and go for a TKO [Technical Knock Out], it looks better on your record!'

CHAPTER THIRTEEN
BLOOD SPORT

'Blood was pumping out and it was coming out black. So when they lifted me up and tourniquet'd my leg, I thought, "Maybe it's pretty serious!"'
- Alex 'The Reidernator' Reid

For most people, the sight of blood is unpleasant, but with ground-and-pounders such as Paul Kelly on the loose, mma fighters have no choice but to take a different perspective. Spilling blood is an occupational hazard and it is virtually inevitable that a fighter will receive numerous cuts during their career. Facial lacerations have the potential to be extremely serious and can cause a fight to be stopped instantly; but, for many fighters, the sight of their own blood will become commonplace over the span of their competitive life, merely a distraction from the matter at hand.

The Cutsman

Whilst the general public might make every effort to avoid looking at cuts or handling bloody situations, Cage Rage cutsman, Paul Marchant makes a living out it. On hand at every event, Marchant can often be seen dashing into the cage between rounds to patch up a bleeding fighter in the precious 60 seconds before the contest resumes. It is in this high-pressure environment that Marchant does his best work; a fact attested to by dozens of fighters who, without his expert help, would otherwise not have been able to continue to the final hooter.

Sealing up cuts as fast as you can and advising officials on the severity of a cut is no ordinary way to make a living, so why was it that Marchant went out of his way to get involved in the misunderstood art of working cuts? 'I've got a couple of fighters who cut really bad' he explained, 'I started off finding out about how to do the cuts then I trained under the British Boxing Board cutsman, Denny Mancini.'

Though the name may not mean a great deal to those outside of his chosen profession, if you are in the cut game, you know that Mancini is a man to be respected. 'He's old school,' Marchant continued, 'he's 60 and he's been a cutsman for years. He used to sell Lonsdale boxing equipment; I used to go to his shop in London and that's how I got into it.'

Working alongside Mancini and a group of pro boxers from London's famous Peacock gym, Marchant took to the delicate art like a duck to water, picking up fight-specific tricks of the trade that no doctor would ever be able to impart. However, to supplement his on-the-job training, the East Londoner has also attended first aid courses and as a result received his British Boxing Board of Control license.

Marchant's quest to augment his skills did not stop there, as he even went so far as to seek expert tuition from accident and emergency doctors and some of London's top plastic surgeons, 'I've got a real thirst for knowledge, I'm all the time asking questions from people who know more than me.'

With a background of training and treating cuts in both boxing and Thai boxing, Marchant is a fountain of knowledge himself and finds himself uniquely placed to assess the difference between the cuts suffered in the various sports. 'They are totally different sorts of injuries really. In Thai boxing you get a lot of cuts from the elbows, elbows and knees cut easy. You get a lot more cuts in Thai boxing than you do in the actual cage fighting!'

In Marchant's view the vast majority of cuts caused during boxing and Thai boxing matches are not from punches due to the larger gloves used in those sports, 'Most of the cuts in boxing are from a clash of heads, or an elbow when you're trying to punch and someone's leant in and got caught. In Thai boxing, it's all elbows and knees; you very rarely get cut off the gloves. In mma it's a little bit different because the gloves are a little bit smaller, so you can get cut quite easily.'

No two cuts are ever the same, so Marchant has to react to the individual circumstances which can vary greatly from person to person. 'It depends, some of the fighters get the easiest cuts, but they are the hardest ones to stop. If they've had aspirin, things like that, if they've taken anything which thins the blood, you know what I mean, Red Bull, stuff like that. It depends, different people bleed differently. You can get the hardest cut in the world and stop it straight away - and a silly little one, it goes everywhere and you can't stop it. It depends on the person and it depends where the cut is, how simple it is. You've got to know what you're doing it took me ages and ages. You've got to be confident.'

Confidence and knowledge is a major part of the puzzle when it comes to staunching the flow of blood from a cut. However, as a licensed cutsman, Paul also has access to adrenaline, a naturally occurring hormone which works as a vasoconstrictor when applied locally - essentially meaning that it causes blood vessels to contract, making it an invaluable asset as he works to keep a cut fighter in the match. As a warning to fighters, however, Paul was keen to point out that the adrenaline solution he uses requires careful, expert preparation which cannot be undertaken by an untrained amateur.

However much expertise and experience you may have, however, some cuts just don't seem to want to close. The first example of this which sprang to mind was, of course, the brutal cut suffered by the accident prone, Alex Reid in his match with Daijiro Matsui at Cage Rage 14. 'Alex Reid was a nightmare', Marchant said with a shake of the head.

As Reid explained himself, the cut itself was not inflicted during the fight, but two weeks before in the gym. 'I was cut thanks to my mate Sol Gilbert', the Reidenator said with a smile. 'We had another war in the gym – we don't spar anymore,' he clarified, 'if we've got a fight, we don't spar because we hurt each other.' On this occasion it was not so much a sparring session that had become a touch overheated, so much as a genuine, and quite bizarre accident. 'We both cut each other! He cut me with a punch and I cut him with a knee to the head at the same time, it was crazy!'

Training around a cut and giving it the best possible chance of healing before a fight is an extremely tricky business as Reid became all too aware. 'A week later it opened again from being knocked, it wasn't a deep opening, but three days later it opened again!' But as the old saying goes, 'Desperate times call for desperate measures' and the Aldershot fighter is not someone to shy away from what most people might see as a ludicrously desperate measure .

'In the changing room on the Saturday night, Paul Marchant super-glued it – with proper glue, super-glue. He did quite a good job, but anyway, the fight starts and it opened yet again within the first thirty seconds! But he did a fantastic job; the fight went the distance, that was a war. He ended up getting facial reconstruction!' Reid added.

'I knocked Matsui out with an upkick, he was on top of me. He actually went out, he fell on me. He recovered while he was lying on me, he slumped on me and then he just came round in seconds. If I had managed to follow up quickly, it could have been an early night for me, but...' Reid paused and let out a heart-felt sigh 'unfortunately it wasn't.'

This is far from the first cut of Reid's professional career, so I had to ask, does he not have any concerns about picking up, potentially very ugly facial scars? 'You know it's funny,' he replied, 'I was thinking about that this morning. It's really weird how my face, my features have changed quite drastically.'

As an actor before becoming a professional fighter, Reid laughed as he did an impression of his casting agent, '"Oh Alexander, oh, what have you done to your face, oh my goodness, your ears, your nose!" My mum always gets upset about my features, "You used to be so beautiful... now look at you!"' Laughing again at their reactions, Alex appeared completely unconcerned by the battle scars etched across his face. 'A few scars makes you look a bit more lived in' he joked.

Referring to his rapidly developing cauliflower ears, Reid continued, 'My ears are not quite Randy Couture yet, but they are half way there. If I could have my ears back to normal, I can't help but think; would I want that? The fact that I've got them is like a little story. This who I am; I'm a fighter, this is what I've chosen to do – and I enjoy it, I'd rather get punched in the face for a living than work on a building site, or sit in an office for 8 hours a day.'

Shin on shin

However, in a fight blood does not exclusively come as the result of facial damage; far more rare yet a concern of any low kicker, bone-on-bone shin clashes can result in some of the very worst cuts in the business. Again, due to endless supplies of bad luck throughout his career, Reid has also been on the receiving end of one such gash after a brutal clash of shins with Chute-Boxe representative, Murilo 'Ninja' Rua.

In the early exchanges, Reid threw one of his trademark low kicks which landed with such impact that Rua was lifted in the air; however, before blast off, 'Ninja' was able to raise his left leg just enough to ensure the strike landed perfectly on the hardest part of his upper shin, causing a cut which literally pissed a stream of blood across the floor of the cage. 'The fight stopped,' Reid recalled, 'I didn't know what was going on. "Why are you stopping it?"' His cornerman, Alexis Demetriades was first on the scene with good advice, 'Alexi said, "Don't look down, don't look down", so what's the first thing I do? Look down.'

'"Ah, it's alright!"' Reid protested, but the doctors were, thankfully, having none of it. '"No, we think you've hit an artery."' They replied gently, 'Blood was pumping out and it was coming out black. So when they lifted me up and tourniquet'd my leg, I thought, "Maybe it's pretty serious!"'

Paul Marchant also confirmed that cuts to the shin are among the most difficult to stop. 'It's a lot different [to a cut on the face]. You can't stop it, depending on where it is. I've had two bad shin ones and each time we've had to call the fight. Each time I've stopped the bleeding, but you can't carry on with both fighters throwing kicks.'

Adding another story of woeful bad luck, Paul continued, 'Do you know my mate Frankie Adams? One of the top fighters in this country, he got stopped in UK-1, I was cornering him. He cut his opponent badly with a kick, but as he cut him his shin went and his shin bled more than his opponent's cut so they called it a no-contest and couldn't carry on.'

'I want to continue!'

Sometimes, however, fighters are able to continue for significant amounts of time with cuts that are both visually quite awful and cause considerable problems. One fighter who has managed to fight on with an absolutely disgusting looking cut is the experienced American Thug-Jitsu fighter, Yves Edwards in his bloody war with former UFC lightweight title challenger, Joe Stevenson.

The cut began on the floor after a vicious elbow from the noted ground-and-pounder, 'Joe did a nice fake,' Yves said, 'he faked like he was throwing his hand behind his back to try and open my guard and I got a little lax at that point and as soon as he did that, he came back over the top with an elbow. He hit me and it's like one of those things when you hit you're head against a coffee table or something. When he hit me, it was like, "That might have cut me"- about two or three seconds later the blood started running across my face.'

Some fighters defending off their back who realise they are cut go into full-on panic mode; for Yves, however, it was simply a cause of irritation and a good reason to fight even harder off his back. 'I was really pissed off that I fell for something like that. I couldn't get away from him or get him off me, but the blood started pouring down and it started getting in my eye, which made it pretty hard to see. I've never had blood in my eyes before and it kinda sucks because when they say you can't see, you really can't see, it's like a big red film over your eye. It's really hard to see and I just didn't want to be in that position anymore, I wanted to push him off and get out and all I could think of was trying to get out of this position.

'When they stopped the fight to check on me and they let me fight, I was pretty glad, so I was able to stand up at the end of that round and in between rounds it really sucked… it didn't seem like anyone was trying to stop the bleeding. There was a cue tip applied to my head, but it was just a cue tip, it didn't have adrenaline on it, no Vaseline, no sealants or coagulants or anything like that and I was kind of upset, but my cornerman pushed the cutsman out of the way and spilled the ice on purpose. I figured he was trying to buy some time, I was kind of happy at that point, but then the doctor called the fight and I was disappointed more than anything else.'

Remarkably, Yves did not feel flustered by the damage he had sustained and remains certain that he would have continued to fight on if he had been given clearance by the doctors. 'I didn't feel like I didn't want to fight anymore, at that point, it was like, "Well, I'm already cut, I'm bleeding real bad; this is about the worst thing that could possibly happen and I'm still in it, let me finish what's going on."

'Other than that, I don't think it caused any psychological damage; it just really, really sucked to not be able to see. I got it cleared after wiping it a few times and turned my head so that the blood would run clean off to the side rather than down into my eyes… but it just sucked, it's a fight I would love to have again. Joe Stevenson is a really tough guy and it kind of sucks that the fight had to end that way. He did do the damage,' Yves scoffed in frustration, 'but because of "safety reasons" and precautions the doctor stopped it, you've got to live with it.'

CHAPTER FOURTEEN
INJURIES

'To do such damage to his leg and not mine, it was a bit of a weird one, I don't think anyone could ever explain why his leg broke and not mine, it's not like I've got super-strong legs that are made of steel or anything like that.'

- Ross 'Angry' Pettifer

For a professional fighter in the world's toughest sport, dealing with injuries is as much a part of the game as putting on gloves before sparring; if you want to train, spar and compete at a top level, sooner or later you will pick up an injury which will force you out of practise. Depending on what is damaged, how badly and what treatment is applied, recovery times can vary spectacularly and, counter-intuitively, it is often during a time away from the mat that a fighter's determination to stay on his chosen path is tested to breaking point.

In accordance with the famous adage that if you go into a fight injury free, the chances are you didn't train hard enough, most fighters will tell you that they pick up the majority of their niggles in the gym. However, sometimes injuries do happen in competition and fighters react in many different ways. When it comes down to it, they have two options; submit, go home and see your family, or think back to the hours of hard training which put you in the cage, grit your teeth and find a way to continue. More often that not, fighters will continue, bravely masking the pain and ignoring the inevitable, agonising consequences.

Broken hand

A common injury among punching pugilists is a damaged or broken hand and whilst most fighters expect to shrug off such an injury in a couple of months, due to the numerous bones involved and sincerely complicated structure of the hand, careers can be ended with a single punch. Thankfully, this is not the case with most hand injuries, but in many cases the recovery process can be long drawn out and lead to painful, on-going problems.

Talented London Shootfighter, Gaz Roriston had the unexpected pleasure of breaking his hand during his 2003 rematch with Mark Day, a meaningful fight for him after facing Day 3 years earlier on the Millenium Brawl promotion. 'That was my first proper, crazy three round fight, it went the distance, I had two black eyes and was banged up at the end of it. That's one that really stands out, that's when I first had to really dig in and try hard. That was the first fight where I wasn't winning just "because I was Gaz". I actually had to dig in and do something, that's what changed the whole way I view the sport of mma. I realised that I need to get some conditioning and need to train like an athlete, not just be happy with having a knack of picking up techniques.'

That fight sounded bad enough, but far worse was yet to come in the rematch. 'I broke my hand in the first round, I'm pretty sure it was the first punch I threw, it connected and something just went, "Bang" and I thought, "That's a huge shot!" but I didn't really do that much damage to him... thinking back, it was probably the point where my hand broke. I became aware that there was something wrong with it during that first round and I went back to the corner – Suley [Mahmoud] was cornering me – I said, "I think I might have broken my hand!"'

Perhaps expecting his friend and cornerman to take a somewhat more sympathetic view of the situation, Mahmoud instead roared back, 'It doesn't matter, you're winning! Slap him if you have to!' Understanding the cornerman's preference for urgency over empathy, Roriston went back to work, gradually clawing his way to an advantage. 'I ended up mounting him, I did try to open hand, palm strike him, but it didn't feel the same as a punch, so I hit him a few more times – and again, that didn't quite feel right because my hand was loose, it wasn't a solid fist because there were things moving around inside. Luckily, he turned to try and escape the mount and I managed to sink the choke!'

I told the welterweight that I couldn't personally imagine the pain of punching an opponent's face with a broken hand; Roriston laughed, 'Neither can I, it's disgusting now I think back on it. When you're fighting it's an altered sense of reality, it's not the same as walking down the road, you know. If someone pinches me, I scream,' he laughed, 'but in a fight, it's completely different.' Sidelined for the foreseeable future, Roriston made the most of the time, beavering away at college to earn a Bachelor of Science degree in sports science.

Rib damage

Another agonizing and all-too-common injury in contact sports is breaking or separating a rib; an intensely uncomfortable experience which can leave the athlete in pain pretty much all of the time as the breathing process itself constantly irritates and exacerbates the problem. Everyone gets a sore rib at some point, but unluckily for Alex da Souza, he received rather more than that, just days before his fight with Andy Walker.

'I fought on Cage Rage 10 with a broken rib.' Alex said, 'I had to fight on Saturday and I broke my rib on the Thursday night, so it was actually proper broken and it was just recently broken as well, just 30 hours before I actually stepped into the cage.' Grimacing at the task he faced, stepping in with an injury of this kind, the jiu-jitsu ace explained exactly how training accident happened. 'There was a guy that I was sparring with he's another Brazilian guy, an instructor from a Brazilian Muay Thai school. I tried to throw a right hand at him and he countered with a knee and the knee landed on my rib. Basically, he dropped me off with that knee, you know, it was very painful. One of my floating ribs mounted on top of the other.'

However, after a previous disagreement with Walker, the fight was something of a grudge match, and although quite seriously injured, da Souza had no choice but to soldier on. Poole Jiu-Jitsu head coach, Andy Walker explained the situation from his perspective, 'I was matched against one of his students, his student pulled out and he came up and I said yes straight away, basically because he hit one of my other instructors in the changing rooms about 6 months before for no reason, just because he's Alex da Souza and he had his entourage around him. He hit one of my instructors and I thought "Look, right, that's not sportsmanship, I don't want to really train with you any more. If you've got any grievances, you settle them in the ring or the cage, not backstage when you've got seven or eight guys behind you."

'I saw the doctor', Alex continued, 'and he told me not to fight, but I managed to hide from the paramedic who was assessing everyone at the event - I only saw him just minutes before I stepped in the cage; I wanted to fight. If he had seen the way I was I wouldn't have been able to fight, so I only had my medicals, literally ten minutes before the fight.'

In great pain, da Souza still had no doubt that he wanted to go ahead and face Walker,

'I just wanted to fight, mate. I just wanted to do it and I went ahead and did. I don't think Andy knew about it because I kept it very quiet. We stayed in a hotel in London and on the first night I just went up to my hotel room. I couldn't sleep, so I had to sleep sat on a chair because I couldn't lie down. The following day I managed to lie down in bed, but I couldn't get up!' laughed the Brazilian, 'I couldn't get up for the press conference and I was feeling so bad. There was pain only when I was moving, but it was very painful, so I took loads of paracetemol, ibuprofen, any painkillers I could get hold of and I just went for it, but still, I could not warm up,' he said, with an air of desperation, 'that was a funny thing. I was feeling so ill that I couldn't even warm up. I had to warm up with Thai oil because I couldn't manage to heat up my body to the temperature that I wanted to.'

Somehow, da Souza managed to drag himself to the cage and take part in a hard fight which lasted over the entire three 5-minute rounds, 'We had a little bit of stand up, I managed to knock him down in the third round, but I didn't have enough power to knock him out. In the first round I put lots of armbars on him, but I didn't have the power to stretch it, you know. I finished the first round with a kneebar on, which he tapped, but after the bell went.'

The pre-existing injury was news to his opponent, but unsurprisingly, Walker saw a different side to end of the opening stanza. 'He seemed pretty fit and OK to me. His movement was pretty good and he did three rounds which, if he had a broken rib, it would have been very, very difficult to carry on after one round! But the most interesting thing for me was that he got me in a legbar at the end of the first round. The bell went and as soon as the bell went, I knew he wouldn't let go, and he held it on for about seven or eight seconds and the referee basically had to drag him off! I know what he's like,' Walker snarled, 'when I heard the bell, I thought, "Right, he ain't gonna let go, he's going to try and hurt me." He didn't, fortunately, but that's Alex da Souza for you.'

'In the second round,' the Brazilian argued, 'I finished in a mount position and in the third round, I had a good round, it was probably my best round of the whole fight, but I couldn't convince the judges. We went for three 5-minute rounds and I lost on a decision. It's on Youtube, search for my name, watch the fight and make your own conclusions. The judges thought that I lost. Afterwards,' he added, referring back to his pre-fight injury, 'I dealt with the problem, but even today, now and then my ribs just pop; it's a recurrent injury which comes back every once in a while. I've just learnt how to live with it now.'

Illness and injury

Living with the frustration and pain of serious injuries is something that energetic American fighter, Kevin Randleman has had to do his entire sporting life. 'To tell you the truth, the only thing you have to overcome in any duress situation, any surgery, any injuries, is your mental state. You can lock a man in solitary confinement for fucking 20 years and still not be able to break that man's spirit because he's like "Shit, I'm here, I've got to deal with this." I do that. I snap at home, I've broken my share of doors, but at the end of the day, when the money's all counted, I've still got to figure out a way of getting better and stronger with an injury.'

Not only has the wrestler had to face more than his fair share of knee and shoulder injuries, he has also come to the brink of death after a string of debilitating illnesses. 'I've had my lungs collapse on me and I almost died,' Randleman noted, 'I had a bad staph infection and they had to remove my pec [pectoral] and my lat [latissimus dorsi muscle]. That almost killed me. I've had knee surgery, shoulder surgery, lots of them. It hasn't made me any less of a fighter; it's made me a smarter fighter.'

In 2007, pictures on the internet of Randleman's staph infection shocked the entire mma community as it became clear that he had simply continued with his training, hoping the infection would clear up. By the time the hole in his side was the size of a decent fist, it was time for a lengthy recuperation process.

'It's taught me how to become more patient.' He continued, 'It's strengthened my will – it strengthened my nuts. My nuts got bigger from that because I wasted three or four years and I don't have time to waste any more. So when I go out to fight now, I go out to devastate everything and everybody and I'm looking forward to fighting guys who have no problem with coming forward.

'I've never really been healthy for the last seven or eight years of my career!' The Monster fumed, 'I've never been healthy. Shoulder, neck, back – my neck has been broke three times. Just lots of little shit that holds you back from going 100%. I just fought three weeks ago knowing my shoulder was messed up going into the fight, but I hadn't fought in 18 months so I just had to see if I was still there mentally.'

Coming through ordeal after ordeal, Randleman is determined to compete once again with the world's top athletes, 'I don't care what anyone says, I'm a warrior. I love fighting. I know this is going to sound real bad for people but understand this, I learned how to fight in the streets. I didn't learn in a fucking dojo, I was a great wrestler, I knew how to box, I did golden gloves, I was already an athlete and I'm always going to be an athlete. I'm going to put myself a little bit ahead of the fucking curve. So I don't have any fear as far as fighting or nothing like that, I just need to be in shape.

'Not being able to lift for three years can be devastating to a person', the explosive fighter announced, 'I walk around at 215-220 [pounds] right now and I'm happy, but it took me three years to build this back up. It's rough, but I've got a good girl. I've been through a lot of shit, and this is a philosophy I live by - Tough times will never last – tough men do. Tough women do. Tough-ass kids do. But the tough times won't last. I live my life that way and all those injuries and all those surgeries.'

Randleman spoke with almost a sense of pride as he discussed a serious lung infection that he picked up, somewhere between the gyms of Brazil and Las Vegas, 'Like I said, I almost lost my life two times – my girl says that I love saying that because it makes me feel stronger, and it does! When I first got sick, I was 230 pounds. I was jacked, I was strong, I was in great shape, I was running everyday. I got down to 189 in four or five months because I was so sick. My lungs collapsed on me, I just woke up in the hospital and they were like, "We need to take out your lung." I'm not going to lie to you, I was crying, "Oh shit! Are you telling me that I've got to change everything that I've been used to for 35 years?"'

The road to recovery for Randleman was yet another extraordinary chapter in his life, 'They scraped my lungs, it was as painful as hell and it had problems healing. Think of if you skin your knee. Think of the scab that's on it – got that picture? Now rip that scab off!' He shouted suddenly, 'That's what my lungs were. My whole entire left lung was one big scab, as they had to pull all that scab and meat off the top off my lungs. So for the next two months, my lungs kept bleeding, I kept peeing out blood, blood was everywhere – but!' he exclaimed of his overdue upturn in fortune, 'they put the lung back in!'

Knee injuries -
A nightmare for any athlete

No stranger to injuries himself, the UK fighter with perhaps the finest nickname of all, Alex 'Reidenator' Reid has previously joked that he has been injured so many times, they keep a bed free for him at his local hospital. 'A week before my last fight with Matt Ewin, I've never been so ready for a fight,' Reid began, 'I destroyed everybody in the gym, bar none. One week before, I did a cage drill with [the aforementioned] Gaz [Roriston] where he would push me into the cage and I'd turn him, he really went for it and I popped my ACL.'

'I screamed on the floor, but I was like, "I'm fine, I'm fine, it's going to be alright", but it came out every single day from then, up to the fight. It even came out in the changing room before the fight and I screamed, but I was like, "No, it's fine, it's fine; it's all good" and I hobbled down the run way with my leg strapped up.

'The fight went the distance; it came out three times in the fight, not bad ones, because it was strapped up. I threw a right cross and it came out, so I didn't want to throw any punches. After the first round, Alexis [Demetriades] in my corner just said, "Sod this, just go for it, fucking go for it". I went yeah, threw the biggest kick I could, it landed, but then my leg went. He looked at me wobble and he smiled, like "I've got you."' It certainly appeared that Ewin was right as he repeatedly took Reid to the floor over the course of the bout, effectively pinning him to the deck in side control and hammering his immobile opponent with punches and hammerfists.

Looking back on the origins of the injury, Reid was fairly certain, 'I think it stemmed from Tony Frykland [at Cage Rage 18]. In the press conference I was stupid enough to ask about kicking on the floor, I wasn't quite sure on

what the rule was, I should have been because I nearly got disqualified for it.'
Alex asked about the penalties for kicking an opponent to the head on the
floor and the example he gave was of a fighter kicking his way out of a
submission.

As if to fulfil his own prediction, Reid found himself in dire trouble on the
mat in the first round of the 92-second bout, 'He had a heel hook on and I
kicked him in the face with a heel kick. Grant said "You can't do that!" and I
actually stopped fighting which is the worst thing you can do and he cranked
the heel hook on properly, really bad. If I was going to commit a foul, which
I did, I should have really gone for it and kept doing it, because I could have
got out. I was stupid, I was foolish, I shouldn't have done that', he said with
a heavy note of regret, 'I've had a bit of a problem since then; it's got worse
and worse.'

'"I'll fucking take it home with me!"' Reid mocked the aggressive
American, 'I was friends with Tony as well before, I went up to him
afterwards and said, "No hard feelings, I'm cool", but I'd like to smash him
up again', the British banger admitted, 'I was owning him, absolutely owning
him.'

Since suffering serious ACL damage himself, Reid now has a rare
perspective on the injury, 'I'm absolutely fascinated now by who has it and
who carries on fighting. Frank Shamrock apparently hasn't got one in either
knee and he fought Phil Baroni and smashed him up! I was like, "Wow". But,
he's suffering, I've researched it thoroughly on the net, he apparently can't do
certain things; he can't sprawl, he could do it, but with pain.'

It's a hard life, Shamrock confirmed, referring to the knee damage he
suffered going into the Baroni fight, 'I tore it completely out; no ACL
whatsoever in the left knee.' That doesn't sound so good. I felt bad to inquire
how his other knee is doing, 'Yeah,' he replied with a sigh, 'that one is starting
to fall apart as well. I think a lot of it is just the leglocks over the years, all the
little tears and stuff accumulate over time and, as your tendons get harder and
your body gets older, they start to fray and tear off, so I fully anticipate that
in the next couple of years my right ACL is gone as well.'

Asked how long before the clash he injured his knee, Frank answered with
the kind of precision you might expect from one of his armbar attempts, 'For
the record, it was two weeks before the fight. In a rigorous sparring session,
a judo guy tried to trip my leg; my foot stayed in one spot and my knee and
body went the other direction. It was immediate, I felt the pain. I also tore part
of my MCL and stretched my meniscus. I was in a motorised cart for about a
week.'

Fighting on with a broken hand is definitely something out of the ordinary,
but to know full well that your knee is in no state to function on any level,

well in advance of a fight, yet to still compete against a concussive puncher like Baroni is definitely bordering on insanity. 'It's just like, I've been doing it for so long,' Shamrock explained, 'you know, my body is used to adjusting to pain or injury, or problems. My mind is really strong, my body is really strong and comfortable with things and I figured out a way to make it work. I just taped my knee up and put a super-brace on and laid on my back for a week and had people punch me in the head. I figured I was either going to come out a hero, or come out a zero, luckily I came out with the first one.'

As unlikely as it may seem, Frank still managed to take some pleasure from the fight, whilst bouncing around on his freshly injured knee, 'I enjoy all my fights, for me, it's the celebration part; for me, it's the party. You spend two months in a gym and what do you get to do with it? I get to go out and fight, entertain and be a part of something pretty cool. A lot of it is gruelling and hard, but when things work and I feel it flowing, it's amazing.'

Fractures

EliteXC really have got their money's worth out of Shamrock. First there was the Baroni fight, then nine months later Frank was back in the thick of things fighting on with a badly broken right ulna in his classic encounter with Cung Le. 'It broke in the first round. I felt it crack and basically break. I misread a body kick and I leaned over with one arm, blocking a kick and that was just a bad move. When you've been fighting, you feel it; they just feel like knife pains, like a big needle went into your knee or your hip or your shoulder, whatever.

'I broke my leg one time in a fight,' he continued, 'and it felt like a needle went through my leg. I had that feeling in my arm and I thought "I've probably just cracked something, it's probably not bad", but the continued kicks to it were a cumulative thing that eventually separated the bone and moved it over. For me, it was a technical error. I wasn't used to a southpaw as much, I was playing around and having a good time and where normally I would block by lifting a leg and an arm, on a southpaw you need two hands and by the time I realised I was doing something wrong, I was in some serious pain.'

With his ulna floating about somewhere in the middle of his forearm, Shamrock still had no compunction when it came to wailing on his opponent with the right hand. 'I smashed him a bunch of times!' Frank laughed, 'The truth is, I like Cung, I think he adds value to the sport. Cung would never beat me in a mma fight; I let him do his work and tried to beat him at his own game because I wanted to challenge myself. Fighting Cung Le again, I'm just going to go in and smash him. That really hurt when I broke my arm.'

'That really hurt' is about as good a description as you could put on the freak injury which afflicted Japanese fighter Tomomi 'Windy Tomomi' Sunaba in her fateful fight with top female UK fighter, Rosi Sexton in the now defunct Bodog mma promotion. 'When the accident happened itself, I was mostly just in shock. It was one of those moment where you could see what's happened, but it's almost like it's happening to somebody else, it' not quite real. You're aware of what's going on and everything but there's this detachment, it was only afterwards really that it hit me.'

The accident referred to came from a twisting sacrifice throw executed by Rosi. As Sexton turned, heaving her opponent to the mat, it became clear that 'Windy's right leg had taken the full brunt of the twisting motion, fracturing both her tibia and fibula, also causing significant ligament damage.

'She was in quite a lot of pain at the time, as you'd imagine' Sexton reported, 'I didn't see anything at all at the time, the first time I saw it was later on, on a picture. I felt it, I felt something snap on the way down, I didn't know what it was or what had happened, I was facing the other way when it hit the ground. I knew something was wrong, so I was basically waiting for the referee to get involved. After that [my trainer,] Karl [Tanswell] pulled me away and I didn't see much else. I knew that something pretty bad had happened both from the noise and from the reaction of everyone around me; it was definitely something bad had happened. She had to have a couple of surgeries on it, but she seems to have made a full recovery now, she's back fighting, fantastic."

As Shamrock hinted earlier in the chapter, shin bones can also crack under the weight of a heavy contact; a possibility which became a shocking reality for Rob Evans in his clash with the then brightest young star of the UK scene, Ross 'Angry' Pettifer. Going into the contest, the promising Sheffield fighter experienced a mixture of feelings. 'I was a youngster, only 18 at the time, I think obviously I'd had a few fights, so I did feel quite confident.' Pettifer began, 'But I think, being a young man in an adult's game, I think you're nervous before every fight, I think you always get nerves, don't you? It would be quite scary if you didn't have them I think, I'd be worried if I didn't have the nerves.

'Have you spoken to the other lad?' Ross asked.

'No, I haven't, unfortunately', I replied.

'No, you probably wouldn't want to either', Pettifer warned, plainly retaining a pointed dislike of his former opponent. 'There was quite a bit of bad blood before the fight, certain things were said at the weigh-ins, and in the back of the event between me and Rob. A lot of it coming from Rob aimed towards me, I think that was nerves or whatever from his side and there was a lot of pre-fight animosity, pre-fight drama between the two of us.'

'Just on the day of the fight, he was a bit of a cocky guy', the Sheffield fighter continued, 'When he came out, I think he had like a ten minute intro, a really extravagant entrance, a really long thing that didn't work out well for him – the fight only lasted three seconds! I was in the ring for quite a while, it literally got to the point where I was looking around saying, "Bloody hell, come on, let's get this over with", I think he was making a big thing of it for his friends.'

When the bout finally began, Evans hared across the cage to land the first and only strike of the contest. 'He ran over for one big right leg kick and I covered it. The funny thing is that I didn't see the kick coming until I checked it because the check was like an instinct. If you watch the fight, the block wasn't the most perfect block by any means. I just kind of like saw it at the last second and reacted, turned my leg and lifted it up slightly and he caught me.'

Evans turned his body as he threw the kick, putting as much power behind the strike as he could muster; unfortunately for him, his lower shin landed on the much harder upper shin of his young opponent, catching him just beneath the knee. In a striker's parallel to the grappling injury suffered by Windy Tomomi, the force of the contact was so great that it instantly fractured both tibia and fibula bones, causing his foot and the detached section of bone in his shin to swing independently from the rest of his leg, curling round to a grotesque angle.

'To do such damage to his leg and not mine, it was a bit of a weird one, I don't think anyone could ever explain why his leg broke and not mine, it's not like I've got super-strong legs that are made of steel or anything like that, it's just the way it happened you know. I think he threw everything he had into that kick, like I said, there was a bit of animosity before the fight a bit of tension, so I think he's just tried to come out and hit me with the biggest kick he's got, so I blocked it and, yeah, his leg broke!'

However, as Pettifer was keen to point out, he did not register that his opponent had suffered a serious injury for several seconds after it occurred, 'I'm one of these people I don't watch people's eyes or their feet because then I'm obviously only watching where his feet are going to go or where his hands are going to go, I watch his chest, like the middle of his chest, then you can look up, you can look down, you can look left or you can look right. I just thought he had fallen over, I thought he had fallen over, tripped, or slipped, so I've run in to go for the kill, kind of.' Diving in to protect the fallen fighter, the referee pulled him away before he could do any further damage, but the injury had been done, 'I looked down and saw his leg was a bit messed up and I still don't think I really realised and I went back to my corner and there were different people telling me what happened.'

According to Pettifer, Evans did not take kindly to suffering such a terrible injury, and went out of his way to get even with his young opponent; as Ross suggests, he sunk to some extraordinarily distasteful depths in an attempt to do it, 'Rob Evans went on the internet after the fight as well and got very personal, slagging off my mum and my grandma, telling me he was going to rape my grandma, rape my mother and things like this. He was told to be at a show that I was then going to attend to discuss this further with him and he didn't attend that show, after he said he would do. Then he went on the internet and done the whole thing about how he wants a rematch and he would have won the fight if his leg hadn't broke.'

'The fight was about five years ago now and him calling me out was about four years ago.' Ross said, 'I answered that back then, if he really wants to fight, he can find a show that's willing to put him on as a fighter and I'll fight him. That's just the fighter's way, to fight any comers. I don't think it would be a great boost to my career to fight the guy but I think that anyone who insults your family in public, you are more than happy to fight.'

A rematch between the two would be enthralling, but is unlikely to materialise; instead, Ross is left modestly pondering the reactions of over 50,000 people who have viewed the fight on Youtube. 'Obviously, yeah, it feels nice, it's nice to have a little bit of recognition. It wasn't that I did anything special; I think he did more work in the fight than me, all I did was block his kick. He kicked and broke his leg. It was quite a decent pay day for a little bit of work. It still gets mentioned now, it still gets brought up; it's flying all over the Facebooks and the Myspaces. It's nice, but it's not like I went out and knocked him out with a big head kick or a big elbow, so I can't really claim a massive victory for it, it was a win, he broke his leg I won, that's it at the end of the day, I can't say I did much more than that. At the end of the day, what did I really do, Jim?' Pettifer asked rhetorically.

'I stood there, blocked his kick, looked pretty, got a bit angry at the end; that was about it!' he laughed, 'The guy did say a lot of negative things the day of the fight and the day before, so when he's gone down, I've gone for him. When I saw his injury I realised that he hadn't slipped and that he was injured so it was left there. After the fight I came back and apologised for trying to get to him after he was injured, but at the time, I hadn't realised that he was hurt.'

CHAPTER FIFTEEN
GRUDGE MATCHES

'If you are going to put two guys who genuinely don't like each other with bad feeling there you got to expect sometimes for that to spill over and you've got to be prepared for that. So, don't cause a reaction and then complain when you get it.'

- Jeremy 'Bad Boy' Bailey

The vast majority of mma bouts are between two emotionally detached sportsman: the cage is simply their workplace and their opponent, a like-minded individual who also craves the excitement and competition of a mixed martial arts fight. However, the sport of mma attracts confident, larger-than-life personalities like no other and with so many boisterous, competitive egos incompatibly vying for the top spots, every so often fighters conflict, tempers flare and a grudge match is born.

It is easily possible to argue that fights of this kind draw negative publicity to the sport and give the casual viewer the clear impression that mma is nothing but a theatre for street-fights. Yet, almost every time harsh words are shared in the run up to the bout, any hard feelings between combatants are released within the rules - and, win, lose or draw, the opposing fighters end up drinking with one another at the after-show party.

However, some fights are different. Sometimes feuds go beyond the point of no return and the fighters involved hate each other with such an undying passion, that even the most vicious contest cannot fully exorcise the ill-feeling. The legendary war between Brazilian fighters Alex de Souza and Roberto Atalla is a prime example of such a bitter rivalry.

Full Contact Fight Night 1:
Alex de Souza vs Roberto Atalla

This mother of all grudge matches, widely described as the most heated fight in the history of UK mma, took place in a venue far away from the spotlight of the big show, instead finding its place on a small but well-supported event in Portsmouth on 11 April 2004.

Incredibly, the source of the bad blood between the two fighters was petty dispute which erupted on an internet forum; as it turns out, the disagreement was so inconsequential neither party can remember exactly how the argument started or ever managed to get so sincerely out of hand. 'I think for some reason, we disagreed on a few points,' da Souza said, straining his memory to recall the details. 'I think I didn't know him and he didn't know me, I probably didn't know what I was getting myself into, same as him. He didn't know what he was getting into as well. We exchanged a few words on the internet and we ended up sorting that out in the old fashioned way.'

'I was happy that someone paid the purse for us to fight – I wish that all my troubles were sorted that way, getting paid to fight someone that you don't like!' the Brazilian laughed, 'That sounded quite good! But to be honest with you I didn't even know how it begun. It was some sort of argument at the time, some bad things that I try to forget really. It started in a silly argument which escalated until it had to be settled that way.'

Atalla's memory was equally patchy, but slightly less hazy, 'The problems started when he called me about a post I wrote on the forums, he was cordial and we finished our talk and he seemed to be pleased and next day he posted shit attacking me and challenging me and that's how it started. I can't really say how it escalated out of control. I believe he thought he was defending the territory. His friends from his city proposed the fight to me and I took it. Now I realize,' Atalla paused, 'it's not wise to take a fight in the guy's place, with his friends doing the event, the chances are that if you do not end the fight, the decision will not be yours. But I really wanted this fight so I didn't care at the time.'

Casting his mind back to the actual fight, da Souza remembered the unique setting for what turned out to be a vicious and bloody battle. 'It was a small ring, a very tiny ring; they crowded all around the ring. The lighting on the show wasn't that great, there was only one light on the ring and it looked a bit like "Fight Club."' He added with a chuckle.

Though Atalla swears that the most significant damage of the fight was caused by a head butt, his opponent disagrees, 'Early in the fight, I landed a right hand on his nose, then there was a lot of blood', he recalled, 'Roberto was on top for the majority of the fight and he dripped a lot of blood on me; on my chest, on my face, I was covered in blood, it was as if I worked in a butcher's shop. It didn't help because I had bleached my hair and it turned pink. My shorts were white as well so they were covered in blood. It looked mean,' he laughed, 'but that's how it was.'

'I was quite angry,' da Souza continued, 'my corner was telling me to do some technical stuff, but as soon as I got in there, technique went out the window. It was a hatred fight really; we wanted to hurt each other, I think that's why it went 30 minutes. In a normal fight, the amount of blows that I threw at him, I think if it's a normal fight and you don't hate someone, if it's a sport, you'd say, "No thanks, I've had enough", but he didn't want to give up as much as I didn't, so that's how it went.'

As one might expect, the fight itself also lives on vividly in Atalla's mind 'Not many people fight so intensely for 30 minutes and both of us went the extra mile, cut or no cut, injuries or not, on that day we gave our lives inside that ring, no one denies that. If anything at all affected our performance on that day, it was the will to inflict injury on the other. Thankfully neither of us had any serious harm and we are both going ahead with our lives.'

After the 30-minute time limit expired, the brutal contest was declared a draw, a verdict that Atalla accepts, but cannot agree with. 'I watched it over and over to try and understand the result but every time I see it again I am sure I was robbed on the judge's decision.'

Da Souza, however, remains to be convinced of this, 'I damaged him more than he damaged me, I wasn't bloodied at all; all the blood was his. He couldn't actually land any clean shots on me. It's difficult for me to comment on a fight I didn't win. He had his merits and I had mine as well. I need to respect him; he fought me for 30 minutes. It's long time to be fighting, 30 minutes, but I could have gone another round, I wanted to go another round; I don't know about him though, he was in pretty bad shape, he looked like the Elephant man at the end of the fight.'

Several years after the fight and with the dust long settled, neither fighter can expect to receive a Christmas card from the other, but they both seem roughly contented to go about their own business, trying their very best to ignore each other's existence. 'No, we're not friends,' da Souza said pointedly, 'but we respect each other. We're not friends, but I've got nothing against the guy. He's pursuing his dreams and going after what he wants in life and the same with me.'

'We have no communication at all,' Atalla confirmed, 'he lives in England and I live in Poland, I haven't seen him or heard much from him after the fight and do not have any feelings, bad or good.' He said, before hinting at a remaining thorn of frustration in his side, 'Just recently he made a highlight of that fight and used the three minutes he was better off and posted it on Youtube. I wrote complaining and he replied, but I am too busy to really care, I have actually left this thing alone and now focus on my gym in Poland and my network of clubs.'

Cage Rage 8:
Jeremy 'Bad Boy' Bailey vs. Phil Gildea

Among the most memorable fights in Cage Rage history – and easily the most hate-filled war I have ever attended – was this classic rematch between the Original 'Bad Boy', Jeremy Bailey and one of the angriest men on earth, Phil Gildea. There was an air of hate around the cage that day that I had never before witnessed, or since seen repeated; both fighters entered the arena intent on doing the worst possible damage to one another and it showed.

Unsurprisingly, the bad vibe between the two fighters stemmed from their first encounter, when Bailey was able to catch his foe in a guillotine at Cage Rage 2. 'In all honesty, I didn't want to fight him again. What happened is, he submitted, he tapped out as was shown in the replay, he then proceeded to make some comment about my younger brother and my mum, which is an absolute no-go; it's not acceptable. So from then on there was bad feeling and to be honest with you, we arranged to have a meet out of the show,' Not a meet up in the sense of, a cup of tea and a slice of cake, 'meet up' in the sense of a vicious, bare-knuckle scrap taking place away from public view.

'Obviously it doesn't sound too professional,' Bailey admitted frankly, 'but we just genuinely didn't like each other, so we arranged to have a meet and basically settle our differences. That didn't come about it didn't happen. I was offered to fight him again, but I turned it down because for me, career-wise in mma, there's nothing for me to gain out of fighting him, I'd already beaten him once fair and square. I credit the guy with the fact that he's strong, he's durable, he got a good chin, very aggressive, but he's one dimensional, unfortunately for him. Big balls will only get you so far… and then it will get you beat and that was the case.'

On this occasion, the Gods of war must have been watching and, as luck would have it, Bailey's opponent for Cage Rage 8 suddenly dropped out, leaving a Phil Gildea-sized gap on the fight card. 'Dave [O'Donnell] and Andy [Geer] offered me the fight,' the Basingstoke 'Bad Boy' said, 'I didn't want to take it, but if I didn't take that fight, I wasn't going to be on the show, so I took that fight. But, as I have said many times before,' Bailey added wearily, 'if you put two guys who genuinely don't like each other, opposite each other to fight, you've got to expect fireworks.'

Jeremy was quick to admit, however, that even before he had set foot inside the building that day, his unusually antagonistic antics in the run up to the fight had played a massive part in whipping up the frenzied, hateful atmosphere between the two combatants. In his pre-fight interview the previous day, Bailey had pushed for the strongest possible reaction from his opponent; 'I know that Phil Gildea is a loser,' he said to the cameras with a cocky smile, 'and that he plays with horses for a living – what kind of a man does that? Last time you tapped out Phil, everybody knows it, the cameras don't lie. This time you're getting knocked out; you're getting stretched out, mate,' he said, before pausing as if to refine his point, 'Tonight, I am going to beat every last little bit of breath right out of your body.'

When Gildea arrived for his interview, it appeared that he had heard Bailey's comments and he did not look at all happy. 'Jeremy,' he fumed, 'all I ask is that you trade hands with me tonight and I will knock you the fuck out!' he shouted angrily, aggressively charging towards the camera to underline his point.

Looking back at a crazy situation, Bailey was philosophical, 'Every fight is a battle and sometimes you can win the war psychologically. As I know that Phil is like myself in many ways, he's very highly strung, you know, he's quite an emotional guy. I think for me, once you've been fighting a long time, you realise that too much hate, too much anger can eat away at you and especially with the build up to a big fight. It's a big show and you've got the TV cameras, your family and friends are there, so I played the psychological game with him as well.

'Because he's so aggressive,' the Basingstoke fighter continued, 'people tend to give him a wide berth. He thinks that's out of fear, I think that's due to the fact that people just don't want to be around him. So I said some things which were basically intended to get his back up, take his mind off his game so he wasn't focussed, he wasn't concentrating.'

'Obviously, I was very psyched up for that fight as well. We got to the centre of the cage and he made another comment and said, "Come on then, do it now", so I did.' Bailey landed a glancing right hand which sent Gildea to the floor, an illegal pre-fight attack which temporarily threw the contest into jeopardy. 'You know, it was wrong, I ended up being disqualified which was the right decision. I won't advocate doing that but if you are going to put two guys who genuinely don't like each other with bad feeling there you got to expect sometimes for that to spill over and you've got to be prepared for that. So, don't cause a reaction and then complain when you get it.'

After taking the punch, Gildea was incensed and began pacing back and forth like a caged animal. 'I'll take a point off,' promised the referee, Grant Waterman, 'you'll have won that round – if you want to fight, we'll start the fight, if you don't want to fight, you don't have to do it.' Gildea, however, needed no second invitation and raised his hands; the tattooed warrior was irate and tore towards his opponent from the opening seconds of the fight. From Bailey's point of view, however, this volatile mindset did Gildea no favours. 'All he could think of in the fight was just pure aggression, hence why he didn't throw any combinations, he stuck to single shots – which is ideal, because if he's not throwing combinations, only single shots, you've only got to move out of the way of one.'

The fight itself was an untidy two round scrap, filled with posturing and wild single shots from both men. At one point, Gildea appeared so overcome with malicious intent that he dropped his hands and walked towards Bailey like a street assailant, but ultimately his unyielding aggression netted him very little genuine success and he was forced to settle for landing a series of ineffective low kicks.

As the fight wore on, Bailey began to see openings appearing in his opponent's defence, as he explained: 'we had basically got through the first round when I realised there was an opening, but I wasn't coming forward. I wanted to wear him down which was my game plan with Phil, to credit the fact that he's strong and he's durable, he looked to me at that point to be in the best shape I had ever seen him. I knew he'd been training with a good gym, he'd been doing a lot of boxing. I know he'd done some bare knuckle boxing, which I've done as well, I've fought some people that he's fought and stuff, I just thought, let's wear him down, we'll mentally wear him down, we'll physically wear him down and we'll pick him off when we're ready.'

Late in the second round, Bailey felt ready and surged forward with a hard right hand which landed flush on Gildea's jaw, sending him tumbling to the canvas once again. 'For me it went exactly according to plan – the only thing was that the redness kicked in', Bailey said in a dramatic understatement. With his opponent writhing on the canvas, trying to shake off the effects of this latest concussive blow, Jeremy launched himself into the air and came down hard with a spiteful two-footed stomp to the face of his dazed foe.

'I honestly, honestly mean this; I don't actually remember trying to stomp on his head.' Bailey said of the flying attack which brought an end to the contest, earning him a fully justified disqualification loss, 'but, I still maintain that I'm a trend setter,' he laughed, 'I got disqualified for stomping on his head, but after that Cage Rage brought in the open guard rule. I think it was more fighter's instinct and as I said, a bit of rage. It was wrong. I should really have left it at the right hand, I think he would have gone, I don't really have any excuses other than I lost my mind and concentration for a short while and was rightfully disqualified, but it was a good knock down!'

Matt Ewin vs. Damien Riccio

Another famous grudge match on the UK scene involves another equally hotheaded character, the infamous Damien Riccio who has been at loggerheads with Range fighter, Matt Ewin for years. Riccio is no stranger to confrontation, he once turned up unannounced at a seminar run by Robin Gracie and unceremoniously challenged the instructor to a bare-knuckle, no rules match and repeatedly head-butted the grappling instructor for several minutes until he submitted under the weight of the blows.

Ewin, on the other hand, is a friendly, mild-mannered fighter; however, Riccio had no trouble in getting under the Gloucester hard man's skin. 'It started when I was fighting Sol Gilbert', Ewin explained, 'My girlfriend of the time, she was watching and he pushed her or something and spat in her face and then went on the internet slagging her off and it all started from there really.'

Ewin was horrified to hear that the Frenchman had insulted his girlfriend in this way, but he was in no position to defend his girlfriend's honour at the time. 'I didn't know anything about it until afterwards in the car on the way home when she told me about it. I was literally in the cage fighting at the time so I couldn't do nothing about it. I didn't hear until later on and I wasn't too happy about it.'

Out to settle the score, Ewin received his chance to gain a measure of revenge over the Frenchman at Cage Rage 8; a bout apparently set up to allow the two seething fighters a chance to settle their differences, whilst at the same time gainfully employed. However, Ewin did not take his opportunity and spent the majority of the 7-minute fight, hovering around the outside, occasionally stepping forward with mild-mannered front kicks, until he walked onto a brutal left hook from the French fighter, sending him to the mat holding his eye in agony.

'In that fight I was messing around too much, throwing all the high kicks which I don't usually do. I was messing around and I got caught', Ewin recalled of the fight, before swiftly moving on to the second meeting between the pair, in the Coventry Skydome on the Cage Warriors... show. "The Hardest" gave his account of one of the most controversial fights held on one of the most talked about shows.

'He started off with a leg kick which took my leg away, so I got back up and took him down and that was it really, I just dominated from there', Ewin said frankly. 'He caught me with an elbow from the bottom which split my eye, it was a good shot that one. The ref stood us up to check [the cut], when we went back down again, he's pulled me in close and stuck his fingers in, trying to open it up a bit more. A big argument and everything else has kicked off with it. Funnily enough, he said he wanted to fight me again, but I haven't heard nothing back from him since.'

Fighting for position in a ground fight next to the cage is rarely a graceful affair, but Ewin is left with no doubt that Riccio intentionally pressed his fingers into the cut in order to dramatically increase the flow of blood. 'Oh yeah definitely, what he was doing was pulling me in and he's pushing his fingers, his knuckles into my eye into the cut, trying to open it up a bit more. I felt it rip, so I knew he did it. I was trying to pull my head away and he was pulling me into him. He tries to say that he was trying to stand up or whatever, but he was pulling my head in and pushing his knuckles into my eye – that's not trying to stand up.' After a heated debate in the cage, the fight was declared a no-contest.

As a result of this unfortunate outcome, Ewin would love to settle the score once and for all, but does not have high hopes for the kind of spectacle a third contest with Riccio would bring. 'I've got nothing against him either way, but

I've heard a few things about having another fight and that would be good! I think it would be a good fight, if he's there to fight, I'll fight him. That's what I'm here for, I enjoy the sport and I'd definitely step back in there. He wouldn't last long, I'm not sure he'd last out of the first round. I've come on a long way since that and I dominated him then.'

Cage Warriors Strike Force 3:
Mike Bisping vs. Jakob Lovstad

Bad feelings between fighters can often simmer for a long time before the characters involved have a chance to square off and settle their differences. In the case of Mike Bisping and Norwegian fighter Jakob Lovstad, it was not until the last moments before their fight on the Cage Warriors promotion that the two fighters suddenly took a dislike to one another, as the UK's most famous fighter, Mike Bisping explained. 'There was nothing before the fight, but backstage just before the fight, we were just a few feet away from each other and we were giving each other the eye – that's just kind of what you do.

'When we got into the middle of the cage, he was pulling stupid faces at me, that got my back up a little bit, he was a bit disrespectful and then he stuck his tongue out at me and he was making stupid noises, I just thought, "This guy isn't taking me seriously, he thinks I'm some kind of chump, with no technique, who's just some kind of stupid brawler." That was the impression I got and I said to him, "You're not going to be smiling in a minute", and he said, "We'll see about that", and I thought, "Here we go, we're in for a good fight here!"

Lovstad immediately shot in for a takedown, but quickly conceded that he had no chance of taking the British fighter down as he flopped to his back and began working his open guard. In a dominant position, Bisping began to demonstrate why he would go on to see such great success in the UFC as he unleashed a furious volley of punches which forced Jakob to turn to his side. The Lancastrian saw this as an invitation and banged in seven unanswered right hands as his opponent covered up. "Within 60 seconds or something he was tapping from strikes! So it just made me laugh a little bit.'

Bisping roared with laughter as he his opponent capitulated and stuck two fingers up at his opponent to let him know who was boss. 'Mike there, keeping up foreign relations with a bit of sign language!' commentator, Ian Butlin noted with a laugh.

'But he's a tough guy…' Bisping added cheerfully, trying his best not to appear disrespectful, with a tongue-in-cheek, but heartfelt compliment. 'I'd just like to say that Jakob Lovstad is an incredible fighter who's been on a roll recently, good luck to Jakob! Make me look good, or I'll hunt you down and chop your legs off!' he warned, breaking down with laughter once again.

Cage Rage Contenders 4:
Sol Gilbert vs. Darren Guisha

Another friendly face on the UK scene is former boxer, Sol Gilbert; but as Essex fighter, Darren Guisha found out to his painful cost, the Brighton fighter is not someone whom you would ever wish to cross. "There was a bit of rivalry in that one', Gilbert explained of their Cage Rage Contenders clash. 'I never really have any bad blood with any of my opponents, but with him I did. He took a liberty with one of my students on another show, UKMMA. I was working in the corner, Jack [Magee] had him in an ankle lock, he started heel kicking Jack to the back of the head from a grounded position and I was like, "Look that's a foul."'

The tattooed fighter's blood came to the boil as Guisha once again tried his best to break the rules. 'Then when Jack had another submission on, he started pulling his hair, real dirty, but because it was in his own local area, Purfleet, he managed to get away with it. There and then I was like, "Mate, you took a liberty with one of my guys, I think you and I should get it on", and he was like, "Yeah ok." Straight away, I spoke to Dave [O'Donnell], Dave managed to sort the fight. I wanted to punish him. I really wanted to punish him.'

Gilbert found the perfect way to make Guisha suffer as he kept the fight at a kickboxing range, consistently landing with heavy right low kicks. 'It's something that I've perfected as I've practised and trained. I try to look at what works best for my style, so I wouldn't necessarily be going for big high headkicks or anything else and I knew that he'd been doing a lot of training at Keddles. So I geared myself towards that, I like a challenge, so I thought "Let's try and keep it standing." I took him down to see what he had on the floor, just to soften him up and see how he was. I knew from the moment I took him down that I could have got a submission or finished him with ground-and-pound, so I thought, "Let's see what he's got standing", and kicked him around the cage for a couple of rounds.'

Mixing punches in with his sharp low kicks, Gilbert bossed the entire contest, dragging Guisha out of his comfort zone and punishing him at every opportunity. The Zero Tolerance Fight Skool founder repeatedly landed a range of shots, 'Especially overhand rights,' Sol explained, 'because of the way he was moving around, he was always moving one side, so I was cutting down the angle. Then I started to mix it up, throwing two or three punches and then finishing with my leg, or start with my leg and finish with my hands, go up and down really. There's a sequence of shots in the end. Still, he seemed really resilient on his legs and he managed to keep going, but every time I was kicking that lead leg, he was wincing in pain, but he still kept going.'

Although he was loving every minute as he meted out his harsh retribution, Gilbert was determined to finish the fight inside the distance, a feat he accomplished mid way through the final round with a stream of spiteful, unanswered punches to the head from rear mount. 'At the beginning of the third round I thought, even though I was enjoying it, it was going to be seen that he's taken me three rounds. So when he came in, I took him down and finished with ground-and-pound. There was malice in that one, you know what I mean? But afterwards, as soon as it had been done, we shook hands and he was, like "Yeah, right, point taken, I understand", and he took it on board, we shook hands and that's it sorted.'

Fighting your friends

In combat sports, there will always be grudge matches between rival fighters and camps, though on the flip side of that coin, by going through the incredible hardship of their gruelling training regimes and knowing full well that their opponent is going through an equally unpleasant time in preparation can breed a deep professional respect between fighters.

Frequently, mma competitors will have met at previous events and socialised with each other or even trained together, striking up a decent rapport before being matched up to fight with their new found friend. This can cause havoc with match-making, as promoter Dave O'Donnell explained, 'In London, fighters are not happy to train in one gym at the moment, so they do Thai Boxing, wrestling, mixed martial arts classes. Training full time, they are nipping into every club they can and guys who would be fighting a bit later down the line, good example of that is Brad Pickett and Ashleigh Grimshaw, ideal fight for later down the line, but they've been sparring partners for the last three months. You know what I mean, it's just a shame because it ruins a good fight, but I suppose they've got to do it to progress and move to the international scene.'

Cage Rage 12:
Mark Epstein vs. Matthias Riccio

However, for the London promoter, this does not always cut out the possibility of two friends being matched up together, as he proved at Cage Rage 12 When two good friends, South London brawler, Mark Epstein and Matthias Riccio, brother of Damien, were slated to face each other. 'We done a couple of shows together.' Epstein remembered clearly, 'You get to know people and you kind of click with some people when you meet people and me and him, we clicked, mate. We were pals straight away. It did feel strange, but it's business', the big punching former-heavyweight said, before promising to beat the Frenchman and 'get a little taste of Frogs legs', in his pre-fight interview.

Epstein was forced to absorb some very snappy low kicks from the Thai boxing Frenchman at the start of the bout, but set about earning his money in typically aggressive fashion; beautifully countering a takedown attempt from his opponent to put Riccio on the floor himself and proceeding to batter the Frenchman with punches. 'The Beast' was merciless, raining down a series of elbows, punches and hammerfists until his opponent's face was a bloody mess; it came to a point however, when Epstein simply did not want to continue and looked over at the referee as if to invite his intervention.

'I looked at Matthias and even though his eyes were open it looked like he was out, a few times. He weren't really defending himself. That's the thing with those French guys they've got great stand up, but the ground game they don't really work on it so much, you know and he paid the price, but I have as well!' Epstein laughed, referring to more than a couple of submission losses on his resume.

'I thought the ref should have stopped it a bit sooner… apparently I fractured his eye socket and cheekbones and stuff. I've given him about three fractures in his face. But I'm not in this to hurt people; I don't get off with hurting people. I do like spectacular stoppages; that's what the crowd want. But I'm not in this to hurt people but it's business at the end of the day, and I've got to do the business until the referee says quit, you know, "That's enough", or the guy gives up, but Matthias would never give up, there's people who would never give up from the ground-and-pound. I think the ref was right, but I would have stopped it sooner.'

Since the fight, it has been business as usual for the two friends, 'I chatted to him after the fight. I still chat to him now on Myspace. We're pals, I talk to him on Myspace and stuff. Yeah mate, he's alright,' Epstein laughed, 'He's alright, he's good stuff.'

UFC 80: Paul Taylor vs. Paul Kelly

One of the most notable friendships between combatants came to the fore in the first UFC fight to take place between two British UFC fighters, the unforgettable contest between the kickboxing machine of Paul Taylor and the ground-and-pounding Liverpudlian dangerman, Paul Kelly. Both fighters had the utmost of respect for one another in the pre-fights interviews, politely passing up my invitation to add some controversy to the fight through some gentle trash-talking. However, with an eye on the healthy UFC Fight of the Night bonus, the two warriors promised to set aside their friendship and go all out for victory.

The opening seconds of the contest provided one of the most exciting passages of action in any UK event as they tore into one another with both fighters swinging for the fences. Paul Taylor came off the noticeable winner of the early exchanges, but his Wolfslair opponent called him into exchange after exchange, shouting to himself as he revelled in his own vitality. Kelly looked back on the memorable toe-to-toe exchanges, promising that he always intended to stand and trade punches at close range.

'That was always my intention,' he began in his thick Liverpool accent, 'if you ever saw me sparring in the gym, because I'm only short you see and to fight a bigger opponent, I need to take away his range. I would have been daft to stand outside of range and try to fight with Paul Taylor at a kickboxer's pace. That's his game isn't it? He's going to pick me off with leg kicks, head kicks and big, long rangy shots - so the game plan from the start was to get stuck right in! I'm quite a durable guy, I do a lot of exercises to my jaw and my neck, every single day before I go to bed, I do 100 neck curls... so I don't really mind getting hit as long as I can hit them back.'

On the night, 'Relentless' Paul Taylor was more than happy to engage his opponent in a close-quarter stand up battle, but it was not something the Midlands fighter ever planned to do, as he explained. 'I think personally, for me, I find I get quite easily drawn into a scrap on the night. If somebody stands toe-to-toe and trades with me, my game plan goes out the window. How do I put it, my ego gets the better of me and I'll stand in front of anybody and just throw shots. It just threw me off my game; it's not how I fight generally.'

His gamble paid off handsomely, however, as Taylor landed some crisp punches in the exchange, backing his opponent up and giving him sound reason to reassess his options in the fight. 'Fair play to Paul', Kelly said, in congratulation, 'He's got a decent chin on him. When you look back on the video, I hit him quite a few times do you know what I mean? Paul has got some hard hands, but from watching that, I was the more technical striker.

'As he was throwing those looping shots – obviously, I come from a striking background, all I'm looking for is straight line, get there as quick as I can and as hard as I can – then get my hands back to cover my head from these looping shots. I think I hardly got hit in that first exchange, it was all on the gloves. He did well to soak up the shots,' Taylor noted, 'but after that he didn't want none of it, obviously, he put me in my worst position which was flat on my back!'

Kelly, however, insisted that he was not hurt in the exchanges, instead playing to his strengths by taking the fight to the ground. 'The game plan with Paul was to get stuck right in and I enjoyed that. I really fuckin' enjoyed us both swinging for the fences and both hitting each other. He did have the better of the exchange, but I wasn't taking him down because he hurt me. I listened on the commentary and they said, "Paul Kelly got caught a few times in that exchange and now he's looking to take it to the ground", that's because, that's my game, to take it to the ground.

'I'm not going to stand there and lose on points, or at worst, get knocked out. If the fight would have carried on like that, he would have definitely have won on points, he was landing the cleaner shots of the two of us', he humbly admitted.

Once grounded, Kelly went to work with punches and elbows from top position, tracing the blue print of a game plan which has helped him cause a great deal of damage to opponents in the past. 'I remember hitting him with five clean elbows square in the face, coming down across his face with the elbow on the top, where the cut began. I hit him about five or six times and I thought, "What's going on? Why isn't he cutting?", and he was going cockeyed as I was hitting him, you could hear the bump on the floor, I was putting all my weight into it. I think that's what softened him up.'

As the contest wore on, Kelly noticed that his steady ground attack was starting to have an effect on the middle of Taylor's forehead, damaging the skin and making it an ideal target for his razorsharp elbows. 'The elbow came over the top, kind of like an overhand right and glanced past his face and that's what cut him. It was already softened and swollen, right in the middle of his forehead.

'You can sort of see the area of swelling', Kelly said, talking generally about the effects his solid strikes have on an opponent's forehead. 'If they don't cut straight away a load of blood gathers underneath the skin, and this always happens, every time. If that goes all soft and tender, it only takes – a big heavy one probably would cut it, but you know that little one which glances past it? And just touches it? That's when I cut a slice right through it. It's like a balloon filling up with water and just nicking it, the water all pisses out, doesn't it?'

Taylor, however, was determined not to take his beating lying down and despite the cut, fired back a series of punches from his own guard. 'When he hit me, all I wanted to do was hit him back, I wasn't thinking about pulling him down and tying him up, which is everything I normally do in the gym, and everything I do when I spar, but all I wanted to do was hit him, I was just out of my game plan.

'To be honest, I've got quite a hard head,' Taylor chuckled, 'so it wasn't terrible at all. I was frustrated more than anything. Especially looking back, I was frustrated with myself for the position I'd found myself in and the fact that I was sitting there trading shots, instead of bringing his head down, tying him to trying to get back to my feet - all this stuff that I drilled in the gym to be honest went out of the window, I just got drawn into a scrap and that's what happened in a fight.'

Both of the granite-chinned warriors absorbed some hard shots, yet after taking the fight to the floor, Kelly was still not in a comfortable position. 'He was fighting for guard and he was catching guard all the time. Paul is a real soldier. At one point, I was butting his elbows, he was elbowing me in the top of the head and I thought, how do I stop these, I've no way of stopping them and I found myself butting his elbows at one point!'

The more damaging blows, however, were landed by the Liverpudlian and once the blood began to flow from his face, Taylor understood the seriousness of his predicament. 'I looked over and see the blood and you can see on the DVD and I said "Oh fuck!", when I'd seen the drip dripping. I just thought, I'm cut, he's going to stop the fight now. Luckily in was in the middle of my head, it stopped bleeding, didn't drip into my eyes. So there was no need to stop the fight. My only concern really, was that they were going to stop the fight. At the end of the day, a couple of stitches later and week after and you're back at it aren't you?'

Whilst Taylor had every confidence his injuries would heal in a relatively short space of time, Kelly remained focussed on the task at hand and had no problem with targeting his opponent, and friend's, cut with vicious punches and elbows. 'I'm not being cold-hearted when I say this,' Kelly cautioned, 'but we're in a fight, you know? This is what you expect. Either way, I'm going to come out the same, I'm not going to change my approach to the way I fight, I'm going to come out and try and be first.

'I've bled in a fight, I bled against Sami Berik, but I finished the fight. He hit me with an elbow on top of the head, it was right on the top of the head and it was pissing with blood. So I knew I had to finish the fight. If I know I'm bleeding, I know I've got to drastically do something or I'm going to lose, it's inevitable.

'I don't feel sorry for the guy,' Kelly continued, 'if he could cut me, he'd most likely cut me… the thing with me is, I'm not a nasty fighter. I don't wish anything bad on anyone that I fight. I'd sooner give them a hug, shake their hand and wish them the best of luck before I go in and in that way, it sort of makes me feel a little bit better especially if they want to make it personal, and they want to keep that head game where they have to be angry with their opponent and a lot of guys do. It sort of knocks them when I go over and give them a hug and go, "Good luck, mate, hope you do well!"'

After sharing the cage for 10 minutes of pure action, the two fighters met one another in the centre of the cage and hugged before resuming their hostile battle, in a virtually unprecedented move. Paul Taylor explained in conclusion; 'I've seen him on the circuit and all the rest of it and it was just a mark of respect. "We've had two good rounds, let's come out and make this another good one in the third!" We got fight of the night for it, so we both come out better than when we went into it. The hug was just a sign of respect, fair play to him, this is the last round, let's keep it in the same vein!'

CHAPTER SIXTEEN
WARS

'We were really fighting, it wasn't like mma; we were really fighting. Now mma is; everybody's going to take you to the ground, put you in an armbar, but there was no technique to that it was just toe-to-toe. Good days you know'
- 'Dirty' Bob Schrieber

The spectacle of a fighter scoring a quick knock out, or the wizardry of a dominant submission fighter sealing another 40-second tap out win is very entertaining to the viewing public and is enough in itself to garner wide interest in the sport. However, close contests in which both fighters refuse to take a backwards step, absorbing their share of punishment in a relentless effort to win the day are worth their weight in gold to a promoter and bring audiences back in their droves.

As the first UFC show to be broadcast for free to millions of homes in America on Spike TV, main event fighters Stefan Bonnar and Forrest Griffin were given the perfect opportunity to showcase their skills and make an impact on this new audience. The incredible back-and-forth contest which took place has gone down in the record books as one of the most entertaining fights in the history of the sport and served as a massive boost to the growth of mainstream interest in the sport in America and around the world.

One American fighter who shocked the world a decade before was Frank Shamrock, who came through some of the sport's wildest and most famous stand up exchanges, coming back in spectacular fashion to claim victory over fearless jiu-jitsu master, Enson Inoue after a famous brawl in Japan.

Japan Vale Tudo 1997:
Frank Shamrock vs. Enson Inoue

'That was a wild and crazy fight.' Shamrock began, 'The thing I always remember most about it was the moment where, in the second round, he kind of folded me over backwards and was elbowing my head. I remember that moment fairly vividly because I thought I was going to die there, it was a really surreal experience and I kind of sucked it up and kept going.'

Shamrock was able to force his way back to his feet and he and his fearless Japanese opponent went to war in some of the wildest exchanges the sport has ever seen. 'It reminds me of a bad movie, where two guys are just clubbing each other and you know that somebody is going to fall soon. I was real lucky that I wasn't that guy', Frank said with an obvious tone of relief.

The pair swung wildly with punches and kicks before Shamrock was able to grasp hold of Inoue's head and send a pair of concussive knees into his Japanese opponent's face. As he stumbled to the ground the American stepped in to pound his fallen opponent, Egan Inoue leapt to his brother's assistance and eliminated the danger by barging Shamrock directly onto his head. 'I wasn't mad at him,' Frank said graciously of an incident which could easily have broken his neck. 'I didn't know what was going on to be honest with you. I knew that something had happened and that I was on my head and I didn't really like it. But I wasn't really mad, I just wanted people to get off me!' he laughed.

UFC 22: Frank Shamrock vs. Tito Ortiz

This incredible battle in the land of the rising sun, however, gained nowhere near as much attention as his a contest several fights down the line with a confident young fighter by the name of Tito Ortiz. The bleach-blonde mauling-machine had been on a tear over his last four fights blowing each of his opponents away inside the distance. However, for a 25-year old Frank Shamrock at the peak of his physical powers, Frank saw the challenge of this rough upstart as the perfect opportunity to demonstrate his skills in full flow.

'That was a fight that I had probably planned and executed better than any other fight that I have ever done' Shamrock said, 'It was kind of a new level for me, just in physical understanding and the technical understanding of the fight. I also knew that, deep down, Tito didn't think that he could beat me and that was a huge factor that I drew on and that's the reason why I mocked him and teased him, because half of the battle was making Tito tired and the other half was convincing Tito that he couldn't beat me.'

The Californian began to show signs of distress at the end of the second round as a hard elbow to the back from Shamrock made him wince and complain to referee, John McCarthy. Frank piled on more misery as he stepped up the intensity of his psychological game plan. 'I was talking to him good and what's hard to see – Muhammad Ali, when he would do fights, he would talk to the crowd and he would talk to everybody and he would talk to himself and he would talk out loud - when I talk to people, I just lean over and I talk in their ear, so only they hear it and they can do what they want with it.

'In the second round, I could tell Tito wanted to say something back, in defence of the talking. I was just telling him that I was going to knock him out and I was just telling him that I was way better than he was and that he wasn't fast enough' - a point which he then tried to reinforce in his opponent's mind which action.

'When I would tell him those things I would move real fast, I'd say, "Look, you're not fast enough!", and I would do a quick movement and make him work a little bit to kind of solidify it. When we stood up in the second round, I hit him with those elbows in the kidneys and the mid-back area and I could tell they hurt, I could hear from his exclamations that I got him good.'

As the fight wore on Shamrock opened up a significant lead with a series of hurtful kicks to the body: 'I was kicking him real good and at that time I was just getting my confidence standing, I was just getting over the hump on understanding that ability. Part of my strategy was to just swing for the fences and scare him a little bit.'

In the fourth round, the action returned to the floor, 'I could hear him breathing hard and he was really tiring. He started talking back to me by then. I was telling him, "You're getting tired",

'...and he was saying, "No, I'm not."'

'I was telling him, "I'm going to get up right now and knock you out",

'... and he said, "No, you're not."'

'I knew that I had him in the psychological realm, he was questioning himself and distracted from the event itself. I was working from a nice open guard and was just waiting for him to catch his breath and relax; you've got to relax some time. He was real tight and real tense the whole time, so I was waiting for that moment and he gave it to me.'

The second Ortiz let himself relax for a second, Shamrock was there to pounce and mid-way through the second round, he swept his way off the bottom, 'It wasn't so much a conscious decision as a reaction as I felt that he had relaxed. When I flipped him over, that quick spin and turn is a drill that we do for getting back into action, a conditioning drill.'

The submission fighter stormed in with a blistering two handed attack, 'I figured I would whack him a few times and he would drop unconscious and I would celebrate in victory, I was pretty surprised when he managed to get me down after that!' Shamrock laughed, 'But I could tell that he was done, physically and mentally and there's that point where I'm front choking him and I wasn't so much choking him and you can't see it, but my hand is open, underneath, and over his nose and mouth, so more than choking him, I was smothering him when he really needed that oxygen and it forced him to push himself over and once he had jumped over – and once he had gave up position, then he was done.'

In the home straight, Shamrock rose to his feet and delivered a savage right elbow before whipping in three vicious hammerfists which forced a battered and exhausted Tito Ortiz to submit. 'I was tired, man,' Shamrock explained, 'that was a hard fight. I was pretty tired, but at the same time, I was just super-exhilarated because, even though I was tiring, I was really excited about the technical game I was playing, I could feel it. It was like I was driving a race car and there was nothing in the way, I could feel it going so well - that was a really nice feeling for me.'

Extreme Brawl 6:
Mark 'The Wizard' Weir vs
Alex 'The Reidenator' Reid

'I did get quite bashed up in that, and I know I bashed him up, we threw a lot of leather!' Alex Reid laughed as he looked back on one of the most talked about fights in UK mma history. 'It was definitely seen as one of the best fights for a couple of years!' Though, after the first lop-sided meeting between the two fighters, not many people gave Reid a chance, least of all, his opponent, Mark Weir.

'That first fight was more one sided,' the Gloucester fighter said, 'in the second fight, I think I was slightly too confident, thinking, "Ah, he couldn't take my punches last time, this should be straight forward." With him, I think he trained even harder because of the way I destroyed him in the first fight. It's a tipping of the scale, my confidence allowed me to be more vulnerable and his determination to erase that defeat make him trainer harder and perform even better.'

Reid started brightly in their clash on Berkshire's Extreme Brawl promotion, landing a powerful right hand directly on his opponent's jaw in the opening seconds of the fight. 'It was a right hand, he came to me', Reid said, explaining his opponent's mindset. 'He thought "Right, I'm going to take him out straight away", because at the time, he was pretty awesome, he was blitzing people. He came at me, I was very tight, very technical. I'd been working on my kickboxing a great deal for that fight because I knew Mark was a stand up guy.

'He stormed at me and I caught him with a straight right, between the acceleration of my punch and him coming onto it, it was very devastating. I was like, "Wicked, I've got him!" and I just didn't manage to follow up. He's tough, because he recovered. You see it so much in mma, someone catches someone and they think it could be the end of the fight and they manage to recover.'

For Mark Weir, making his way back into the contest was a matter of pride, 'As soon as I went in I got caught, right on the chin. I remember being shook and thinking, "There is no way this guy is going to beat me!" I remember thinking about the humiliation if he had won!'

At the time, however, Reid genuinely felt that the fight was his, 'I really thought I had it, but my success was also my downfall in a way because I went into "War mode", but I'm usually a much more technical fighter than that. I kept trying to really take him out, brawl him, which is very exciting for the fans, but strategically, as a fighter, "Take a hit to give a hit?"

'You want to be giving the hits and not taking them; standing in front of each other and seeing who's the toughest is great fun when you're in the heat of the battle, but there's only so much that your body can take and I think it's those sorts of fights that make your longevity in the sport a bit less. Look at Wanderlai [Silva], he's just bashed his body so much, your body can only respond like that for so long.'

At the time, however, Weir, the usually elusive traditional striker, was more than happy to stand at close distance and exchange punches. 'I remember thinking, "If he wants to trade then we'll trade, I'm not going to back down." I thought I was going to be the last man standing. I believed that I had the stronger of the two chins as well and because I had my kicks, which always seem to be my saviour. That in the end is what tipped the scale, a few heavy round kicks to the face, the bridge of the nose, but he was really durable that day, he was really determined.'

Weir's kicks had a telling effect as they opened up Reid's face and forced him out of the contest, 'The bugger caught me with a nice kick, I had to have nose reconstruction surgery after that!' the London Shootfighter protested, 'He cut my nose so bad, the bone was showing, pretty disgusting, but you don't worry about getting a scar at the time, you don't worry about anything like that.'

Cage Rage Contenders 4:
Lloyd Clarkson vs. Dan Mohavedi

In a lesser known battle, but one in which both combatants went all out for victory was the brutal four minute war between Poole Jiu-Jitsu trained Lloyd Clarkson and Elite representative, Dan Movahedi. 'I felt nervous obviously,' the Londoner said as he chased after his first win. 'I had a good corner with me, no problems, I just felt really good and just let it all hang out in there – I enjoyed it. I can't remember much of the fight; when I watch the DVD I go, "Oh yeah! Did I do that? Phoar!"'

The two fighters went toe-to-toe through the fight in some of the most exciting exchanges ever seen on the Contenders show, however, at one point it appeared that Clarkson was using rope-a-dope tactics, an extremely risky move in mma. I caught up with Lloyd at the weigh-ins for his clash with Adam Greener at FX3 and asked him why he chose such a risky strategy. 'He's bigger than me, I knew he was more cut than me and I wanted to wear him out so the plan was to wait till the second round – because I can take a hit – now that I've said that I'm going to get knocked out tomorrow, it's all your fault!' He laughed.

'It's a big one, taking hits', the Poole fighter said, 'I thought I'll wait, see if he wears himself out in the second round and I felt him blowing after about two minutes in I just covered up and let him work.

Movahedi banged in a varied assault, ranging from short hooks and uppercuts to solid knees to the body and low kicks; he appeared to hit his opponent with every strike in the book. 'Yeah', he agreed reluctantly, 'but they weren't good shots. I wasn't putting my hips into it and using my pivot – all credit to him, any other guy most probably would have gone down. With those first few knees, all I was thinking was, "Why aren't you going down?", and when he didn't, that's what made it a good fight. I personally really enjoyed it.'

There's no wonder Dan had fun, for the first two minutes it was one-way traffic, 'I remember seeing Grant to the side of me and I'm thinking, "He's got to stop it surely he's got to stop it now; his nose bleeding, surely he's got to stop it." Even with the leg kicks, I would kick him and kick him…' Movahedi said exasperated. 'I admit it, because I was going full out, I felt a bit gassed. Everyone said, "Ah, your cardio wasn't good" – it was! But you imagine 2 and a half minutes, full pace, knowing this guy is not going to go down so you're putting everything into it and he's coming back."

Clarkson was irritated by the suggestion that he was anywhere near being stopped. 'I was pretty happy to take the punishment. I'm not the most technical of fighters, so my plan is always to take 'em on, see what they are like after a couple of minutes. That was my theory for boxing as well, I've only had one fight where I've won in the first round, the rest have just been, crack on and wear them down, let them wear themselves out.

I was a bit pissed off really because I read a report that Grant was gonna call it when I was up against the side, I was like, "Man, I was nowhere near!"'

I may have been the author of the report in question, and in my defence, it was hard to see a way through for Clarkson at the time as Dan was seemingly throwing strikes as fast as his burly frame would allow him, and the vast majority of the blows were landing heavily on Clarkson's head, legs and body. Impressively, however, the Poole fighter held on to his competitive spirit, carefully picking his moment to throw a damaging counter punch.

'I waited for it; I'd been waiting and waiting because I practise it as a counter. I was waiting for him to come in, I was thinking that he was going to throw a right; he didn't, he just flinched, so I counter-punched that instant. If you get two big fighters toe-to-toe, it's just luck isn't it? So you just wait for the right moment.' Clarkson said, in an extremely humble assessment, considering the effort he was put in to capture victory. 'At the beginning of the fight he was covering up, I threw a few and they weren't hitting him, so I thought I'd just wait. Two or three minutes later, he was down, he was breathing heavily in the Thai clinch, I could hear he was shattered and just thought, any minute now, when you're like that, your arms come down… and I just waited.'

Battered, but unbowed, Clarkson whipped his left hook across, landing squarely on Movahedi's jaw, stopping the Elite fighter in his tracks. The stunned and exhausted Elite fighter tumbled backwards and out of the contest. 'At the end of the day, my safety comes first, if I wasn't defending myself, which I can't say I was, for a second I did go out, so I'm not going to complain about that! He could have landed another couple of shots that could have stopped me from ever fighting again. He got his credit, I got lazy, dropped my right hand and he hit me with a left hook, I can't take nothing away from him.'

However, that is not to say that the persistent Londoner would back down from a return challenge with his former conqueror. 'He'd definitely bring a different game; it would be a good fight and if they can get it on here again, I'd take it - why not?'

Cage Rage 7 & 9:
Mike 'The Count' Bisping vs.
Mark 'The Beast' Epstein

Long before he became a UFC star, Mike Bisping suffered from no lack of confidence as he strolled into the weigh-ins at Cage Rage 7, set to face South London hard man, Mark Epstein. The Clitheroe fighter was unimpressed by the footage he had managed to gather on his opponent and felt even more sure of himself having set eyes on his opponent. 'At the weigh-ins I thought, "Ah, I'm a bit taller than him," but he is a very well-built, stocky fella and having a bit of bravado, you know.' However, in fairness to the Clitheroe fighter, making his debut on a London show and surrounded by an army of muscular cockneys, Bisping did well not to show any sign of nerves at the press conference.

However, come fight time, it was a different story, 'When I walked in and the cage door shut behind me, first time and he was standing across from me. It was my first time in the cage, so I think that was playing with me psychologically. I remember hearing the cage door clink shut and I thought "Oh shit, this is a bit different to a kickboxing ring!"'

Bisping also had a live opponent to keep his attention; what the South Londoner lacks in stature, he more than makes up for in aggression, punch-power and durability; hardly the ideal opponent to be locked in with for your debut fight. Epstein also suffered from no lack of confidence, as his Northern opponent was about to discover.

'I've always known I had that one punch knock out, since I was a kid' The

Beast recounted, 'When I was out there playing naughty stuff in shops, trying to get this and that, store detectives, "Bam!", they're over; big guys, you know. I surprised myself, but since I was about 15 I knew I had that one punch power, it's just collecting it.'

However, in the first meeting between the pair, Epstein was unable to land his power shots and soon found himself running out of gas. 'I shot my load in the first round; second round I didn't have nothing. I'm not going to make no excuses, he finished me; I can't really say nothing, he's done his job. I was a bit gutted - well, I was very gutted, but I only had myself to blame.'

'It was good,' Bisping said, looking back on the Cage Rage 7 contest. 'It was the first time I'd been put under pressure in a fight, in the first round, but he didn't really do any damage at all. He took me down, tried to ground-and-pound, but I didn't sustain any damage. So once I got back to my feet I just thought I'd let it all go and I did and stopped him.'

Seething at this loss in front of his army of local support, Epstein trained like a man possessed for the rematch on the promotion and was in top fighting condition when he got in the car to travel to the venue. 'The thing is, I live in South East London, I started off in South East London going towards the Blackwall tunnel, I get to there and it's shut, so we've had to drive all the way from fucking West London, Paddington, some long thing. I've got there 15 minutes before the fight, I didn't even have the chance to warm up, wrap my hands, nothing. Just got straight in there, pretty much cold and got jabbed.'

Bisping used some vastly improved footwork to skip in and out of range, implementing some good head movement as he peppered Epstein with jabs. The future UFC star smashed him to the floor with an uncultured left in the first round and cruised into a clear lead in the second round behind a series of lunging jabs, right hands and inside low kicks.

However, after two bright rounds, Bisping's confidence began to get the better of him and he began waving his arms and playing to the crowd. 'He was being too cocky,' Epstein explained, 'he was winning the fight, I'll give him that, he was winning the fight clearly, but when someone takes the piss out of you that's a bit disrespectful, but that is Mike being a showman I suppose but, I found it a little bit disrespectful and it kind of give me a little bit more hate. I thought, "You what? You cheeky cunt"' Epstein used that thought to land one of the most effective low kicks of his career.

Bisping was happy to admit that he felt the chopping right low kick, 'I was doing really well, landing lots of good combinations and then in the third round he caught me with a real good leg kick, I walked onto it and he threw a great kick, not taking any credit away, but I walked onto it as well which gave it extra impact and, yeah, it really hurt! He'd seen that he'd hurt me and so he threw it a few more times, so I was limping around a little bit.'

'I knew I hurt him, it was nice after what he did before!' Epstein said laughing at the way his opponent reacted to the strike. 'He was standing on his tiptoes dancing at me. I caught him with a couple of those and things changed, it was nice!'

Not quite so nice from current UFC fighter's perspective; 'I could see his confidence was growing because I was landing the leg kicks, but I thought, "Nah it's alright, I've got this under control.' In obvious pain, Bisping appeared to shift gears and did an incredible job of checking the ensuing deluge of right low kicks thrown by the Londoner and kept on his bike behind a stiff jab. With the steely look of concentration back in his eye, the Count followed one of his fast jabs, stepping in with an overhand right which caught Epstein full on the temple, sending him crashing to the mat. A further right hand from Bisping was all that the referee needed to see as he stepped in to save the battered and apparently unconscious London Shootfighter. 'Thankfully I landed the right hand and knocked him out cold, sealed the deal...'

Epstein, however, disagrees with that assessment and protested angrily, 'He hit me with a nothing punch!' he raged, 'I slipped over! I spat some water on the floor at the end of the second round and I've fucking tripped over on my own fucking...' he tapered off, 'I'm not making any excuses, he had won the fight, but I was hurting him with the low kicks.'

'I was fucked, I was I admit it. I was fucked, I was exhausted, but he never knocked me out.' Epstein said defiantly, 'But you know what, I wish Mike Bisping all the best in the world, good luck to the fella, I hope he goes all the way. But I know I gave him a hard time and I'd still give him a hard time with the right training - I'd love a third one with Mike. I know, if I hit him with a right hand, full on, he'd go. In the first fight, I was going backwards and I hit him with a right hand and dropped him. If I hit him stepping forward, he'd be out. I hope he goes all the way, but if he's thinking of fighting Anderson [Silva], I think he'll need a couple of more years yet.'

2Hot2Handle 4 Simply the Best: 'Dirty' Bob Schreiber vs Gilbert 'The Hurricane' Yvel

'Dirty' Bob Schreiber is a former street fighter and also one of the most experienced mma fighters on the Dutch circuit 'I have many memories.' Bob said, looking back on his professional exploits; however one encounter stuck out in his memory more than all the others. 'The fight with Hugo Duarte, that was a very memorable fight as he was a very arrogant prick and he didn't want to shake my hand. Later on, I knocked him out in the ring; it was a very good experience! Duarte is a very good submission fighter', Schreiber

233

qualified, 'He brought me to the ground and I escaped and then I came on top and I smashed his face!' the Dutchman laughed cheerfully.

Yvel was also in laughing mood as he looked back at the youthful confidence which allowed him to take on a monster like Schreiber after only competing in mma for six short months, 'I was like the puppy, you know? They gave me Bob Schreiber. I think the people in Holland like all the big names and all the promoters were like, "This black guy is unstoppable, let's put him onto Bob, because he's the guy from the streets; "Terrible" Bob, he can probably stop him." They had problems with me because this one big promoter in Holland had all the good fighters, he had a bit of a monopoly going on, then came this small black guy and he destroyed all his fighters, so at this point they give me Terrible Bob.'

In the first fight, a tiring Yvel caught Schreiber in a straight anklelock in the second round and cited sensitive family problems for his KO loss to the infamous brawler in the rematch held two months later in Amsterdam. However, the final fight in their trilogy is widely regarded as the most entertaining of the contests as the two proud fighters exchanged punches and kicks for 13 minutes, battering each other in a relentless turf war.

'When Bob and me met for the final time, oh, that was a hard fight!' Gilbert said, exhaling deeply, 'I was fucked up, he was fucked up, he was bleeding out his eyes, out his nose, out his mouth, out his head; everywhere there was blood.

'When you are fighting a guy who will never go down or be knocked out, I fight him two times first and then I give him knees, kick him on his head I landed three straight knees on his head and he was still fighting so it was a really mentally difficult fighting an opponent like that.' Gilbert said, obviously quite pleased that the two are unlikely to ever meet again in competition.

As the contest progressed, Schreiber's face started to display signs of a serious beating. 'After 13 minutes, Bob's face like, there was no face anymore, he was like one big mess of blood and they decided to stop the fight. It was lucky for me because he didn't really want to stop, "Ah man, let me fight", but his wife was telling him – "You know Bob, you'd better stop, right now." When his wife told him to stop, he realised something was really wrong. That was my luck because I was fucked up, tired!'

Bob remembered the incident fondly, 'My wife is always in my corner and I have a rather hard head and I can take a lot of punches in my head. During the fight, my wife shouted to me, "Keep your hands high because your face looks like shit!" he laughed, 'Almost at the end of the fight, the referee stepped between us and the doctor came in the ring and my wife said immediately stop the fight. And I said, "No, no, no, no why stop the fight?"

But I couldn't see anything out of my left eye and only a little bit with my right eye. Later on, in the dressing room, I was standing in front of the mirror and I thought, 'Yeah, OK, it was a good decision...'

Schreiber looked back on one of the most memorable and damaging scraps of his life. 'He knows that I'm a very hard headed,' Bob said very seriously, 'He knew that he couldn't finish me off with punches; after the fight, he told me he was very happy when the referee stepped between us.

'We were really fighting, it wasn't like mma; we were really fighting. Now mma is; everybody's going to take you to the ground, put you in an armbar, but there was no technique to that it was just toe-to-toe. Good days you know', he reminisced, before finishing with a laugh, 'but I never again want to fight in the cage or in the ring... maybe in a discothèque or a bar, but never in the ring or a cage!'

UFC - The Ultimate Fighter 6 Finale:
Clay Guida vs. Roger Huerta

Clay 'The Carpenter' Guida is known as one of the UFC's most exciting fighters and has a habit of putting on performances which have the crowd in their feet. Guida had the perfect chance to shine as he went up against Sports Illustrated poster boy, Roger Huerta, in an eagerly anticipated bout. Despite a passage of slick kickboxing by his Mexican opponent in the first round, Guida controlled the first round with his neat wrestling before really piling it on in the second.

During a frantic exchange of straight punches both fighters threw wildly, each putting real spite in their punches as they threw with bad intentions. After catching a couple of shots himself, Guida caught his opponent with a stinging left hook which left him open for a right hand, straight down the pipe. Moments later, another hard right hand off a failed shot attempt left Guida feeling comfortable going into the final round.

'I remember I won two rounds pretty handily. It was a pretty close fight, but I know that the UFC had me two rounds up to zero and it went to the third round. People say that they were some of the best exchanges in MMA history, we were just standing toe-to-toe and throwing everything. I tagged him, I think I hit him with probably 90% of my strikes, that's a pretty high percentage when you've got 4oz gloves on and for him not to get knocked out... that's impressive on both ends!'

In the third round, however, things rapidly changed around for the Chicago fighter as a couple of hard knees from Huerta rocked his world. 'I remember catching the knee; it was kind of in slow motion. It's not like it hurt, when you get hit like that, it doesn't hurt, it sends you into a state of mind where you don't remember much.'

235

Guida instinctively surged forward for the takedown, but in his discombobulated state, the attempts lacked the precision they needed and a six-punch combination from Huerta only made matters worse for the long haired Illinois puncher. 'I was kind of reeling, he took my back, he hit me with another knee I think and another couple of punches and took my back. Yeah, he did what he came to do, that's to fight.'

Though his opponent was able to seize control of his neck, choking his way to victory one minute into the final round, Guida still received a standing ovation from the Las Vegas crowd. 'To be known as one of the UFC's most exciting fighters is an honour, you know. I'm always about having fun and winning. It's an honour at weigh-ins to have people on their feet cheering – even when I'm on the undercard I get a louder response for the undercard fight than we did the main event, against Samy Shiavo.' The wild-haired wrestler duly went on to pummel the Frenchman inside the first round of their preliminary bout.

CHAPTER SEVENTEEN
BEATDOWNS

'£25? £30 on the door? You want to see someone getting filled in for that!'

- Anonymous

Unsightly beat downs can take place as a result of optimistic, or ill-considered match-making, but often enough, a fight can look even on paper, only for one of the combatants to pull out something extraordinary, bringing the fans to their feet as he sends his opponent crashing to a heavy defeat.

For the crowd to enjoy watching a fighter taking a beating seems, on the surface, to be a somewhat guilty pleasure; but the losing fighter rarely looks for sympathy, instead working as hard has he can to escape the tight spot and overturn the adversity. However, even if there is no way through, fighters who receive a beating one day will train harder for their next contest in the hope of dishing out a beating himself at the soonest opportunity - such is the circle of competitive life inside the cage.

Beatdowns in the gym

However, in the mid 90's - back in the very early days of the sport - Frank Shamrock found to his detriment that not every beating takes place in the cage as he tried out for a spot on the team of the world famous, Lion's Den. At such an early stage of the development of training techniques for mma, Frank's brother and UFC Hall of Famer, Ken Shamrock placed a heavy emphasis on testing his student's survivability in the most arduous of circumstances. Therefore, in the late 90's, the character of many Lion's Den fighters was forged in the high-pressure crucible of exhausted, full contact mma sparring.

'It was the old crazy initiation where we'd do 500's – and then you have to fight somebody for 20 minutes.' The dreaded '500' involved 500 squats and leg lifts, followed by 250 nausea-inducing push ups; 'Then I was lucky enough to fight Ken,' he continued, 'not that I was lucky, but I ended up fighting him. He broke my nose, tore out my knees, broke my ribs, basically either got me ready – or not ready to fight.'

Such an incredibly injurious initiation seems ludicrous by anyone's standards, but Frank brushed off the tendon-snapping ceremony as part of the earlier days of sport that has since come on a long way. Speaking with the stoic acceptance you might expect from an empty-netted Inuit fisherman, he explained; 'I never was angry with Ken because for me that was just the way that we did it, I didn't know any different, I didn't know any better. It was tough, it was definitely tough, but that's how I was raised in fighting. I didn't know any different, I just thought that everybody beat the crap out of each other all the time!'

Another training group known for exceptionally hard sparring is the lesser known but equally as formidable London Shootfighters. The twin pillars of the West London gym, Alexis Demitriades and Paul Ivens, are fascinating characters, dedicated to learning and developing new techniques and strategies as they prepare a room full of professional fighters for competition.

To this day, the London Shootfighters insist that if any of their students are bound for the cage, they must first test their mettle in tough sparring; however, these sporting, but intense sparring sessions are gentle in comparison to the in-class scraps of yesteryear, when people would literally walk into the gym and challenge members of the team to a fight.

Soon after the formation of the training group in the late 90's, a visiting tough guy made such a challenge as he unexpectedly took issue with one of the group's most gifted fighters, incredible kickboxer and counter-wrestler, Michael Johnson. Amazed as he looked back on the events of the day, Paul Ivens explained what happened, 'We once had this South African guy that really wanted to fight Michael Johnson. It was the first day he came here to train and he kept saying, "I wanna fight him, I wanna fight him." Don't know why.'

'To be fair, the guy was South African', Alexis interjected with a wry smile, 'and Michael was the only black guy in the class at the time... He kept asking and we finally stopped the class, we made a circle and they fought.'

The fight took place using mma gloves; however, there were precious few rules to adhere to. 'They did elbows, headbutts and everything.' Ivens recalled, 'For a few beginners it was a bit shocking for them, one guy started screaming for them to stop the fight! Michael smashed his face in; he was bleeding all over the place.'

The disrespect shown by the visitor earned him the beating of his life, 'When we say "Smashed his face in,"' Alexis clarified, 'we don't mean like a normal fight nowadays. We were the referees at the time and, to be fair, we didn't give a shit. It was like the guy had two heads on him, absolutely smashed to bits. His face was unrecognisable, Elephant-man standard. Michael spun out for an armbar and broke the guy's arm as well - and we ended it.'

As the reputation of the gym grew, an increasing tide of muscle bound hardmen began making their way to the gym, intent on making a name for themselves in the quickest possible time. One such meathead who stepped through the doors of the London Shootfighters old facility in Kilburn was an American who – for reasons best known to himself - wanted to fight one of the gym's most dangerous fighters who would go on to fight in the UFC, 'Lightening' Lee Murray.

Paul laughed as the memories flowed back, 'He came in and then said, "I want to fight him [Murray]. I want to spar with him right now." Basically we had this security guy call up and say they had this guy who's hot shit, "Can he come to your gym so you can have a look at him?" We said yes. The guy turned up, jacked up, juiced up bodybuilder, we lined five guys up in a row and said "Who do you want to fight?"'

Laughing almost uncontrollably, Alexis took on the story, 'We've all got our shirts off, everyone's a bit big, Murray's the skinny white kid in the corner. If you don't know him, he doesn't look like a fighter; if you look at his hands, he looks like a fighter, but if you look at his body, he looks very, very skinny and scrawny, so the American picked the skinny kid which was probably the wrong move!'

As one might expect from the former street fighter, Murray was in no mood to be picked on and quickly set about making an example of the unwelcome doorman, giving him a taste of his own medicine as he ejected him the tough way. Paul summed up the quick but agonising fight, 'We used to have these huge double doors and he ended up getting punched out through the doors into the concrete and dragged back in by his head. He got knocked out three times in a minute.'

World Vale Tudo 9:
Gilbert Yvel vs. Fabio Piamonte

Within the realm of mma competition, an absolutely stunning one-sided victory from the early days of the sport took place in Aruba on the old World Vale Tudo promotion. WVT was as old school as they come, allowing all of the traditional nasties; headbutts, downward elbows, kicking and stomping to the head of a downed opponent, the lot. Under these rules, you would need to be near-on certifiable to take on a fighter from the legendary Chute Boxe academy in Brazil.

However, when Dutch kickboxer, Gilbert Yvel made his way to the beautiful island to take on the academy's top student, Fabio Piamonte, not even the mind games of a Chute-Boxe trainer could shake Yvel's confidence. 'He first said to us, "He's a good fighter for Gilbert, Gilbert will probably beat him", but it was a set up, Fabio was supposed to be a really good fighter and the same trainer told us right before the fight, like "Gilbert doesn't have any chance." Because this Fabio was supposed to be this big, champion guy, he felt a little bit bad because everyone was talking about me and how good I am before the fight. I gave all the interviews, he gave no interviews.'

This was just the tip of the iceberg when it came to pre-fight sabre-rattling. In what seemed a laughable set up, WVT camera crews miraculously appeared poolside at the hotel where all the fighters and trainers were staying. Arriving just in time to witness the rivalry heating up, they would have us believe, the cameras picked up a stilted exchange of intimidating looks between the fighters, punctuated by Piamonte making his way over to Yvel as he chatted to some girls.

'You'd better get out of here.' Piamonte said, 'If you don't do that I'm going to kick some ass before the time. You are an asshole!'

Watching the disagreement for the first time on video, it appeared to be complete sham, reminiscent of a cringe-worthy WWE promo. However, unlike most threats of terrible violence delivered within earshot of a camera crew, this exchange of words was very real. 'At the pool, we were eyeballing each other and he said something to me... I was angry; at the fight, it was hard to keep my temper and I lost it a little bit.' Gilbert said, chuckling to himself. 'A nice thing I remember was right before the fight started,' he added, continuing to giggle like a schoolboy, 'the bell went "ding" and he said to me, "So, now we are going to find out who is the real champion", and kicked me, it was so funny!'

As you may have gathered, Yvel did not appear in the least bit concerned by his opponent's posturing and threw himself headlong into a war with the Brazilian, fighting wildly at a dangerous punching range. 'The first one or two minutes were just fighting,' he said, 'no plan, just try to hurt your opponent and it was like my first mma fight. I fought before, but I knocked the guy out in seconds, so it was like the first time I was fighting on the ground and was allowed to give elbows and punches to the face.'

Yvel landed some hard punches and knees and, though his Brazilian opponent was not without success in the stand up himself, his punches caused Piamonte some disorganised moments as he desperately shot in for the takedown. 'I remember getting mount and trying to give him an elbow and missed it really hard. My ground skills were really bad so I got up, give him a knee, give him some more knees and he fell to the ground and I finished it off.' The Hurricane battered his fallen opponent with knees to the head and a series of downwards elbows which prompted the referee to the stop the contest after 2-and-a-half minutes of one-sided action.

UFC 38: Mark Weir vs. Eugene Jackson

In what was an incredibly ambitious move for Zuffa officials, after taking control of the Ultimate Fighting Championships in 2001, they almost immediately turned their attention across the pond, and took a tremendous gamble by deciding to host UFC 38 in the prestigious setting on London's Royal Albert Hall. This bold and unprecedented move even managed to stir up interest among Britain's mainstream press; providing a layer largely negative, but nonetheless extremely useful coverage to the fledgling UK mma scene.

For Mark Weir, one of the UK's best fighters at the time, appearing on the card came as a very good opportunity to not only demonstrate his skills, but help to present the sport in a positive manner. 'Obviously, I am from a traditional background,' he said, referring to his years of experience in top flight Tae Kwon Do competition, 'the main thing that was nice because I've tried to keep progressing in the martial arts as a whole, Everybody had a funny idea about mixed martial arts. They'd seen it as a thug's sport, but because I was traditional, I didn't see it that way.'

As an Olympic sport, Tae Kwon Do has a reasonable following in the UK; however, the numerous contests and exhilarating successes under his belt that he carried to the octagon could not prepare 'The Wizard' for the nerves and anxiety that he faced that night. 'Fighting in the UFC is just not the same. The lights, television coverage – it was a live show as well, there were people all round the world watching, people from my town. But I just kept focussing on what I had to do on the day.'

His opponent, Eugene Jackson was less likely to be suffering from big fight nerves. We're talking about a fighter who not only competed in some of the earlier UFC shows, but who also flew to Brazil in 1999, to engage Wanderlai 'The Axe Murderer' Silva in a bare-knuckle brawl. Taking a complete kicking in that contest, the idea of facing a gangly traditional martial artist from the idyllic English city of Gloucester must have seemed like stroll to his local Walmart in comparison. Understandably, Jackson looked fired up and ready to cause damage as the pair of fighters touched gloves to begin the contest.

Weir wasted no time and almost immediately whipped a stunning hook kick straight past his bewildered opponent's face. 'I've got very long legs,' he recalled, 'it was hooking past his hand it actually pulled his arm down slightly. I just wanted him to be wary that I was coming forward. He didn't see that I was following up with a punch though, which was very lucky. It's a combination I'd done for years. I always follow up, when I step forward, I hit. The main thing is to also keeping your hands up as well. But I'm not being funny, but it's like, if I didn't land on him first, and he's landed on me, then I know that one of us is going to go down, so it was a race. I was using the one edge I had over him because he never kicks. I've seen him wrestling, I can wrestle back, but the main thing that tipped the scale was the kicking side of things.'

The knockout blow landed with devastating force, sending Eugene crashing to the floor and causing 'Big' John McCarthy to call a halt to the proceedings at only ten seconds, a new UFC record at the time. 'I think that because he came into it, he generated the power even more so.' Weir explained, 'It felt like I hit him, but it didn't feel overly heavy, but it's just because I connected right on the chin as he came forward. He was properly out before he hit the floor to tell you the truth. Obviously, because you usually tend to carry on fighting on the ground, I didn't switch off and I think I gave him maybe another couple of hits before the referee jumped in, which I was glad for. As a UFC debut, it was great; a nice, easy, quick introduction into it. It was nice.'

UFC 38: Ian Freeman vs. Frank Mir

That very same night, less than 90 minutes after Weir's hand was raised in victory, another pillar of the UK mma community, Ian Freeman made his way to the cage to face rising heavyweight prospect and future UFC champion, Frank Mir. Tipped as the next big thing in the sport, the American jiu-jitsu expert arrived in London full of confidence that he could easily submit the tough Sunderland fighter as he had done his previous two UFC opponents.

As a heavy underdog in the fight, Freeman still felt under extraordinary pressure to perform well in front of his fellow countrymen. Knowing that the vast majority of the fans at the Royal Albert Hall would not have seen any of his previous victories, Freeman was all too aware that they would judge his worth on this contest alone – a contest in which he faced one of the most talented young submission artists the sport has ever produced.

With his pride and reputation at stake, Freeman took a giant leap out of his comfort zone in preparation for the bout, making his way across the pond to train with Josh 'The Babyfaced Assassin' Barnett. 'He was pushing me to the limits. I'm sure he was trying to break me at one point, that's what it felt like.' Freeman said, looking back at one of the toughest training camps of his career. 'But obviously, afterwards, I realised that it was for my own good. The harder the training the easier the fight becomes – and my training was so super-hard that when I got in there I just knew there was nobody alive who could have beaten me that night.'

However, it was not simply his hard preparation for the bout which gave 'The Machine' this incredible surge of determination that night, as he explained. 'My main motivation was my father dying from cancer. But my father used to be the ABA boxing champion when he was 18, I think that was in 1941. He had just been diagnosed with brain cancer and had two weeks to live. I didn't want to fight, I wasn't even going to bother going in for it, but my mother says "Look, your dad used to be a boxer, he was so happy when you became a fighter, the best thing you can do is go in there, win the fight and come back and tell your dad, it would be the best going away present ever."'

'So that just inspired me,' Freeman said, reliving the mixture of emotions he felt on the night, 'that was the mental side of things. I was so fired up, I honestly believe to this day, that whatever man you put in that cage beside me that night, I'd have beat the crap out of them, just so I could go back and tell my dad. I went in there and just felt invincible, unbeatable; I just went in there and I knew, no matter what shots he threw, that I would beat him.'

Predictably enough, it was not long before Mir shot in for the takedown. 'I sprawled and I thought,' prophetically, as it turned out, '"You're not getting back up from this", I just knew, "You're not getting back up from this."' Live opponent that he was, however, the American refused to go down without a fight and tried every trick on the book to stay in the contest, yet Freeman refused to be distracted from his task. 'He caught me in a reverse kneebar at one point, he could have snapped my knee off, but I would have still kept on fighting. I was just so positive. That's what drives you, you know, if you've got 100% positivity in your mind – along with skill level, like – nobody's going to beat you. It's only when you start to get beat on and you think, "What am I doing here? I want to get out of here." That's when you get beat.'

In an enthralling passage of the fight, Mir took control of Freeman's ankle; with his hands tightly clasped together, in order to prevent his opponent from escaping, the jiu-jitsu expert began to apply a nasty inside heel hook. However, after training with one of the best leglockers in the business in Josh Barnett, Freeman set about relieving the pressure by cupping his opponent's head and pulling it towards him. With one hand free to punch, the former doorman went to work, laying in a series of hard, chopping shots to Mir's exposed head. Under heavy fire, the youngster refused to give up the submission, cranking on the ankle for all he was worth.

'People have asked me about this before' Freeman explained, 'and they've said, "What a stupid man, why did he do that?" and I said, "No, it wasn't stupid because the heel hook was on!" It was on, and at the end of the day, he's a submissions expert, he knows whether his submissions are on or not. So it was definitely on, it was a reverse heel hook as well, which is the most dangerous. He knew it was on, I knew it was on, but luckily, I was pulling his head forward and by pulling his head forward, it kind of released the pressure on me – even though it was hurting, it wasn't enough to make me tap out. It wasn't a stupid thing, people say "You were punching him in the head and he was still going for the heel hook", fair enough, I was punching him in the head, but that heel hook was on! He wasn't being stupid. He was hoping that

I would have tapped or my ankle would have cracked, that's what he was going for.'

After taking years of flak for refusing to give up the hold, Mir reflected honestly on the tough situation, without a hint of regret. 'I was using the wrong part of my arm and at the time, I didn't know better', he explained of the ill-fated submission attempt. 'When Ian was punching me, he was hitting me more on the top of the head, I could feel the impact, but it wasn't like he had caught me on the chin. After the fight, you could see it in my nose and my upper brow, but so far the only time I've really been dropped was when I fought Brandon Vera. He caught me in the chin and that took my legs out from underneath of me. With Vera punching me, I've come to realise that being hit on the top of the head doesn't really matter. When I had Ian Freeman in the heel hook, he was hitting me on the top of the head and I really didn't acknowledge it. "OK, so what if you're going to hit the top of my head?" I didn't feel good, I wouldn't volunteer for that, but at the same time, I was really determined to rip his knee.'

As the stream of punches began to morph into a tidal wave, Mir began to show the affects of this sustained beating as he slumped from one position to the next on the floor, eating punches at every turn. After 4-and-a-half minutes, the American was barely able to stand, leading Freeman to believe the contest should have been stopped earlier. 'I was a little bit disappointed with John McCarthy, I'll be honest with you. The number of chances he gave him to continue. He spat his mouthpiece out, he stopped the fight, got his mouthpiece, got it washed off, went back to him, "Do you want to continue? Do you want to continue?"

'I was standing waiting, get ready to fight again, thinking, "This man is fucking unconsciousness! He's out, he's gone, he's finished – and you're asking him so many times if he wants to continue." He was trying to feed the gumshield back into his mouth; I was thinking, "What are John McCarthy's instructions? What has he been told? How many chances does he have to give fucking Frank Mir before he realises that he's just not going to continue?" I just felt a little bit let down by that.'

This bitter note to the end of the fight did little to dampen Freeman's spirits when he was declared the winner, though a far more serious matter immediately confronted him, 'At the back of my mind, if you watch the video at the end of the fight again, as soon as I'd won the fight I jumped up on the cage and everything, but I've walked back to my wife in my corner the first words I said were "is my dad alive?" He was so close to dying, I told everybody when I went to London, no matter what the story, whatever, just don't tell me, I just want to go in there, win the fight and go back and tell my dad. I didn't want to be so close to a fight to have someone ring me up and say, "Oh, by the way, your dad has just passed away." So I wanted to see if she already knew or not. They were the first words when I get back to my corner, you can actually hear it on the video.'

With the highest of highs and the deepest of crushing lows potentially colliding around him, Freeman rushed back stage to phone his mother, '"I'm sorry son," she said, "but your dad died yesterday", so from being on such a high, I went straight down to a low. It was unbelievable, you just can't describe, although I was on such a high, I couldn't take it in that my dad was dead, I didn't even get upset, it was like being in shock. It's hard to explain. You know your parents are going to die one day, but when it actually happens it's a weird feeling.'

Hard-punching brawler, Mark 'The Beast' Epstein

Mark 'The Beast' Epstein is a fighter who never steps in to the cage hoping to win by decision and, as a result of his determination to avoid going to the judge's scorecards, he has been in some of the UK's most memorable wars, delivering and receiving hard shots all day. Employing such a no-nonsense attitude to his ring craft, it comes as no surprise that he has battered numerous opponents into the floor, and also paid the price for his marauding style on more than one occasion.

'There have been a couple of guys who have knocked me out,' the Woolwich fighter said with a tone of complete indifference, 'one of them was my second fight, it was my first fight in the cage, Craig Amer; he knocked me out, him and [Evangelista] "Cyborg" [Santos]; Bisping never knocked me out, I was never KO'd against Bisping, exhausted, yeah, but not KO'd.'

In a harsh learning experience, 'The Beast' was sent crashing to defeat in only his second professional contest, 'Craig Amer knocked me out real quick; it was my first time in the cage, my second fight, I wasn't even supposed to fight him. I was supposed to fight someone else the promoter changed the fight on me, didn't even tell me, phoned me the night before asking about ticket sales and didn't tell me he'd changed the fighter. I got there and he told me, "You're fighting this guy". I thought, "Who is this, I don't even know him!" I'd seen him fight once, I'd seen him fight Andy Langdon. Him and Andy Langdon came out, I'd never seen anything like it, double KO.'

Slightly put out by this sudden change of opponent, the memory of that shocking finish on the Extreme Brawl promotion gave Epstein a much-needed, but illusory boost to his confidence, 'I thought, "If I can bang this fella, I'll knock him out." I trained for a tear up, it was my second fight. Lee [Murray] went to me, "You can't fight this fella", I said "Fuck it, I've seen him fight, I've seen him get sparked out, if I hit him, he'll go." But he'd had like 40 Muay Thai fights and three mma fights, I wasn't ready for Craig Amer', the South Londoner admitted.

'I went in there, he caught me with a left hook about 15 seconds into the fight, I was out, mate; he proper KO'd me. Proper; that was naughty. I was out for about two or three seconds; nothing major, mate, but I just weren't ready for Craig, I should have listened to Lee, but I didn't 'cos I wanted to fight - I'd been training for 6 weeks. I'd seen him go, I'd seen him put over; that Andy Langdon, he come out windmilling and just caught the fella and they both went.'

A few years later and after accumulating a string of knock out wins himself, Epstein squared off with the appropriately nicknamed, Dave 'Death Wish' Legeno at Cage Rage 17 in a fight that was set to rank among the most emphatic knock outs in the domestic game. In contrast to the vicious fight which was to come the next day, Epstein and Legeno laughed together like old friends at the pre-fight press conference, belying the murderous show of aggression which was to follow.

Things started to go wrong for Legeno before he had even made his way down the runway, as an interesting choice in entrance attire helped Epstein to dissociate himself from any feelings of goodwill towards his opponent. 'Dave is alright. I didn't really know him that well before the fight and when he came in, the entrance and all, it pissed me off a little bit to tell you the truth. He came in as a priest and that and it kind of got my back up, you know. The entrance was long and it was all theatrical and I thought, "You know what, this is bullshit."'

Dressed in black and surrounding himself with ring-girls kitted out like a gaggle of sexaholic nuns, 'The Beast' was furious that Legeno had apparently tried to attach devilish overtones to his nickname. 'He was trying to link me to some kind of satanic rites, you know what I mean; I'm not down with that shit. I thought, "Nah, mate, this geezer..." you know, "I've got to make him pay for this."'

Epstein was able to stamp his mark within the opening moments of the contest as he took the centre of the cage and began unloading wild hooks as the pair went to war. Just as the commentary team noted that technique had gone out the window, Epstein landed a hard kick, following in with punches. 'I caught him on the forearm with the kick, but the left and the right, they were clean. Right on the jaw, both sides of the jaw; I love that, I wish I could bust that out every day!'

The left hook connected with such power that Legeno was out cold before he hit the ground, yet, before he could meet with the comparative luxury of the soft canvas, a right hand crashed home on his jaw. 'I knew he was sparked out, I knew he was out, but I just thought I'd help him over.' Epstein said, with a sly chuckle, 'He was sitting into the fence; you know, I just wanted to put him over, I didn't want to put nothing too major into it, but I wanted to put him on the deck. It weren't like I disliked him. It was just the heat of the moment and I just wanted to finish it off, put him over, rather than leave him sleeping on the fence. That's quite a nice bench mark that little knock out.' He added of the 45-second finish, 'I've got some really good knock out highlights now!'

Pride Fighting Championships 34:
James Thompson vs Don Frye

Facing a legend of the sport is always going to be hard enough, but when that legend also happens to be your hero, the task at hand immediately becomes that bit more difficult. However, while James Thompson showed all the respect in the world for his idol, Don Frye at the pre-fight press conference; on the night of the fight, however, it was a different story.

The two locked horns in an intensely physical head-to-head stare down, either fighter could easily have sustained a broken nose as they met face-to-face, alternately pushing forward with their foreheads. Thompson's trademark 'Gong and dash' bull rush came to nothing as he charged onto a kick from his opponent and was sent to the floor with a hard right hand.

However, Thompson recovered quickly and pushed into the lead in the fight with some heavy shots in the clinch. As Frye retreated into the corner of the Pride ring, 'The Colossus' released an avalanche of punches on his role model, hammering the resilient warhorse to within an inch of his life. Asked how he was able to remain standing through the barrage of technically-rugged, but highly effective blows, Frye let out a deep and cheerful laugh, 'Beats the hell out of me. He just hit me fast enough, knocked me left, knocked me right and kept me up! I grabbed the ropes a couple of times there to hold myself up. That guy is as big as a damn ox, I'll tell you, he was powerful too, I was impressed with him.'

Some referees in Japan have been accused in the past of letting big name fighters take an incredible volume of punishment and give them every chance to make what quite often would need to be a miraculous recovery. Thompson, however, did not have time to engage the referee in a discussion, and kept pouring on the punishment in the hope of taking home the win. '"Just keep going"', Thompson said to himself, 'I was getting tired at that point; it had been quite a fast-paced fight. I just thought, keep going, keep going, don't stop. That's all that I thought. Really, I should have stepped back.'

Don, however, was suffering under the attack, as he quite openly confessed, 'Oh I lost consciousness, he came up and kicked me in the face with a shin – I was out there. That's the thing about heavyweight fighters, they'll knock you out with one punch and wake you up with another punch. That's what happened, he knocked me out - woke me up, knocked me out - woke me up, it must have happened about four times!'

'I thought it was very honest of Don to say that.' James said, in a heartfelt mark of appreciation for his hero. 'He could have just said that he was tired or that the punches didn't have much affect. He could have said any number of things, but I really respect that he just came out and told it like it was.'

UFC 75: Jess Liaudin vs. Anthony Torres

Going into only his second fight for the UFC and sporting quite a patchy record, Pancrase London fighter, Jess 'The Joker' Liaudin was in many people's minds a firm underdog ahead of his clash with seasoned American wrestler, Anthony Torres. The talented submission fighter, however, did not see it that way at all and entered the contest brimming over with confidence.

'I didn't see myself as the underdog at all. I was training at Team Quest and doing the same preparation as Dan Henderson who was training for Rampage at the time. I was doing exactly the same cardio work out, exactly the same sparring. They had the whole gym to train Dan, so Matt Lindland was there, a whole bunch of people, so I was getting the same training as him. So I was very confident, physically and mentally, I'd been training with very good people and I knew that he wouldn't be able to take me down. I saw him fight before and his stand up wasn't that great, he was more of a brawler; but I knew that he was good and that his wrestling was OK, but I'd trained with world-class wrestlers and I knew I could counter him and let my fists do the talking, stand up with him and try to go for the knock out.'

That's exactly what Liaudin did, firing off a quick succession of punching combinations with a genuinely mma-specific style. 'Obviously, I do my sparring sometimes with the big gloves, straight up boxing and things like that,' the Frenchman explained, 'but I do a lot of sparring with the small gloves because the striking technique that you use for mma is slightly different to boxing, obviously your posture would be slightly different, your blocking would be different, but there's also a lot more gaps and things like that. I think the secret is that I do a lot of sparring with the mma gloves. I can throw punches and kicks and control them, so I can afford to use a lot more striking in my mma training.'

'I was training at Team quest at the time,' he continued, 'but before that, my combinations were very restricted. It was one-two, hook-cross, always the same thing, so that's what the coach had me working on, being a lot more fluid and throwing a lot more combinations and that's what I've tried to keep up since then.'

In addition to the near-continuous flurry of shots the Frenchman threw at Torres, he also added some meaningful low kicks which had the wrestler grimacing. 'I didn't throw too many middle kicks because he was set up for me to start using my punches. I didn't throw as many kicks as I usually do, because I didn't want him to grab my leg and take me to the mat. So for this one, I was mainly concentrating on my boxing skills, but I would throw the occasional low kick, because if you start throwing the same thing all the time, over and over again, he's not worried because you start to become predictable. So sometimes you have to mix it up a bit and that's what I was doing, throwing the occasional low kick.'

Torres soaked up the punishment like a sponge, a feat which surprised Jess at the time, before later finding out a possible explanation. 'Later on he tested positive for steroids, I don't know if that had anything to do with it – I don't know very much about steroids, I never took any in my life, but I don't know if that would help in any way shape or form. He's definitely a tough guy,' Liaudin added respectfully, 'he's from Hawaii and I've never seen a Hawaiian guy who was a pussy, they are always very tough.

'In that fight, I was going for a lot of very fast shots, I wasn't going for a big overhand right or anything like that which would knock him out cold. I think a lot of them were dazing him and not necessarily putting him down. I still had the gas to keep going and throw those very fast combinations, bunches of punches over and over again because once again I was looking for speed over power.'

Taking Torres off his feet three times with punches during the first round, Liaudin kept his head, rather than rushing in and making a mistake in an attempt to bring an end to the contest. 'I didn't really think about it. Every time I dropped him, I tried to keep my composure and my concentration and not get over-excited. Every time I put him down, I didn't try to do anything tricky, just control again and try to finish him off. At any point until the referee went in between, I didn't feel that I won the fight.

'He caught me with a few punches, a couple of uppercuts in the clinch, every time that I got overconfident and not keeping my guard up a few punches went in. They had an affect on me, but nothing that was really that dangerous.' Liaudin assessed, before highlighting what he considered to be the most damaging shots of the contest which ultimately led to his impressive knock out win. 'I think the ones that people don't realise was all the uppercuts I was throwing from the clinch. Once again, those are things that I learnt from Dan Henderson, I worked a lot of dirty boxing, using the clinch and collar tie. That started the damage from there, he started to get a little bit tired and that allowed me to throw a lot more combinations and catch him later on.'

Cage Rage Contenders:
Sami Berik vs. Mark Smith

A fighter who has seen more than his fair share of crushing defeats is Sami Berik - whilst mentioning that about a fighter can sometimes seem impolite, the hired gun from North London understands the fight game on a different level. 'Each one of my fights is the extension of a verbal argument, the best way to settle it is to just be relaxed and in the state of mind where you're prepared to argue it. So I always try to gear myself towards being relaxed and confident before each fight.'

Fighting almost every week during the less active periods in his career, Berik often blows hot and cold; one day, a tired-looking Sami falls to a quick submission defeat to a fighter no-one has heard of, the next day he bombs out a noted contender with the ruthless efficiency of a young Mike Tyson. You really never know quite what to expect; on one occasion, Berik started a match with an attempted flying knee, but simply ran straight onto a haymaker of a punch. The mixture of pain and indignity must have been excruciating, but showing the mental toughness of an artic explorer, Berik came back to hammer his opponent later in the first round.

On 2 February 2008, the more focused version of 'The Hun' arrived at his office and things went badly wrong for Mark Smith in nine short seconds. Fighting out of a bizarre, almost Kung-Fu looking stance, Sami exploded across the cage with a heavy left high kick at the start of the contest, catching Smith full on across the jaw. 'That made contact, it was more like a "clonk" hit, it shifted his centre of gravity and it was the follow up from the punch which shifted him even more and clocked him really hard.'

With his opponent visibly shaken, Berik stepped in range and lined up a left hook powershot which seemed to come from the back of the building. 'The punch was one of the hardest I have ever landed on someone. I whipped my left hook across and it landed real nicely with enough leverage on it. It landed on the side of his temple.'

Another short punch went in as Smith slumped to the floor, lying prone as Berik swooped in to finish the deal; however, exhibiting unbelievable presence of mind, Sami pulled his potentially career-ending punch just inches from his fallen opponent's face. What did he see which prompted this incredible display of self-control?

'It just didn't feel right.' Berik answered: 'In my fights, yeah, I'm never scared because I go for it 100%; so I'm not scared and I feel good. But when I hit him twice as we were falling, I was getting ready to punch, but I arrived at the evaluation point.

'When I kicked and punched, it was like a flow of moves, but as we were falling to the floor, I was re-evaluating and when I got ready to punch, I felt

250

scared. Not scared, but on the road to it, if I threw that punch I would have been. It felt wrong so I didn't execute the punch. It's awareness' he said, summing up his understanding of mma competition, 'I see it like a duel. We don't play for keeps, there's a point where it ends, and we both acknowledge that. I make sure I stop when I'm supposed to stop and that shows control, rather than thinking it's the ref's job to stop it.

'It's how we carry ourselves and how we do the little things, how we don't resort to biting or other nasties. Even the little things like grabbing the fence, I know the ref says "Don't grab", or whatever but on the times when I instinctively grab it, to let go and not stay grabbing and do what the ref is telling you. For me, I see it as an extension of sparring.' Berik concluded, 'For me to justify punching someone, that's the only time and space I ever fight, in the cage and - outside - I specifically stop fights. That's what people don't understand as well, I don't express anger or anything outside of the fights; that is the only time I do it. So if anything goes on, I take full responsibility. When the fight is over, I'm up for his safety. I never ever put on heel hooks in my fights, ever. Just in case I ever pop anyone's knee. I might punch them up, bruise them up and everything like that, but I'll never pop a joint.'

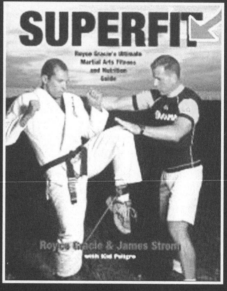

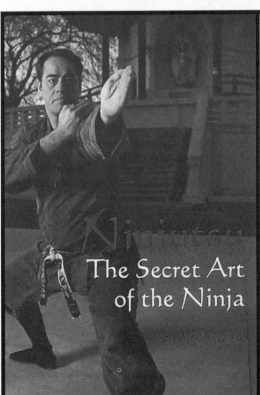

The Secret Art of the Ninja

Simon Yeo has trained in martial arts for more than 30 years and has practiced Judo, Kyokushin Karate, Tai Chi, Pk Mei King Fu, Tae Kwon Do, traditional Jiu Jitsu, and Brazilian Jiu Jitsu. He has studied Bujinkan Ninjutsu under the Ninja Grand Master, Masaaki Hatsumi, and holds a 10th degree black belt in this art.

His new book Ninjutsu - The Secret Art of the Ninja covers all aspects of the art of Ninjutsu, and reveals the secrets of how to develop power through body movement and how to effectively remove an opponent's balance.

A wide-ranging introduction looks at the history of Ninjutsu, as well as mental and physical attitude. Featuring additional subjects such as training advice and pressure points, this essential guidebook will promote harmony between the reader's mind and body, a balance rarely examined from a 1,000-year-old martial arts perspective.

Available from all good bookstores